FROM THE PULPIT

Sermons and Poetry

By Jerry M. Self

Copyright 2024 by Jerry M. Self

ISBN: 978-0-9962558-6-8

Dedicated to all of you who listened over the years

AN INTRODUCTION

This collection of sermons has been selected from 3,000+ preaching events delivered over 64 years. Just re-reading that sentence wears me out. Most of these found expression in six pastorates and two interims. While a senior at Hardin-Simmons University, I pastored Valley View Baptist Church in Paducah, Texas. As a student at Southwestern Baptist Seminary, I pastored the Baptist Chapel in Hillsboro, Texas which was a mission of the First Baptist Church. From there I moved to Ada, Oklahoma to pastor Immanuel Baptist Church. The Sunday (April 7, 1968) following the assassination of Martin Luther King, Jr. I preached the inauguration sermon for Austin Heights Baptist Church, Nacogdoches, Texas. Their response to my sermon linking MLK's life to their intent to provide a witness against racism led them to call me as pastor. Many of these sermons came to life during my ten years at AHBC. While working for the Tennessee Baptist Convention as their ethics consultant, I was an interim pastor for Bear Cove Baptist Church, Sparta, Tennessee and then at Gum Springs Baptist Church, Gum Springs, Tennessee. After Southern Baptists moved to the theological and political right I took a position as pastor of the Donelson Cumberland Presbyterian Church in Nashville, Tennessee for three years. I followed that with a two year pastorate for the Mount Denson CPC in Springfield, Tennessee. After that I taught courses in ethics and religion. That cut down on preaching opportunities to some extent.

The title <u>From the Pulpit</u> suggests a book of sermons, but is somewhat ironic. For ten years at

Austin Heights I preached without a pulpit because I wanted a more direct relationship with the congregation. That also meant I never used notes or a manuscript. I wrote a manuscript of the sermon before delivering it. Those manuscripts have made the production of a book somewhat easy. The road from manuscripts to a published book has required considerable typing and editing by my wife, Maralee. Her much appreciated contribution to this volume is enormous.

PEOPLE OF THE STAR: A MOTHER'S COURAGE - MARY

… Then Mary said, 'Here am I, the servant of the Lord; let it be with me according to your word.'
Luke 1:26-38

Someone has said that the oldest relationship of people is the relationship we have between an individual and God. The second oldest relationship is the relationships that exist between a man and a woman. And then comes the relationship of the parent and the child. This is what we discover in the first chapters of Genesis: God creating humanity, establishing a relationship between Adam and Eve and their having children and then dealing with those children.

I want to talk about Mary, the person we have just read about and her relationship with Jesus. Not so much the relationship any of us would have with Jesus as a relationship to our Savior, relationship to Jesus Christ who is the Son of God, but her position as the mother of Jesus and her relationship with her son. And whatever that might mean for his specialness and whatever it might mean that she was the mother of the Messiah, she was a mother, she was a parent. She was a nurturer. And in some way, all of us, male or female, married or not, with child or not, all of us understand some kind of relationship with someone who is dependent and whom we nurture. I am struck that it seems to me that the first thing that we see in Mary and one of the most outstanding characteristics we see in her is courage.

Now courage is something we typically understand is what it takes to take a gun and go into battle and face an enemy, confront that person, and it be a your life or mine situation. Certainly that is true. But it seems to me one of the outstanding characteristics of a mother is her courage.

Now, of course, if you were about14 years old, a young Jewish girl, in the first century Palestine and were inexplicably (is there another way to put it?) pregnant, there would be a certain need for courage in your life. But apart from all of that, if you are bringing new life into your life, courage is needed and called for. If you are bringing newness of any kind into your life, you know, a puppy or a kitten, courage is called for. Courage seems to describe Mary to me. This is a courageous woman.

Her courage comes out in a variety of ways. One of those ways is JOY. Mary and Elizabeth meet and Elizabeth says to her, "Oh, how happy you are!" You know, the interesting thing is a pregnant woman often betrays her pregnancy not nearly as much by her form as by her face. Often people will guess, ah, ha! And the form has not betrayed her. Why is that? Simple joy. These two women meet and they are overjoyed, one 6 months pregnant and one barely so, and they rejoice in their common experience and they are courageous to do so. Sometimes, joy masks our courage, but none the less, it is there.

It is a little easier to see courage in something else I find in Mary and that is the mystery of her relationship with Jesus. The same mystery that is found with every parent and child. There is one of the songs I love to sing at Christmas time, a haunting melody, beautiful hymn and lyrics: I Wonder as I Wander. The second verse begins:

When Mary birthed Jesus 'twas in a cow stall,
With wise men and shepherds, and farmers
and all.

Now if that is not a mysterious place to deal
with a baby! Those first two years, the wise men
didn't come immediately, those first two years of
Jesus growing up with all these strange things said
and happening and all these strange people coming,
it is indicative of all the mystery involved in being a
parent. Just who is this kid? This is asked more
often than not by some wondering father and there is
a great deal of mystery in having children and in
watching them grow up! Sometimes it is exciting,
sometimes it is challenging, sometimes it drives you
crazy, but it is always mysterious. How did they learn
that? Where did they get that? There is a great deal
of mystery going on in the story of Jesus growing up.
And paradox. When Jesus is 8 days old, they
take him to the temple for circumcision. There in the
temple is a man named Simeon, who has been
waiting to see the Messiah for years—he is an old
man. When he sees the Messiah, he rejoices and
praises God, but one of the things he says to Mary is,
"Sorrow, like a sword will pierce your heart." What a
thing to say to a mother with a week old baby! But
that is part of the mystery of having children—the
paradox involved. How one child will bring so much
joy and so much pain—sometimes they do it the
same day and sometimes with the same event. One
happening with a child can be a happening that
overjoys you and yet sometimes you want to spank
that bottom. A child that is lost and then found, you
are so glad they are found and safe and happy that

nothing happened, and boy, when I get you to your room . . . That is the paradox of the parent-child relationship. Raging, competing emotions are so hard. It is part of being parent.

Christmas is a good time to see the paradox involved in parenting—it is nearly midnight and you have been trying to put together that blankety-blank toy. You are so excited about their getting the toy and so angry that you decided to put the thing together—the competitions that in your mind and your being in being a parent.

Courage for the mystery; courage for the paradox.

There is one other thing about Mary. All through the Gospels, we see Mary in five basic stories. In every one of these stories is the need for courage for Mary to release her son. There are the birth narratives. And then the next time we read about Jesus, he is a 12 year old boy who has come to the temple—this is a big event, a large crowd, people traveling in groups. Mary and Joseph leave—all the kids are over here with Aunt Jane who has got a dozen cousins and surely Jesus is with them, but no, he isn't, so he must be over here with Uncle Ben; no, he isn't with him. Where is he? He's still BACK IN JERUSALEM!!! They go back to the temple and find this 12 year old boy in the temple and he is talking to all of these learned leaders of the whole Jewish denomination. These are the top learned guys and he is asking them questions and they are asking him questions. Mary and Joseph ask him, "Where have you been? We were on the way home." Jesus responds, "Didn't you know? I had to be about my father's business?" Mary is puzzled and challenged by this. We understand that she treasured what happened in her heart. There was something she took out of that moment and treasured, hidden away. There had to be courage for her to face that event that happens to every one of us—there is a little bit of me in this child and that is me acting that way—no, that's my spouse—and then all of a sudden, wait a minute, I don't recognize that person. It isn't either one—it is a third personality here—it is somebody different! That is quite a recognition and it calls for courage, and it usually comes before the child is 12, but it will come then as well.

Jesus begins his ministry and there is a wedding; they have run out of wine. And Mom, the stage manager Mary, like mothers across the century says, "My boy can fix it!" And her boy says, "Mother, I can take care of it myself. Back off." How rude! It is something the child has to say. Children have been saying this to their parents since time began, since Cain and Abel. "I am me, and I can take care of myself. Thanks a lot. Leave me alone." And Mom needs courage to be able to hear that, accept and back off.

The next event is when Mary and Jesus' brothers come to where Jesus is teaching to get him. They have come to get crazy Jesus and take him home and hide him. He doesn't know what he is saying. Mark is the harshest one in telling that story and it comes across very clearly. They think he is nuts and they have come to get him. Luke probably heard the story from Mary herself, probably heard several things from her and he covers it over, smooths it out, tries to make a nicer story, but it is still Mom and the boys going to get crazy Jesus, to protect him, to hide him. Jesus says, "I'm not going. I know what I am doing. These people believe in me. They can be my family. Leave me alone." Mom has to go home. Who is this guy? He's somebody else. I don't understand. It takes courage.

Boy! The last story. Jesus is on the cross. Convicted as a criminal. Punished to the ultimate. Hours, maybe only minutes left to live. Jesus says, "Mom, this is John. John, this my mom. You know each other. John, take care of her. Mom, I'm dying. This is goodbye. You can't prevent it. You can't stop it. Let John take care of you." A hard thing to face; to let go, ultimately, completely. It takes courage.

Jesus isn't your son. Mothering Jesus, maybe it was different. But in much of the walk in that family, it wasn't that different. What we read in Mary is encouragement for us all. Parent, teacher, friend, neighbor—whoever you are and however you live, you touch and nurture other lives. Courage.

The babe Jesus who grew to be the Master, Teacher, Healer, dying and risen Savior, the reason for the season, stands before us today and calls each of us to know his work, his values, and his salvation. Let's all commit ourselves to discovering the power of the resurrection in Jesus Christ and using that power and that grace to turn toward others.

Preached at Immanuel Baptist Church, Ada, Oklahoma 12/08/1965

AN ENTANGLING ALLIANCE

... But wanting to justify himself, he asked Je-
sus, 'And who is my neighbor?'
Luke 10:25-37

Don't want to get involved? Have you any choice?

Jesus' parable is a radical call to relate to one another. A lawyer/scribe comes to Jesus for a discussion about fulfilling rules. Maybe he wants to catch Jesus in some argumentative trap or maybe he simply enjoys hearing himself talk. Whatever the motivations, Jesus takes hold of the opportunity to tell a story which has a radical impact upon the hearer. To illustrate just how radical the story is, consider how we try to explain it away. Don't we usually tell this story with a patronizing disclaimer that the story is valid in a simple society, but it is too dangerous for men with family responsibilities to pick up hitch-hikers or some such explanation that says good stewardship means the parable of the Good Samaritan doesn't apply to the middle-classes?

I am beginning to wonder: If I have so much valuable property that I am suspicious of anyone with a day-old beard and a five year old jacket, maybe I have too much property.

The parable is radical in impact if you are willing to hear it all the way inside of you. Perhaps just reading a parable of Jesus is enough sermon, but be patient for two points.

You are a person not a category.

Victim/Priest/Levite/Samaritan: One of the things Jesus is doing with his story is attacking labels. Jesus' question at the end is "Which man . . .?" not

which category is acting as neighbor. We are so
prone to generalize about one another on the basis of
employment. Perhaps we are moving away from
racial stereotypes and religious stereotypes but pro-
fessional generalizations are no better.

"John this is Bill. Bill meet John."
"How do you do, John, Glad to know you."
"Pleased to meet you Bill. What do you do?"

He has to ask, doesn't he? How else can they
carry on a conversation unless they can put each
other in the proper professional box?

"I want you to meet my friend over there."
"Oh?"
"Yes, he's a lawyer from Philadelphia."
"OHHHH!"

What if he is a hamburger cook from Dime
Box?

The priest and the Levite would be identified by
their clothing, their haircuts and certain items which
they wore or carried. The Samaritan would have
been identifiable by clothing, features and speech—all
exteriors.

But exterior things are what we use as keys to
help us generalize about people. I wonder what the
crowd thought who first heard this story as Jesus in-
troduced the Samaritan. Did they think he was bring-
ing in a villain who would kick the man who was
down? But wait! I had better not generalize about the
listeners.

Time out for an aside. If anyone generalizes
about this church, assuming that all the members are
very much alike, that person, whether one of us or

someone else, might be right about some exterior matters, but essentially is wrong! This is a very diverse group. Time in.

The story says you are a person and not a category and the point has meaning for each of the perspectives represented in the story.

The victim. Victims fall into categories rather easily. He quickly will become a police statistic, and insurance claim, a medical/clinical term, or even a pastoral visitation category. "I'll visit Baptists. You visit Methodists. The chaplain will visit the non-affiliated. Oh, yes, you are the non-affiliated, third-party claim, contusions and abrasions in room 307."

The priest. The Levite. According to Numbers 19:11, "Whoever touches a corpse is ritually unclean for seven days." Suppose that man over there in the ditch is dead. If I touch him, I wouldn't be able to perform the ritual which I am on my way to Jerusalem to perform."

The problem has to do with concentration. Concentration is what makes a professional. A recent study has indicated that people who make it to the top, have a keen ability to concentrate. They can isolate attention in one area so well that, in effect, they can slow things down. Imagine how well you could perform or understand if you could change to slow motion? The ability to concentrate is the ability to turn off your multitude of senses to enhance one sense. Can you imagine the discipline it must take to become a Talmud scholar? All of life is turned off. Only Talmud is on. And that is what it takes to become a professional anything.

But the problem is forgetting to switch on again your sensitivity to life. Sometimes the switch can stay off so long you forget where it is.

I have seen quite a bit of it lately: someone can be professionally pigeon-holed so that care is eliminated from the job-description. Oh, the rules all make good sense. We can't have MD psychiatrists doing intake interviews. We can't have Ph. D.'s with full professor status teaching introductory survey courses. There are reasons for the rules and they make sense. A seven day expulsion from ritual will give you time to consider the implications of the corpse—handle grief if appropriate. But sometimes the rules are an escape from caring. "I'm sorry I cannot help you. I'm overqualified and you are not important enough." Maybe there is a step above full professor, above president or chairman of the board, above proprietor/employer. Maybe it is an invisible step, an unnamed title, an intangible promotion called death-in-life. It comes when the ritual of the routine wears away your personhood and you become the category. And the tragedy is that it is such a subjective thing that you don't notice the silent promotion.

The priest and the Levite needed the grace which this parable extends by virtue of its insight into life.

The Samaritan. Of course, the Samaritan already knows the point. Whether he hears the story or not, he lives it. But it occurs to me to ask: What is a Samaritan doing this close to Jerusalem? Evidently he was not imprisoned by stereotypes or geography.

In my more lucid moments, I believe this point strongly: I am not a Baptist preacher, not a white-Anglo-Saxon-protestant, not a doctor of theology, not a lot of things some people would call me. Oh, they may all be true descriptions of what I have done or am doing. But they are all categories. I am a person! Not a category! And so are you!

Christianity is a way of life, not a set of answers.

The lawyer pursues a philosophical question which can lead to wasted hours of talk unmatched by life. But instead, it leads to this story. And it is a dramatic story. The picture Jesus sketches has great impact. The road from Jerusalem to Jericho drops from 2000 feet above sea level to 1000 feet below sea level in a space of twenty miles. It was winding and treacherous and notorious for bandits.

The story is gripping but it is not used to elicit a general rule about neighbors nor salvation. It is used to touch life with life.

The lawyer's response to the word "neighbor" is defined by adjectives and nouns: Jew, relative, friend; or more precisely, respectable Jew, close relative, congenial friend. The definition is static, consistent, and frankly boring.

The Jesus response to the word "neighbor" is defined by verbs: going, healing, helping, caring, providing, planning. It is attitude and action rather than distance and blood lines. The definition is mobile, portable, unpredictable, and exciting.

Category thinking raises walls between categories and limits interchange. You cannot see between the walls. It is inappropriate to know or relate to anyone beyond the walls. But you cannot care for someone you do not know. And you cannot know a category. Categories are never neighbors.

Preached at Immanuel Baptist Church, Ada Oklahoma 5/1/1966

WISDOM FROM AFFLICTION

I have uttered what I did not understand,
things too wonderful for me which I did not
know.
...
I had heard of you by the
hearing of the ear,
but now my eye sees you;
therefore I despise myself,
and repent in dust and ashes.
Job 27:5-6; 28:20-23, 42:1-6

Affliction has many faces. Job seems to have worn them all. Grief, financial loss, loss of health, uncertainty about friends, doubts about God, questions for himself. Affliction has many forms. It may be visible, as visible as undernourished children or Job's sores. It may be invisible, as invisible as headaches, ulcers, or Job's anguish of soul.

Affliction always seems to bring questions. Here is a book full of questions. And if affliction has any redeeming values, maybe those values are found in the pursuit of questions. Will a man serve God for nothing? What reward is required to make God's way worth following? Here from an anguished heart are basic questions, impertinent questions, fighting questions, staggering questions.

In affliction we question ourselves.

The council of Job's friends sought to do this task for him. He rebuked them and their challenges. Still, he does question himself.

Early in the book we see that he performs as the head of his family during affliction. In chapter 31, he describes his action as a responsible citizen. He faces the questions of personal integrity and they are hard questions.

What is the nature of life? It is hard service. If a tree is felled, it may sprout again, but if a man dies, will he live again? Here during his bout with tragedy, this question carries frightening weight and he probes the darkness with great uncertainty. With all of his probing, Job concludes that his conscience does not condemn him. He has lived properly and his affliction is no cause to regret the good life. His vow is that he will not give up his integrity. So what if nice guys do finish last? Would you hold to your integrity, your righteous life, even if there are no mundane rewards? Will one serve God for nothing?

Affliction may show your caliber. Whether others discover what kind of person you are through affliction, is questionable, (Job's friends seem to have misjudged him) but you will surely discover yourself. It seems wise to become the kind of person who can stand up to severe self-scrutiny.

George Frederick Handel came to the place in life where his money and health were gone. His right side was paralyzed and his creditors threatened prison. It was at the time when he was most sorely tempted to give up that Handel composed *The Messiah*.

In his sermon on shattered dreams, Martin Luther King, Jr. said, "Some of us, of course, will die without having received the realization of freedom, but we must continue to sail on our chartered course. We must accept finite disappointment, but we must not lose infinite hope."

In affliction we question God.

And how Job did question God! And what vital questions they were too! "If I sin, what do I do to you, oh watcher of men?" There is a great question. From his agony, Job asked, "Why haven't you pardoned my iniquity?" That is basic. And then there is the impertinent but ever present question, "How can a man duel with God?" It just isn't a fair fight by anyone's standards. Job exclaims "If it is a contest of strength, behold Him!" He complains that God is not a man; therefore, they cannot come to trial together as equals. Listen to his challenge to God: "I need an umpire between you and me."

There can come a time in a person's struggle when God seems wrong and the person right. If you have the courage for it, then that is the time to go full speed ahead and challenge God.

Martin Luther thought that God made his own rules as he went along or maybe that God has already decided everything so that we are locked into a road toward heaven or hell with no choice. Luther was devastated by the thought that God might not be just. He cried out,

> "Is it not against all natural reason that
> God out of his mere whim, deserts men,
> hardens them, damns them, as if he delights in
> sins and in such torments of the wretched for
> eternity, he who is said to be of such mercy
> and goodness? This appears iniquitous, cruel,
> and intolerable in God, by which very many
> have been offended in all ages. And who
> would not be? I was myself more than once
> driven to the very abyss of despair so that I

wished that I had never been created. Love
God? I hated Him!"

Staupitz appointed Luther to earn his Th. D.
and teach Bible. In his study to prepare himself to
teach the Psalms, Galatians, and the Book of Ro-
mans, Luther came to a new appreciation of Christ
and the truth that the just shall live by faith.
Job questioned himself, and because he was a
man of character, he found that his life could bear
scrutiny.
**When affliction drives us to question God,
what happens? God seldom answers but always
provides.**
Now, is that fair to conclude? Here are the
great questions. What are the answers? No answers
come, just great questions. It sounds paternalistic.
God seldom explains himself to us and why should
he? Or better, how could he? Have you ever found a
satisfactory answer to a child for questions like, "How
are green beans good for me?" or "How much longer
before we get home?" God seldom answers but he
always provides. Job called for an umpire and in Je-
sus Christ, such an umpire-mediator is provided. That
answer has usually satisfied me. But I wonder what it
meant to Job? It feels helpful for me to believe that
God provides. Certainly sounds glib just to say it.
Job questioned God and then God questioned
Job. No answers, just staggering questions:
"Where were you when I laid the foundation of
the earth? Can you bind the chains of the
Pleiades, or loose the cords of Orion? Have
you entered the storehouses of the snow?
Who has cut a channel for the torrents of rain,

and a way for the thunderbolt? Have you an arm like God?"

And on and on the questions go. No answers but the assurance that God has the answers to all these questions. The assurance that He who is capable of managing constellations is present in the midst of consternation. No answers—but the presence of a friend. You know, a parent's kiss never lessens the pain nor does a kiss explain the hurt; but somehow, it is better than answers and explanations.

Martin Luther King, Jr. spoke of his first twenty-four years of life as trouble free and full of fulfillment. Then came the Montgomery bus boycott. There were phone call threats and other discouragements. One night, late, after an anonymous call, he went into the kitchen and prayed over a cup of coffee. "I am here taking a stand for what I believe is right. But now I am afraid. The people are looking for leadership, and if I stand before them without strength and courage, they, too, will falter. I am at the end of my powers. I have nothing left. I've come to the point where I can't face it alone."

From that night, there came courage. Three days later his home was bombed and the black crowd was volatile. A riot would have started for certain except for the fact that Martin Luther King appeared before his neighbors as the calmest man in Montgomery. He had no answer to segregation, violence, hatred, but he did have a provision from God.

Questions and debate fill more than thirty-five chapters of the Book of Job. The flash of devotional insight barely covers six verses wherein Job repents in dust and ashes.

Someone has said the striking of a match makes more noise than the rising of the sun. But can there be any doubt where the true power lies?

Preached at Austin Heights Baptist Church, Nacogdoches, TX 4/13/68

WHAT DO YOU MEAN?

> Then Samuel went to Ramah; and Saul went up to his house in Gibeah of Saul. Samuel did not see Saul again until the day of his death, but Samuel grieved over Saul.
>
> 1Samuel 15:13-35

At a Christian Life Commission Workshop, I was a reactor to Foy Valentine. Afterwards, a man challenged one of my remarks. I admit that I had not been too clear in what I said. About that time, James Dunn walked up and told this man that he had misunderstood me. The last I saw of them, they were explaining to each other what I meant.

Consider 1 Samuel chapters 13 through 15 as seen through the eyes of Samuel. He had made Saul king by his theological-ecclesiastical authority. He shows up to give the official sacrifice before a battle and finds that Saul has impulsively sacrificed and that the men are thoroughly undisciplined. As a king, Saul is constantly in trouble and only Samuel's prayers help. Samuel brings the word of God to Saul concerning a new battle. Thorough instructions are given but Saul cannot follow them. Samuel discovers that men and animals are yet living in spite of instructions to the contrary. Samuel makes a profound point: God would rather have obedience than sacrifice. Samuel prophesies Saul's loss of position and then goes home to mourn Saul's misuse of his potential.

That's about the way you have read it, isn't it? That fairly well represents the attitude of the author of this area of the Bible. Have you considered Saul's perspective? Listen. Read between the lines. Listen to the echoes and the shadows.

The people needed and wanted a king, because the prophet Samuel was a poor administrator attempting to do too much by himself. Shortly after becoming king, Israel needed Saul to lead them into battle quickly. They needed the element of surprise, because they were outnumbered. Saul conscientiously would not begin the battle until proper sacrifice was made. So they waited for Samuel. They waited beyond all reasonable time limits. The men lost spirit. Some hid while others just went back home. Originally, they were outnumbered ten to one. Now, it is fifty to one. It was an intolerable circumstance. Surely God had better battle sense than did his servant Samuel, and so surely God would accept the sacrifice of a responsible and conscientious king. Samuel shows up only in time to castigate Saul.

What a set up preachers have! They can be as derelict as they please. But since they preach the sermons against sin, they get to choose who the sinners are. Later, Saul issues some battle orders that his son doesn't even hear and when he does hear, Jonathan scoffs at his father's orders. Saul receives more commands from the pompous prophet and follows them as best he can only to discover that he has omitted some minor detail. He is subjected to another tirade. The sneakiness of those whom he has most respected keeps him off balance. His suspicious nature is a symptom of the deterioration of his undermined social self. And who knows but what Samuel is responsible for Saul's decline?

Does that version sound familiar to you? Probably not. But the hints of that version are there. And after all, it wasn't Saul's friends who wrote the book.

Samuel is tardy, prophetic, hard-nosed, and compassionate. Saul is religiously well-intentioned, pragmatic, and impulsive. What we have here is a failure to communicate. A failure between king and prophet, father and son, a general and his troops, and even between the Bible and the reader.

Sometimes it is difficult for our religious selves to speak to our political selves. The family could well learn better communications. Employee-employer or superior-subordinate relations often suffer due to muddled communications. And sometimes, even God seems to stutter.

We usually read these stories with Samuel as hero and Saul as the goat. I hope you can see that this is not entirely the case. Each of us has been wronged and each of us has been wrong at the point of communications. It is important for us to see the checkerboard quality of our lives. Samuel is so very right much of the time. He is the Lord's prophet. His remarks on obedience over sacrifice show insight. They are profound. But this does not prevent him from being very wrong. A point which we tend to ne-glect. Saul is so very wrong much of the time. He was an arrogant, impetuous man. But, this does not preclude the possibility of his being right occasionally. A point which we tend to neglect.

How can we do a better job of communication? Two suggestions which are neither as obvious nor as easy as they will seem.

Learn to listen.

Listening is hard work. It is a skill to be devel-oped. It is a talent to be practiced. This is so be-cause we need to learn to hear more than just the words.

Learn to listen with your mind. We don't hear with our ears. We hear with our brains. The ears simply send the signals which our brains interpret as sounds. But I didn't say learn to hear with your brain, You already do that. Learn to hear with your mind. The brain interprets what the sound says. The mind interprets what the communication means.

Counselors sometimes use a question as a diagnostic tool. One such question is "Why are you telling me this now?" You, me, this, now, are the four keys in that question. Any one of them might unlock the troubled message which the client is sending.

Listening with the mind enlists all the senses. What do you see? What do you hear other than words? What do you feel? What do you expect? What do you remember?

At one Christmas family reunion, a cousin brought one of her deaf students to share the holidays with our sprawling family. Somewhere during the raucous celebration, my brother and I attempted some magic tricks. We never fooled the deaf girl. In fact, she sometimes did not even get the point of the trick. Our problem, not hers, was that we could not distract her with our words. Listening with your mind means that you do not let what people say distract you from what they mean.

"Can I go over to Joel's house?"

"Yes."

"Then can I go over to Stephanie's house?"

"Sure."

"Well, can I go over to G.B.'s house?"

What is being asked of the father? Maybe permission to play with friends. Maybe a definition of the boundaries. Maybe an indication that I love him enough to say, "No."

Learn to listen with your heart. To care is the first secret of listening. Words seldom mean what the dictionary says. They mean what the heart declares them to mean. I am often surprised at what people heard me say in a sermon. Sometimes, my heart expands the words I use. I hope not too often does my spoken message contradict my lived message. But it happens. And, of course, sometimes the hearts of the listeners are tuned to a different wave length and they hear what they need to hear even though I did not directly say what they heard.

A man told a counselor that in fifty years of marriage, he had never known his wife to admit a mistake. With patience, the counselor was able to lead the couple to recognize her massive insecurity which would not allow such an admission. What a difference listening with the heart would have made!

How many times Saul must have reached out to Samuel! But Samuel only hears him at the end, if even then.

A second suggestion is equally obvious and equally difficult.

Learn the value of sharing yourself.

If you do learn to disclose yourself to others, there will be two profound discoveries.

You are worth sharing. Paul's expression "my gospel" says so much to me. It says that our slogan "Jesus saves" is an incomplete testimony. It is meaningless until I confess "Jesus saves me." "We are bought with a price." That declares our worth and it says that we are worth sharing.

Why is obedience better than sacrifice? Because obedience is a more direct and personal relationship than is sacrifice. And God values us. He wants to be with us and hear from us. Until you hear the gospel with your insides—that is until you value yourself—you will not be able to share yourself.

"She asks such silly questions," he complained. "She already knows the answers." She doesn't want answers. She wants him.

"Where are you, Adam?" What are you doing here, Elijah?" Silly questions if all God wanted were answers.

Others are worth the effort. It is difficult and risky to share yourself with someone else. But people are worth it.

Samuel runs in long enough to give an order. He rips Saul for the poor job he is doing. He tells him how God will curse him if he bungles the next assignment and runs off. Nothing shared. No companionship. Saul needs a share of Samuel. Must he be only God's messenger? "And what about you, Samuel? Speak for yourself. Will you despise me if I goof up this assignment? Haven't you got time for coffee? What's your hurry?" How often did Saul cry out for help? But, of course, he was head and shoulders above every other Israelite and big boys never cry.

What if one day Saul said, "I'm afraid that somewhere out there is a Philistine who is bigger, stronger, and quicker with his weapons than I am. What am I going to do, Samuel?" And what if Samuel responded, "I know how you feel, Saul. Because, you see, I was afraid you were going to ask me that and some days, I just don't know what God wants us to do. And it scares me."

Who knows—they might have become good friends.

There are a few who find communication a talent. Most of us find it a task. All of us should find that it is a necessity.

Preached at Austin Heights Baptist Church, Nacogdoches, TX 9/20/70

THE GREAT I AM
God said to Moses, 'I AM WHO I AM.'
Exodus 3:13-14

Comedian playing Moses: Who are you?
Voice off stage: Tell them I am what I am.
Comedian: Well, I'm glad we got that cleared up!

The line is funny to the audience because they never have understood that verse and they enjoy sharing their sense of puzzlement. Well, today I am going to explain it to you. We may not have time left over for questions.

The answer given Moses sounds like non-sense to some. It seems to be a profound philosophical comment to others. Whatever, it is basic to the Old Testament understanding of God. It is foundational in any discussion of the Exodus people. From this passage we can say at least three things about God.

God Is The God Of Revelation.

Contrary to gods which men make and to whom we give characteristics, God comes to man and shows himself. God reveals himself in the constant process of acting out his name. There is a sense in which this name is an anonymous name. It is not a name like Mars or Zeus or Apollo or Ra. It is a verb. It is one form of the verb "to be." In this verse it is translated "I am what I am" or "I will be what I will be" or "I cause to be." It shows up in other parts of the Old Testament in variations. For instance, in Exodus 33 God says to Moses: "I will show mercy on whom I will show mercy."

The Name "I am" is just the first name and God is showing us constantly his middle names. I am the God of Abraham, Isaac, and Jacob. I am the Lord who brought you out of Egypt, out of the house of bondage. This is not an abstract, philosopher's god. This is not the kind of god that sophomores fabricate in a bull session. This is the real God who reveals himself.

Moses has to be able to say he represents a God who can do what he claims. He must bear credentials that vindicate his claim to lead an Exodus. God says, "Tell them that I can say I AM." No other god can do that.

God reveals himself by saying to us I am active in your life. I am your heritage. I am your present. I am your hope. And yet, as rich as that revelation is, God is yet a mystery. This revelation is open to so broad and so deep an interpretation that we must realize immediately that the concept of a real, live God who comes to us is beyond our comprehension. The Atta Nisa, a Jewish prayer for feast days makes the point.

> Thou art!
> The hearing of the ear,
> The seeing of the eye
> Cannot reach Thee;
> No How or Why or Where
> Can lead us to Thee.
> Thou art!
> Hidden is Thy secret,
> Who may fathom it!
> Deep, so deep
> Who can find it!

The mystery of God reminds us that God has to be a God of revelation because there is no other way man can know God.

God Is The God Of Relationship.

Before Moses asks about the name of God, God was already revealing that name when he told Moses that he could depend upon God's promises: ". . . for I will be with you." The name of God is often posed in such a way as to bring out this vital truth. God says to us, "I am active in some way related to you." As you read and as you experience the Exodus, you learn some of the words that describe our relationship with God.

One of the words is **sovereign**. The Exodus treaty which we call the covenant was a treaty between a sovereign and his vassals. Now, we rejoice in the idea Jesus has given us of God as Father. That is such a warm concept. But let us not deny the value of the Old Testament picture of God as sovereign. Against Pharoah, we need a greater sovereign. Against the bandit chieftains of the desert, we need a greater leader. We need the experience of knowing one with sovereign authority and power.

Another word that describes the relationship of Exodus God and Exodus people is **election**. We have used the word already and will continue to use it as the Exodus is discussed. Purely put, the Exodus is nothing more than an act of election. Here it is again: I am saying that God reveals his relation to us in the scandal of particularity. You want to know about a God who loves everybody and loves everywhere and I say that God chose to be active in the Exodus and he lives with Exodus people.

But don't you see? This is not to say that God is capricious. To say that God is everywhere as a starting point for a philosophy is the same as saying that God is nowhere. With great purpose in his action God says, "I am the Exodus God. I am in this place at this time for this purpose. I am with you." Only if I am convinced that God is with me—only then can I hope to try to convince you that God can be with you. Eventually, that thought can expand our minds to the realization that God can be with anybody, anywhere. It is through the "scandal" of coming to particular people that God chooses to come to everybody.

Do you see the awesome implication in this concept? We have been taken in as junior partners in the task of revelation. We are responsible to know God and to share our taste of the divine. That brings up another word that describes the relationship: **obedience**. The Ten Commandments are not so much a set of rules—and certainly not a set of arbitrary rules. They are further revelation about God and instruction about our relationship.

"I am the Lord God who brought you out of the land of Egypt out of the house of bondage"—this tells us something of God's name. The text continues with a definition of who we are:

> You are those who have forsworn other gods.
> You are those who do not carve pictures of that
>   which is not photographable.
> You are those who do not casually bear God's
>   great Name.
> You are careful stewards of God's time.
> You are the respecters of God's representa-
>   tives in your home.
> You do not wrench life from your brothers.

You do not abuse marriage.
You do not take another's property.
You do not rob another of his reputation.
Your hearts are not drowned in selfish greed.

That is somehow all the middle names of God.

God is the God who is related to us—and yet the Name of God fiercely preserves his independence. If Moses says to God, "Well, I can't go running around acting important without a god's name. We have got to have a name for you. What shall we call you?" God responds, "I am what I am!" "I will be what I will be!" or as the margin of the American Standard Version has it, "I am because I am!" No one in all creation can make that kind of independent statement. James speaks of our salvation which is according to the counsel of his will. Who is God's counselor? The will of God. How is God's will determined? By listening to his own advice. God is as he determines he will be. And that gives assurance to us. Our relationship is that of the weak leaning upon independent strength.

God Is The Living God.

History is the process of learning God's name. God is yet revealing to us exactly who he is. He is the God of Abraham, Isaac, Joseph, Moses, David, Isaiah, Amos, Jesus, Paul, Augustine, Calvin, Luther. He is the God who brought us together. He is our history. That means he is a living God.

That means that this is neither a static nor a dead universe. That means that history is not about to play out on us. That means purpose and meaning can still be found. That means that we—who are yet an Exodus kind of people—we are going someplace. God is the living God.

I hope that I have whetted your appetite for learning more about the significance of the Name of God. It is a foundational concept for the study of the New Testament. But more than this, it will open up the New Testament to you. We usually hear it said that the New Testament helps to explain the Old. Actually, the reverse is true. For instance, consider the importance of the repeated Old Testament theme of God's name beginning "I am . . . ."

Now read the book of John.

The woman at the well says that she knows that one day the Messiah will come and Jesus says, "I am he, the one speaking to you." To the crowds he says, "I am the bread of life." And "I am the light of the world." The religious elite claim to be descendants of Abraham so Jesus fires their anger by saying, "Before Abraham was born, I am." In John 10 we find Jesus saying, "I am the door of the sheepfold." And he says, "I am the good Shepherd." Beside the grave of Lazarus, he says, "I am the resurrection and the life." In his final moments with the disciples, he says at one point, "I am the way and the truth and the life." He also says, "I am the true vine and my father is the vine dresser . . . I am the vine and you are the branches."

Always the expression "I am" is an emphatic form. It is not the casual term as when one would say, "I am hungry, I am tired, I am here." And the ones who heard usually understood that Jesus was using a form of expression that belongs properly to God as revealed in the Old Testament.

Perhaps this helps interpret that scene in Gethsemane. Here they come, armed as though they were going to storm a Black Panther's apartment. Jesus asks of them, "Whom do you seek?" And they respond, "Jesus, the Nazarene." He says to them, "I am (he)." They fall away from him and he has to encourage them to arrest him if he is whom they seek.

What irony! One Exodus commentator makes it clear that the Exodus God was constantly reviled yet was always Lord. Jesus stood there affirming the Exodus revelation. What we learn of God through Jesus Christ confirms the Exodus experience. Our God is a living God who reveals himself as related to us.

One of the Johannine * "I am" passages especially parallels the Old Testament formula and makes clear what our relation to God through Jesus Christ should be.

> I am the vine, you the branches. Those who abide in me and I in them bear much fruit, because apart from me you can do nothing. [John 15:5]

> *But Moses said to God, "If I come to the Israelites and say to them, 'The God of your ancestors has sent me to you,' and they ask me 'What is his name?' what shall I say to them?" God said to Moses, "I AM WHO I AM."*

*Johannine: relating to the apostle John or to the Gospel or epistles of John in the New Testament.

Preached at Austin Heights Baptist Church, Nacogdoches, TX 1/31/1971

TWO CHEERS FOR DAD

We see plainly that the Lord has been with
you ...
Genesis 26:12-35

My grandfather was meeting a train carrying
the governor of Oklahoma. Grandfather Trammell
was the representative of the Chamber of Commerce
who was to officially greet the governor. When "Al-
falfa Bill" got off the train, Clark Trammell decided that
he was not greetable and walked off the platform leav-
ing the governor there. My grandparents were some-
thing else.

I would love to tell some stories about my chil-
dren. They are something else, too. Sometimes I feel
that I am only a historical pause between ancestors
and descendants. Something like an Isaac.

Have you ever read what the commentaries
say about Isaac? He is called the patriarch without a
history! "An ordinary son of a great father and the or-
dinary father of a great son." One commentator says,
"Isaac's wife Rebecca was ambitious, energetic and
shrewd and she managed her husband to her heart's
content." Another writes, "Isaac, who can scarcely be
described as a memorable personality in his own
right, is important chiefly as a link in the patriarchal
chain. Continuity is essential, but the vitality of the
line will now depend on the woman who is to become
Jacob's mother."

Do you know how to outline the book of Gene-
sis? Chapters 1-11 concern Primeval History. Chap-
ters 12-50, the remainder of the book, concern the
Patriarchs. And those last chapters are divided in
three sections: chapters 12-24 tell Abraham's story,

38

chapters 25-36 tell Jacob's story, and chapters 37-50 tell Joseph's story. Notice anyone missing from the outline? Old Isaac. He is sort of a pause between acts1 and 2.

And something else about Genesis. In chapter 26, there are some anecdotes about Isaac, we didn't read them all, which are identical to stories about Abraham. In fact, the story about the patriarch telling Abimelech that his wife was his sister is told once about Isaac and twice about Abraham. I don't have time to go into details, but scholars seem to feel that the incident really happened to Isaac and is only attributed to the better known personality of Abraham. How about that? He didn't do much but someone else gets the credit for what he did!

Here is a man with an illustrious father, a shrewd wife, and unmanageable children. The text is a story of him not standing up for his rights and of him redoing what his father had done before him. He is good subject matter for a presentation of the decline of dad. It is an occasion of honoring father, but it is difficult to rouse three full cheers for the old man.

Well, I want to tell you something. I think old dad is a better man than he gets credit for. I think Isaac had a lot of good things going for him. I believe he was a man of quiet integrity and could be a model for us.

Isaac possessed a quiet strength that did not have to be brandished about in a display of power.

He could have drowned himself in a sea of self-hatred because he was not the hero-man-of-faith-friend-of-God that his father was. He could have longed to be the daring and resourceful masked rider that was his younger son. But he did not pine away for either a past or a future life. His own life had its own attractive strength.

Many of us neglect our strengths while wishing for one power that belongs to someone else. You must ask yourself, "For what reason do I want power?" An honest answer would be, "I want the power to be able to make things go my way." We usually see power as the ability to manipulate. To have power means to be able to make people do things my way either because of my physical strength, economic power, sexual hold over another, or through any number of various shades of tantrums.

Isaac had the strength to be able to allow the other man to have his way. How easy it would be for the son, or wife, or neighbor, or enemy of a man like Isaac to say he is weak. He has given in. He will not stand up for his rights. Ah, but that is not the case. Isaac has a rare strength. And we could use more like him. He had the power to voluntarily relinquish his rights.

A closely related asset was Isaac's quiet self-assurance which did not require flamboyant notoriety.

You know, some people who are so publicly cocky are really crying out for acceptance and assurance. They are saying, "Does everyone know I'm here? Please look at me and say that you think I am important." Isaac was not so insecure that he had to parade to get attention.

Larson and Osborne open their book <u>The Emerging Church</u> with a story about a business man who would calmly ignore the phone during conferences with client. His explanation sounds like that story of the New Englander. "It is there for my convenience—not to tyrannize me." Few people are this self-assured, this free from the insecurities of life.

The first point about Isaac asks the question, "What do I want to do and am I able to do it?" Now we are dealing with the question, "How do I view my struggle toward my goal? Am I doing an adequate, inadequate, super, or dumb job?" In other words, whose approval am I seeking? Is it my goal to say something meaningful or is it my goal to be commended for having said something meaningful? Is it your goal to do something significant in terms of ministry or is it your goal to collect accolades? If you can be honest with yourself, and learn to accept yourself and live with yourself, you can free yourself from some of the anguish of social insecurity.

I give Isaac a good cheer for his two quiet strengths and his acceptance of himself. I could almost give a third cheer. **Isaac possessed a quiet love of his family.** Unfortunately, this does not seem to be well communicated. It is too quiet. His love is seen primarily in the pain which they caused him.

There seems to be so little communication in the modern family. Again, I believe we must ask, "What do we want of our families?" As a parent, what do you want of your children? Do you want to manipulate them or to guide them? Do you want the kind of children that are convenient for you to have around or do you want them to fully become themselves?

And from the other side of it. As children, let's learn a little caution in judging parents. Let us learn from Abimelech that there may be more to the man than meets the eye.

To be a father means that one has a link with the past and with the future. You have received and you give. Yet you cannot enter either the past or the future except in a very limited way. Integrity means to be the man you are in the time you have. If our sons are generous, they will appreciate our integrity. If not, well, integrity doesn't have to be commended to be valid.

Preached at Austin Heights Baptist Church, Nacogdoches, TX 6/20/1971

SIBLING RIVALRY

What if Joseph still bears a grudge against us
and pays us back in full for all the wrong that we did
to him?
Genesis 50:15-21

In one of O. Henry's stories, two parties to a
feud find themselves the sole survivors when the
smoke clears away. Bereft of relatives, Cal Harkness
disappears from the Cumberland Mountains and gets
a job driving an express wagon in New York City. A
year later, Sam Folwell, discovering his new place of
residence, follows him to cancel out the Harkness
clan once and for all.

Sam starts out on the New York sidewalks
looking for Cal, his pistol strapped to his side and feud
hate-red in his eyes. He walks the busy streets all
morning, darting nervous glances over his shoulder,
fearful that Cal may be waiting in ambush behind a
door or window to shoot him first. At noon, Sam
stands at the corner of a giant intersection. People
rush at him from four directions. No faces turn toward
him and no voices confirm his presence. Suddenly,
the foolish fear that he is dead and disembodied
seizes Sam.

"Nobody can see me," he cries, as the city
smites him with loneliness. There is no response.

"The Rankin's hog weighed more'n ours," he
shouts at a plump passerby. The fat man hurries on
and buys a bag of roasted chestnuts to mask his
alarm.

A club tickles Sam in the ribs. "Move along,"
says the cop. "You've been loafing here long
enough." As Sam retreats across the street, an auto-

mobile grazes his knee. A cab bumps him with its hubcap. The cabby purples the air with threats and profanity. A streetcar motorman clangs his bell and a newsboy joins the fray by pelting him with banana peels.

About this time, Cal Harkness, whose work is over for the day, turns the corner. There, three yards away, he faces his blood enemy, the last Folwell, who has come to obliterate the last Harkness. Unarmed and unprepared, Cal wavers, but Sam's sharp eyes pick him out of the crowd. Sam rushes toward him and reaches——but not for his gun. He reaches for Cal's hand. "Howdy, Cal, I'm darned glad to see you." At the corner of Broadway and Fifth Avenue, the Cumberland enemies shake hands.

[*Squaring the Circle* in <u>The Best Short Stories of O. Henry</u>, Modern Library (New York: Random House, 1945).]

In O. Henry's story, these enemies learned what we all must learn; they learned that we are all brothers and sisters on the tiny space capsule we call Earth. But within this lesson, we must realize that our close ties to each other should create community rather than competitiveness and rivalry.

The story of Joseph begins with sibling rivalry and ends with community. Joseph was an obnoxious, boastful tattle-tale. And it was no surprise to anyone that his brothers did not wish him well. As a matter of fact, some of them wished him dead. While Joseph was imprisoned in a well so that the brothers could decide his fate, a group of travelers stole him and sold him into slavery. You know the story of the peculiar circumstances that brought Joseph to prominence in

Egypt as an overseer charged with the responsibility of seeing Egypt through the coming famine.

You remember how the brothers then come to Egypt in search of food and, completely unaware that Joseph is even still alive, they are easy prey for Joseph's games. Finally, however, Joseph cannot continue the games and he reveals his identity to them. There is a reconciliation but it is not complete. There are nagging fears which are brought to light later when Jacob is dead. Has Joseph really forgiven the brothers? Or was he merely accommodating his father?

As the Book of Genesis closes, we see the rivalry between these brothers renounced and community achieved through open communication, the acceptance of humanity, and gracious realism. Let me explain.

One avenue to community is open communication.

The brothers were very much afraid of Joseph. But they did not keep this to themselves. They immediately let Joseph know how they felt.

Learning the truth and speaking the truth is a risk. But neither is so great a risk as attempting to build a relationship on speculation or deception.

It is usually a mistake to play the code and guessing games which most of us employ. Humpty Dumpty's remark to Alice characterizes too many of us: "When I use a word, it means just what I choose it to mean—neither more nor less." We might rather say, "When I put on a mask, I am what I appear to be —neither more nor less." The brothers didn't do this. They were afraid and they said so.

Things might have gone better if Joseph had learned this earlier. Several times in the story, he has to leave the room so that no one will see him weep and guess his identity. He is like the New Englander who said to his wife, "You just have no idea how hard it has been to keep from telling you how much I love you."

I enjoy Calvin Coolidge stories. He is supposed to have said, "If you don't say anything, you won't have to repeat it." I have often felt that was good advice. But it isn't! Harold Bosley advises preachers to speak out. And his comments could apply to any human relationship. Bosley writes:

> If he belongs to the great tradition of preaching, he will know that it is better to be wrong than to be silent in the face of the problems that are tormenting the thoughts and lives of his people. It is easy to explain mistakes, for all honest men will understand and sympathize; it is impossible to explain silence, for none will listen.

Communication is vital to community. But it is difficult. You may need to say something several times in different ways before you have properly shared yourself with someone else.

Robert Leslie tells about a conversation where a young man was moaning about the fact that he and his bride had not had the proper time to celebrate their fourth anniversary. They had been married four months. Another man commented that when they had been married longer, they wouldn't be so concerned with such insignificant things. Leslie sensed how that was received and so asked the younger man how he felt about the remark. He was quite hostile in reply. Leslie then asked the older man to repeat what he had tried to say at first. It seems that when the second man had been married four months, his wife was discovered to have T.B. and was subsequently hospitalized for two years. Leslie asked him, "Why didn't you say that in the first place?" The man responded, "I thought I had."

Open communication is something you must work at. But it is worth it. Imagine the false sense of security which the brothers felt at Joseph's banquet. Then imagine how that sense of security was devastated when they found that things were not as they imagined. It shouldn't be too hard to conjure up that feeling because it happens all the time. Open communication is insurance against such falls.

Another avenue of community is acceptance of your humanity.

The brothers are quaking before Joseph when he says to them, "Don't sweat it. I know I'm not God." What a fantastic insight! Earlier, he had been testing them to see if they would again sacrifice a younger brother to enhance their own position. Now, he renounces such a god-like role. He says, in effect, "I realize that I am a man, too, and do not have the prerogative of vengeance."

Isn't this what stands in the way of the realization of community for us? Someone has to play God. Someone has the attitude, "I'm always right. I know who is wrong. I know the proper punishment. My opinion must be sought and honored."

John Claypool tells a story that brings home the force of this insight:

I once knew of a father who had real trouble in adolescence, developing personal honesty. He had a strong, dominating mother who made unreasonable demands on him, and he learned to cope with her by telling lies and thus almost lost contact with reality. After several near-tragic experiences, this man worked back to truthfulness through real struggle and fashioned his adult life on this basis. When his own child entered adolescence and was caught telling a falsehood, this father debated at length on how to respond. His own experience made him doubly anxious about the pitfalls of this habit, and the easiest thing to have done would have been to pick the fruit of his struggle and go in with a lot of abstract lectures on why lying was wrong. The trouble is, the stance of the advice-giver always seems so remote from the problem and the person in need assumes he really cannot understand. After much thought, this father took the other road and dared to share his experiences of lying and his struggle back to integrity with his son. It had a very powerful effect in putting the two closer together . . .

I submit to you that this may sound like a new way for fathers and sons to relate together—weakness to weakness—but I believe it holds great promise. I, too, believe there is great promise in being able to step away from playing the role of God. Relating weakness to weakness, accepting our humanity, is a way to communicate.

The final route to community indicated in this story is gracious realism.

Joseph says to his brothers, "You meant wrong but God worked it out to be good." Joseph was realistic. He did not ignore or deny the evil intentions of this brothers. But he was not caustic either.

Haven't you known people to try to ignore or cover up ugly reality? I went to visit a lady in the hospital who had a hopeless problem in a medical sense. We had had some good visits though and I was prepared to have a conversation again. But her sister was there. She introduced herself, asked me to say a little prayer and literally pulled me out of the room. She could not tolerate her sister's condition and would not allow me to accept the reality of it either.

It doesn't help to cover up reality. People do this with apologies. So often people cannot tolerate apologies. They will attempt to destroy the reality that is there before them. Joseph's model was a good one. Gracious realism: you meant wrong but things are good now.

Rivalry marks many a family, many a church, and certainly this town. Open communication, acceptance of our common humanity, and gracious realism could help. What are you going to do about it?

Preached at Austin Heights Baptist Church, Nacogdoches, TX 7/30/1972

49

ON LOSING THE TUNE

> … Then the Lord was angry with Solomon be-
> cause his heart had turned away from the Lord the
> God of Israel.
> I Kings 11:1-13

In the book <u>The Autobiography of Charles Dar-
win</u>, Darwin tells of the pleasure he received from po-
etry up to his early 30's. He enjoyed the graphic arts
but even more, music. However, Darwin came to the
point where he wrote:

> But now for many years, I cannot endure to
> read a line of poetry. I have tried lately to
> read Shakespeare, and found it so
> intolerably dull that it nauseated me. I have
> almost lost my taste for pictures and music.
> My mind seems to have become a kind of
> machine for grinding general laws out of
> large collections of facts.

As a young man, B.F. Westcott was a fine
singer whose talents were often recruited for choral
work. But later, as a bishop in the Church of England,
he had no time for singing and lost his sense of tune.
Norman Hope says of the bishop, "If he ventured to
join in a hymn, people could never tell what tune he
was singing."

Hope also tells of William Graham Sumner who
began his teaching career with a fine Christian testi-
mony. However, in later years as he immersed him-
self in his lectures at Yale, he lost interest in formal
religion. Sumner observed about himself, "I never
consciously gave up a religious belief. It was as if I

had put my beliefs into a drawer and, when I opened it, there was nothing there at all."

There is a pattern in these three lives, a pattern of the loss of their gift or gifts. It is a pattern that can be traced in the life of Solomon. We have a positive picture of Solomon due to the fact that the writer wants to put Solomon in a good light. So, as the story reads, the problems of his life are minimized and saved to the last. But, to the writer's credit, they are presented and those who read the whole story cannot miss the significance of the final chapter on Solomon's life.

Solomon ascended to the throne at the time of Israel's greatest prosperity. The borders were extended to the maximum. The people were at peace. In many respects, it was a time of great promise.

But there are somber overtones to the story. Under Solomon, Israel reached a high point of luxury and extravagance. A large number of the people were in the employ of the government. And Solomon practiced foreign policy by marriage. For each of his wives, he found it necessary to provide facilities for their national rites and customs. Ultimately, this meant the dulling of his own religious convictions and led him into the practice of idolatry.

Solomon ended his reign under pressure from three sides: Hadad of Edom organized a revolt aimed at cutting off Solomon's trade from the Gulf of Akabah. Rezon of Syria seized Damascus to endanger his holdings in the North. And Jeroboam of Ephraim, employed by Solomon as collector of taxes from Ephraim, saw the abuses and oppression of the people and agitated for revolution.

Solomon is known for the wisdom cult, magnificent buildings, thriving commerce, and an era free from war; but he was also responsible for religious stagnation and political and economic oppression.

What happened? **His life countermanded his prayers.**

He had prayed first for wisdom so that he might lead his people with insight and justice. Yet the direction of his life was toward selfish novelty and indulgence. He turned his back on the very people he had intended to help.

He prayed, secondly, at the dedication of the temple that it would come to pass, that worship would become the central reality of the kingdom. Instead, his actions led in the opposite direction toward idolatry.

Why did Solomon invalidate his own prayers? **His life contradicted his acts of worship.** This happened because he mishandled, or abused, or neglected his gifts.

Solomon stumbled over his success. He was irresponsible with his prosperity. He had the answer to his first prayer: the gift of wisdom. He also had the bonus gifts of wealth and power. But the blessing of a gift can become a curse if it is mishandled, abused, or neglected.

The gift of wisdom brought competing commitments into Solomon's life. Most cultures of his day had a wisdom school. These wisdom schools were in touch with one another. There is a universality to wisdom. So the sages of one nation had communications with those of other cultures. Politicians and prophets tend to emphasize borders but businessmen and philosophers cross them. There were no prophets in Solomon's court, only men of commerce and sages.

We applaud Socrates because his philosophy was greater than Athens. Some men can handle the gift of universal wisdom but it brought problems to Solomon. Trafficking with those of other cultures put him square in the middle of the tornado of competing commitments and he lost his grip on the worship of the true God.

The Masoretic text of the Hebrew Old Testament names one of the idols Solomon worshiped, "Ashtoreth," but the correct spelling is "Astarte." Astarte was a fertility goddess. The reason for the change in spelling the name was the practice of the Masorets of substituting the vowels of the word *bosheth*, meaning shame, for idolatrous names. The gift of wisdom became the cause of shame for Solomon.

Solomon possessed the gift of wealth. Because Christianity has been historically a religion of the have-nots, our tradition is suspicious of money. There are good reasons for this. Unfortunately, our suspicion of wealth is too often our undoing. We have seldom seen the development of a strong doctrine of responsible stewardship. Maybe that was Solomon's problem. At any rate, he did not fully appreciate the debilitating nature of wealth. He mishandled this gift and it brought him to ruin.

Another gift was his position of power which meant to him prestige, prowess, notoriety or fame. This can be a most useful gift. Numerous theologians, ethicists, and sociologists have emphasized the value of influencing those who have the vantage point of power. Ah, but the wine of prestige-power-fame is intoxicating. And Solomon went on a binge that soiled his good name.

The perversion of his prayers was in the mishandling of circumstances where he could have brought to bear his wisdom, wealth, and power.

Recently I quoted the late Rabbi Abraham Heschel who wrote, "Mankind will not perish for lack of information; it may collapse for want of appreciation." We have the gift of a quantity of information; but is it possible that we lack an appreciation for both the potential and the danger of our gifts?

Just as fire can be a useful tool or a destructive, consuming master, the gifts which we possess can enhance life or devour it.

The gift of organization can produce ordered living or programmed monotony. The gift of communication can be used for teaching and sharing or for despotic harangue. The gift of worship can enhance living in grace or deteriorate to the chains of superstition. The gift of imagination can make for a creative living or for unprincipled fiendishness. The gift of a heritage can provide structure and meaning or can be perverted into the suffocation of lifeless, antiquated, reactionary traditionalism. The gift of commerce, the ability to make money can be used for the enhancement of personality and the extension of the powers of life; but the perversion of the gift of making money leads to the worship of the gods of acquisition and statue.

There lies within the gifts which you have the promise of hope and the danger of death.

Only the inspired genius of humanity could produce Handel's Messiah,

                A Bach fugue,
            A Frank Lloyd Wright building,
            a sewing machine,
            Parliament,
                libraries,
                    ocean transport vessels.

        Only the perverted genius of humanity could
produce the attack on Pearl Harbor,
        Dacau,
            My Lai,
                the Daisy Cutter anti-personnel bomb,
                    Houston's homosexual murder ring.

        The gift you possess enables you to achieve
greatness, or foulness, or—or perhaps even worse—
mediocrity.
        Ross Coggins, once a missionary to Indonesia,
for a while on the staff of the Christian Life Commis-
sion, stirred my thinking with the remark, "An individ-
ual has the privilege of choosing mediocre living; but
there is a cost for lesser loyalties." Another way to put
Coggins' point would be: when you pervert or restrict
your gifts rather than enhance them, you are commit-
ting suicide.
        Ross Coggins concluded a sermon one night
by taking a flower from in front of the pulpit and count-
ing the various excuses we give for delaying a serious
look at the stewardship of our lives. With each ex-
cuse cited, he tore a petal off the flower. Finally, with
but one petal left, he spoke of the decision to be re-
sponsible about life. But it is a decision of too little,
too late.

Well, it's your life. What are you going to do with it?

Preached at Austin Heights Baptist Church, Nacogdoches, TX 9/23/1973

ANYBODY HOME?

Then the Lord God said, "It is not good that the
man should be alone ...
Genesis 2: 18-25

Kenneth Wilson tells of his son learning to be a
ham radio operator. One of the interesting things
about radio is the code language used. For instance,
if you wanted to talk to just anyone on the radio you
would send the code letters CQ followed by your own
call letters. Wilson comments on this:

How the letters CQ came to be used for this
purpose, I do not know. Judging from some
other radio amateur code abbreviations, I
wouldn't be surprised if once upon a time it had
something to do with "Seek you." Anyway, that
is basically what it means. Is anybody there?
Will somebody let me know I am not alone? I
am seeking you.

Wilson goes on to speculate on the number of
CQ's that are sent out daily, not just the amateur radio
kind, but those requests or pleas that all give or re-
ceive which say, "Is anybody else there?"

In every part of our lives we are on one side or
the other of the plea for relationship. CQ, CQ, CQ,
the signal is in the air all about us. Unfortunately,
there are too few receivers either turned on or tuned
in to the signal. Well, sometimes that is the way it
must be. We are not capable of receiving all signals.
Some messages must be tuned out if others are to be
tuned in. So it isn't necessarily all bad that some
messages are not communicated. That's the way the
world is. And besides, for most of us, if the big bad

world doesn't want to listen, then we can go home to the warm and receptive environs of the family. And there we will be heard.

Today, at a time of emphasis on the family, I have planned to talk about the question, "Anybody home?" That question is warm and cozy in my memory. The only fitting response to it, that is, the only response that feels comfortable to me, is, "We"—or "I"—"We're in here!" It's a cheery greeting that locates the family for the returning member. Of course someone is home. Although the surface meaning of the question assumes two possibilities: (a) someone is home or (b) no one is home, the real intent has nothing to do with (b). It is an announcement which says (1) I am home, (2) I know you are here, but (3) I don't know precisely where, (4) so respond that I might find you.

To prove that this is what is meant, think about that rare possibility of the house being vacant. No one is home. In that case, again, I can only think of one response: "That's funny! I wonder where everybody has gone?" In other words, I'm stumped. This is an unexpected alternative.

Well, from this beginning I anticipated building my remarks around the concept of "being home to one another." However, there are some problems with the concept. In the first place, none of you ever stay home, so you wouldn't know what I was talking about. The second problem is more complex and devastating to the concept.

Recently when Henry Kissinger got married, a writer in TIME magazine made the comment that now he had someone to come home to. As you might expect, a letter to the editor charged that such a statement was sexist and betrayed a male chauvinist attitude, etc.

And it is true that the image, which is a part of my memory, is that Mother was always home. That is a warm and comfortable memory for me. But it is a concept which can be an entrapment and problematical for my wife. Occasionally, the husband/father is the one at home in our household.

Well, as you can see, I have had some second thoughts about what I wanted to say to you today. And after second and other subsequent thoughts, I have found that what I really wanted to say to you at first is what I really want to say to you now.

My point has nothing to do with the gender of the person waiting or the one returning. Incidentally, it has nothing to do with coming home in the physical sense of walking in the front door. My point has to do with the description of humanity in Genesis 2 where the profound insight is stated: "It isn't good for a person to be alone."

Every man needs a woman—which is not a sexual statement although that element cannot be ignored. And I do not choose to ignore it. At the heart of it, the text says that **every person needs a correspondent.**

God senses the loneliness of Adam and says I must make him a partner, literally a counterpart, one like unto, a complement, or one who corresponds to. In all creation there was no one who could respond to the man on his level and to whom the man could respond on par. The individual person needs a corresponding person.

This statement gives a high view of human relationships. It is followed by a chapter which tells us that the Fall of humanity into sin is the source of alienation. We make much of the fact that sin led to the killing of brother by brother. But even before that, a gulf is indicated in the ability of male and female to reconcile themselves to one another.

The whole of the Bible reflects on this estrangement. Along side the lofty insights of Genesis 2, there is the Old Testament reflection of a patriarchal society. Within that society the woman was not much more than a womb: a source of fresh males, or a pitfall: the way to destruction for the unsuspecting or careless males. Even the lofty passages of Proverbs speak of women in functional rather than relational terms. The whole of society centered on the patriarch and the women in his life gained their value and identity from him. Even in the New Testament the radical attitude of Jesus in relating to people and the stereotype shattering cry from Paul that in Christ there is neither Jew nor Greek, bond nor free, male nor female, are easily lost in the cultural baggage which surrounds them.

The same is true today. Many people are making and remaking the great discovery of the ultimate value of personhood. But the priests and priestesses who preside over the rituals of the discovery of personhood within womanhood, bring along their own excess baggage of frustrations, taboos, or esoteric structuring.

Why is it necessary to show women can be equal to men by proving how foul-mouthed or obscene a woman can become?

But let me say again, my point is not whether a woman can pursue certain careers, or any career. It is not who stays home and does the housework. The point is surely unrelated to clothing styles. It isn't a matter of who is waiting behind the door and who returns to go through the doorway. The point is in the meeting beyond the doorway—whenever and wherever such meetings happen. The question which addresses itself to the point is: Do two people greet each other and correspond to one another?" Do they, in effect, say to one another, "You are bone as my bones, flesh as my flesh, we are suited for one another?" Do the two stand—or lie—together eye to eye with the shared realization: "you are to me as I am to you."

The heart of the Genesis passage can be applied to any human relationship but let me simply apply this point to the marriage relationship with two statements.

First, it is not good to be alone; therefore, share through communication. By communication, I mean far more than talk. It takes work, a lot of work, to develop communication skills. You must work at giving and receiving through hearing, seeing, touching. We are sensual creatures; that is, we live through our senses. We communicate in many ways other than just the concepts we express in words. It is popular to say that the female needs a lot of touching. I'm not so sure that there is anything exclusively feminine about the need for correspondence with all the senses.

Jim Croce sang:
When I tried to tell you, the words just came
out wrong.
So I had to say, "I love you," with a song.

Now think about the fact that some of us don't talk so well and don't sing so "purdy." So if you can't correspond with someone with all of your senses, then you are missing a lot of "I love you" in other messages.

I am appalled at the number of times I have missed the point simply because I only listened to the surface meaning of someone's words.

Second, it is not good to be alone. If you would have a partner, that means you must share on par level. Have you heard about the child who wrote, "The Christian religion allows a man to have only one wife. This system is called monotony." Well, that is all too true in any one way relationship.

If a couple forces themselves into some narrow role expectations, then their relationship will be a monotonous one indeed. But there is no need for a good healthy relationship to be monotonous. If two people are growing together on a corresponding level, then they are always new to one another and the relationship is alive and fresh no matter how many years it bridges.

Of course, it takes work to realize a correspondent relationship. We are programmed otherwise. David Edens says that we love girls because they exist. We love boys because of what they will become. Upon boys, we place the burden of proving themselves. Upon girls, we place the burden of attractability. Listen: "What are you going to be when you grow up?" "How fast can you run?" "My aren't you pretty?" "You certainly look sweet." "Who made your dress?" You see we get programmed into roles which we play. We need to be drawn out as persons and relate.

If we could learn to relate on level as adult to adult, then we wouldn't play parent-child games. At Interpreter's House, James told me, "I think you've been playing father to your wife and she wants a husband." That was true of me and is true of many a married couple. We can make room in larger social circles for the perennial parent or the constant child. But there isn't room in a healthy marriage for a mother/son or father/daughter relationship. Oh, you might get by with it. But it is far from best for you.

Kenneth Pepper tells of struggling to get a discussion group going with some young married couples. Finally, he got something generated by asking what they did for Christmas. He says he knew that would shake something loose because it involves the dynamics of debating whether or not we are adults or still children. Do we have the autonomy of our home or must we dutifully parade back to our parents as their children? That dilemma is never adequately resolved until you learn that you can go back home and face your parents, also on a corresponding level—adult to adult.

The secret to corresponding relationships is learning the reciprocal nature of relating to people. One way relations are at best unproductive and at worst destructive. You can give and receive from anybody. Consider this: Jesus became his mother's Savior. Now that is startling. We seldom expect that our children have anything of value to give us. And let me carry that thought a little further: if you relate to your spouse as parent to child, you probably don't expect anything creative, original, productive or of value out of your child/mate either, do you?

Is anybody home? CQ, CQ, CQ? Ask the question. You might find yourself in an exciting conversation.

Preached at Austin Heights Baptist Church, Nacogdoches, TX 5/12/1974

SMILES

Smiles do not die immediately.

They linger in the cheeks and eyes

And slowly shoulders realize

The calming gift will soon depart

To find its rest within the heart.

I've caught your smile

And for awhile

I will be brighter,

Taller, lighter

Jerry Self

5/22/79

AMNESTY FOR US, TOO

… Making her stand before all of them, they said to him, 'Teacher, this woman was caught in the very act of adultery. Now in the law Moses commanded us to stone such women. Now what do you say?'… 'Let anyone among you who is without sin be the first to throw a stone at her.'
John 7:53 – 8:11

How I wish that there was some wonderful `
   place
Called the Land of Beginning Again,
Where all our mistakes and all our heartaches
And all our poor selfish grief
Could be dropped like a shabby old coat at the
   door,
And never put on again.
<u>The Land of Beginning Again,</u> Luisa Fletcher

I can imagine that if you were caught in the act of adultery, you might also wish for a "Land of Beginning Again." At first glance, this is a simple story: she is caught. She ought to be punished. But we quickly get beyond this superficial simplicity. The motivations of her accusers are not religious nor are they moral. The are politically motivated. Notice she was caught in the act. There would have to be eye witnesses in order for it to be proper to call for the death penalty of stoning. So where is the man? He isn't brought forward. Why? It was not uncommon for a man to quickly excuse another man for an action which is scandalous for a woman. The Old Testament called for the same punishment for them both.

It is quite possible that the whole scene shows the callous use of this woman as a pawn. Her spiritual or moral state is of no concern. She is merely a suitable bait secured to trap Jesus. The absence of the man suggests a possible moral degeneracy which would go to the extreme of plotting with him to set up a trap for her, allowing him his freedom in exchange for cooperation and then, having seined for bait, successfully gone hunting for bigger game.

At first, it is clear that she is guilty and the sentence is the appropriate punishment. Righteousness demands stoning. But as the surface appearance gives way to full reality, we still see her as guilty, but guilt becomes the common denominator.

Guilty? Yes. But how shall she be sentenced? What response can Jesus make to the challenge? The difficulty here needs to be detailed for us. If Jesus had called for a strict adherence to the law and demanded death, it would have meant a separation between himself and the "sinners" who were learning to trust him. Besides that, it is probable that such a decision in favor of Jewish law would have been opposed to a Roman law which may have been instituted about that time, taking capital punishment out of the hands of the Jews. On the other hand, to recommend leniency would have flagrantly encouraged lawlessness.

Leniency would have been unpopular with the strict Jews and, evidently, was unpopular with the early church. This story was, it appears, a part of Luke's gospel; but the ease with which Jesus forgave the woman was a problem for a young church which was attempting to discipline itself sternly. Augustine wrote that the story was suppressed because "some were of light faith" or they wanted "to avoid scandal."

What was Jesus to do? Strict adherence to law would jeopardize his ministry to the outcasts. Leniency might show moral laxity. He scribbles in the dust. He delays. His tactic causes the woman's accusers to puff up even more in their self-righteousness.

The law required the eye witnesses to initiate the stoning. Jesus quotes to them the law. Only . . . not quite. Let the innocent do the stoning. Oh, Jesus! That's too subtle. There is always some obtuse graduate assistant around who, in self-righteous cockiness, will grab rocks and start throwing. You're too subtle! But what happens? One by one, the older ones first, they disappear.

Jesus has walked a narrow tightrope in his response which acknowledges guilt on all levels but disarms dishonest, inequitable revenge.

This scene is often repeated. Jesus came to save, not to condemn the sinners of this world. Yet his very presence becomes the catalyst by which the self-righteous are led to bring judgment upon themselves.

So, the story leaves no question about the woman's guilt but raises the question of the appropriate response to that guilt. And the reason such a question is raised is the reality of the guilt of others.

It is not difficult to see applications on a national scale. As we go through a period of debate on the issue of amnesty, the question,"Who is guilty?" has no common agreement as to the answer. We could easily become a nation of cartoon characters and stereotypes. On the one hand, is a disheveled hippy stoned on drugs belligerently yelling across the Canadian border that he doesn't want our stinking ex-pletive-deleted forgiveness? On the other hand, is a beer bellied VFW commander obstinately refusing to forgive? It would be easy to conjure up such a scene, but isn't it a caricature? Is that a true picture of America?

Well, to be sure, we could find some individuals who fit the roles I have described. But basically, those are stereotypes each side has drawn of the other.

One might more sympathetically describe the Marine lieutenant giving his testimony before numerous Baptist churches. His story is full of courage, loyalty, responsible concern for his men, and sacrifice. You discover he is only 75% of the physical being he used to be before Vietnam. We would like to believe that he represents courageous America.

Or you read of Daniel Ellsberg who was shaken by his Pentagon Papers research which revealed the deceit which hid the fact of "just one war, continuously for a quarter of a century . . . an American war almost from its beginning . . . after all, a foreign aggression. Our aggression." We would like to believe that those who opposed the war were all responsibly opposed to moral evil as they saw it.

We are in danger of becoming the cartoon. Rather than a group of self-righteous men ready to stone an adulteress, we are more like two sullen camps circling one another and the question is, who will be the first to stone whom?

It is self-righteousness that says, "I don't need your forgiveness. I'll stay in Canada." It is self-righteousness that says, "You can't have our forgiveness. Stay in Canada."

We have a tendency to hurry past the unpleasant matters of life and once past them, to pretend they were not there. This is an induced amnesia, not amnesty. And it is socially destructive. Those who will not learn from history are doomed to repeat. If we must divide into two camps with all the right on our side and all the wrong on their side, then we have learned nothing in the century that separates us from the Civil War. A house divided against itself cannot stand.

Henlee Barnett, ethics professor at Southern Seminary, has two sons. One is a conscientious objector and one has served with distinction in Vietnam. That, to me, is a parable of our national scene. There are divergent opinions and diverse actions among us. But we are brothers and sisters.

On the surface the national picture is simple. They are guilty. And the punishment is clear. But reality shows us that guilt is more common and the response to such guilt is more complex. Yes, they are guilty. What is the response to guilt? Mohammad tells us in the seventeenth chapter of the Koran:

> Every man's fate we have fastened about his neck. And we will bring to him on the day of Resurrection a book which shall be offered open; 'Read thy book; thou thyself art accountant enough against thyself this day.'

I've never heard a better description of hell. All right, so amnesia is socially destructive. Isn't there some possibility of responsible forgetting? Can't we find some way to acknowledge guilt and then put it aside?

As a matter of fact, that is exactly what is needed. Let us acknowledge guilt, responsibly face it. And then we can redemptively put it aside.

Rollo May has commented,
> With all its evil Vietnam may, daimonically*
> indeed, represent an occasion in which
> America could achieve an insight into life
> that will be essential to its future. This
> could come about by our gaining a tragic
> sense, an awareness of our own complicity
> in evil, our own participation in automatized,
> dehumanized destructiveness.

We need to update the insight of John Bradford when he watched the criminal on the way to gallows and exclaimed, "There, but for the grace of God, go I."

One by one, beginning with the older ones, they gave up their mission of vengeance. It was Goethe who commented, "One need only grow old to become gentler in one's judgments. I see no fault committed which I could not have committed myself."

There is no question of guilt. The only question is how does one respond to guilt. Robert Jay Lifton is a psychiatrist who has worked extensively with veterans psychologically wounded by war. In his book <u>Home From the War,</u> he talks about two ways of responding to guilt. In my terms, not his, he talks about suicidal guilt and redemptive responsible guilt.

Suicidal guilt is what happens when you become numb, frozen, or desensitized by guilt; or when you lacerate yourself with your guilt. Guilt can be turned inward in a murderous way.

Redemptive responsible guilt is coming back to life through your guilt. It employs the ability to see beyond guilt to a new potential. It accepts responsibility for the past and moves on. Jesus never denied the reality of guilt in this woman. He simply said to her that she should not allow her guilt to destroy her future.

Amnesia is destructive because it ignores reality. But grace, God's doctrine of amnesty, allows the facing of reality with the redemptive ability to set it aside.

We are concerned with the national debate on amnesty because it is important in its own right and also because it is a reflection of personal and local realities. What will be President Ford's program for war-resisters? Was his pardon for Nixon wise or proper? What about other Watergate defendants? Of course, we are concerned about how and whom the president pardons. But more to the point: will we pardon one another and ourselves?

There is not a one of us who has so degraded himself/herself as to be lower than the rest of us. There is not a one of us who has so distinguished himself/herself as to be above the rest of us. We are on one level. In our personal, individual ways we are commonly guilty. The question is, how do we respond to our guilt? Let us accept God's grace for ourselves and deal redemptively and responsibly with personal guilt and then, perhaps we just might be inclined to extend to one another, the graciousness of forgetting grudges.

Jesus told a story about a foreman who hired laborers all during the day and promised them a day's wages. At the end of the day, everyone received the same pay and those who had worked longer complained. One commentator observed that if Jesus had been teaching economics, he would have had the foreman pay the workers proportionate to their work. After all, smaller denominations of currency were available. But Jesus was teaching a lesson on grace and there are no small denominations of grace.

*daimonic: from Greek literature referring to inner warnings and urgings from the gods, or a pointer to one's destiny or character. As a psychological term: represents an elemental force with an irrepressible drive towards individuation. As a literary term: refers to the dynamic unrest that exists in all people, which can lead to self-discovery or self-destruction.

Preached at Austin Heights Baptist Church, Nacogdoches, TX 6/6/1974

PEOPLE OF THE STAR: A FATHER'S CHARACTER - JOSEPH

Her husband Joseph, being a righteous man
and unwilling to expose her to public disgrace,
planned to dismiss her quietly....
Matthew 1:18-25

In two weeks we are going to have the parade, but between our Sunday Advent service and the parade there will be a wedding in here. It isn't anyone you know, maybe you will if they come to church here, but in between the two events we are going to have a wedding. It isn't going to be anything like what we just read about. In fact, what we just read as we understand weddings and engagements and all that kind of thing—what we just read is confusing. Early in the text it says, "Her husband Joseph" and then all through the rest of the text, it is a debate about whether or not he will take her as his wife. Now, how can you be a husband if you aren't married yet? In that day, you could. Marriage involved three steps: engagement, betrothal and the taking of the wife— there is the marriage.

Engagement in that day was when a young man asked a young woman to marry him or parents arranged the marriage. Now you know about that kind of thing. It still happens today, maybe in some ways. You know somebody, I am sure, that if you are honest about it, you would say, "The parents kind of pushed that." Anyway, engagement starts when the decision is made that these two people will get married. We understand that.

The third step, taking the bride, was when the man went to the home where the bride lived, took the bride from that home and took her to a new home and established a family. We understand that. The hard part is understanding what betrothal meant in that time. It was a period of time where there actually was an understood contract between the two. To break that contract required a bill of divorcement. The only way you could get out of betrothal was to divorce someone. If, during that time, Joseph had died—he hasn't married yet, but is engaged and betrothed—Mary would be referred to as Joseph's widow. They didn't live together, there were no marital relations, but there was an understood contract between them that was almost as good as being married, legally and socially. Now it is during that time frame, that Joseph finds out his bride to be, his betrothed, is expecting a baby. This is a very serious concern for him because as the text says, "Joseph was a righteous man."

The Jewish historian Josephus tells us that a righteous person was understood to be someone who was obedient to God's commands, someone who was an upright person, and an individual of character. So here we have Joseph who discovers his betrothed is pregnant and he is a man who wants to be obedient to God's commands, he is an upright person, he is a man of character. Now somebody else who was not righteous might have had several choices. But in Joseph's mind, he understood a righteous man, obedient to God's command, upright, a man of character, would only have two choices. Surely there is a third. But Joseph only understands two choices: one public and one private.

The public choice is to make it public that Mary is pregnant and that would bring public judgment and stoning. The private choice is to give her a bill of divorcement privately and no one mentions anything about it. However, the private choice isn't absolutely private because you have to have two witnesses sign the bill of divorcement. Probably there is an extended period of time here where Joseph is trying to find two people. Now remember, this is a righteous man, a man of character, trying to find two people who would be discrete about this bill of divorcement.

I will bet you that wasn't an easy task. He doesn't consider the stoning, the public side, and probably very few people did. It probably didn't happen. But can you imagine what a powerful, parental tool that is? "I want you kids to behave yourself. I don't want to find out that you are going to have to be stoned! Oh, it would break a mother's heart to have to see her baby stoned. You don't want to do that to your poor mother, do you?" Now maybe nobody got stoned, but boy, is it a whip! It might bear bringing it back, not because I want to see anybody stoned, but the power of saying that to a child. "You behave yourself. I'd hate to have to see you stoned in public." That probably didn't happen much. And as I said, other less righteous people probably found other alternatives. But Joseph only sees two. Now surely there is a third. Joseph sees two and chooses out of his care and concern, chooses the one that will be private and protective. But isn't there really a third option? Somehow, Joseph finds a third option: to marry the girl and take that child as his own.

We do an awful disservice to children. We call children ugly names when a child has no choice about his parentage. A child doesn't choose how it gets here in this world. But there are ugly names for children. And Joseph finds a third alternative that will mask those ugly names.

How do we come to those kinds of choices in life, especially for those of us who are trying as hard as we can to be obedient to God's commands and to be upright and to be people of character? When faced with difficult circumstances, how do we come to choose some creative alternatives, coloring outside the lines, but are still obedient to God? And yet, it isn't according to the rules that we've learned before. Joseph spiritually discerns in a dream, hears from an angel that there is a better, creative option here.

Now, Joseph, I suppose, could have said to his buddies in some discrete way, "Well, he's not actually my son. You see, the Holy Spirit came upon Mary and she conceived."

"Is that what Mary told you? And you bought it? Would you like to buy a bridge in Arizona?"

Now Joseph didn't tell people those kinds of things. I am sure it put a strain on Joseph; I am sure more than once, somebody close to the family observed, "Tenth anniversary. Wait a minute. Jesus is going to be 11, isn't he?" I am sure there were whisperings, and murmurings, and Joseph had to live with those, had to deal with those. But he took the woman as his wife, raised the boy as his son and was still a man obedient to God's commands. An upright man, a man of character.

He taught Jesus. I don't know what all he taught him. I don't think they had Frisbees then, but I do know he taught Jesus carpentry and he gave him a trade. And he raised that boy never having real proof—I mean what could he do? Go to some lab somewhere and say, "Here's a tissue sample. Will you do a DNA test and see who the father is?" No, he didn't have any kind of proof of this. All the evidence suggests Joseph is dead by the time Jesus is baptized, conducts his ministry, is crucified, resurrected. Joseph never saw any of that. He lived a life without any kind of proof. He just knew the growing boy as his son. One thing – I am just so convinced of this – that I think he must have given his son was an attitude toward women. I don't think it is accidental.

There is a story out of Jesus' ministry where some very upright, and uptight individuals bring to Jesus a woman caught in adultery and call for her to be stoned. Jesus successfully turns them away and ministers to this woman. Jesus was a revolutionary individual all through the Gospel in his treatment of women. Now where does a boy learn how to treat a woman than from his dad? I think we see here that evidence of Joseph's obedience to God's command, his uprightness and his character.

I notice four things about Joseph. One is his INTEGRITY. Here is a man of integrity. He faces a questionable situation, a difficult moral choice and comes through it with his integrity intact. Jesus is born in a day when it appears quite obvious that the politicians of that age, just like the politicians, many of them of this age (I don't want to paint everybody with the same stroke), learned their ethics in a barn. They learn to deal with life like a couple of donkeys bouncing against each other, fighting for the hay in a stable and leaving the bi-product of their existence to stink up the surroundings. It is not a coincidence that Jesus is born in such a stable reminding us that God's visits to us are very conscious of the reality of the world in which we live. And yet even in that environment, Joseph is a man of integrity and makes the right choices to honor God. I doubt if there was ever anyone outside of Mary in all of Joseph's life with whom he could discuss his real relationship with his son. I imagine that there were whisperings that he had to live with and bear and no one, particularly no male friend to whom he could say, "Here's the truth and I want you to believe it." What a mark of integrity he is! To live a life of character, whether anyone else understands that's what you are doing or not. That is integrity.

Joseph was a man of COMPASSION. What a compassionate decision he makes. Creative beyond the rules that he had learned. Compassion in action. First of all, simply to go through with the marriage. And then to live as father to Jesus all those years. Why do we celebrate Christmas on December the 25th? I doubt that that was the day that Jesus was born. Well, we celebrate Christmas at that time of year because the ancient world had pagan rituals at that time of the year, trying to appease false gods to bring the sun back. And Christmas at December the 25th is a compassionate redemption of the winter sol-stice celebration. A compassion found in those deci-sions in life that take ugly and difficult and awkward things and re-color them, re-design them, re-fabricate them so that they are beautiful and meaningful and honoring God. There is Joseph saying, "Let's go on with the wedding."

Joseph was a man of FAITH, a believing man. You know, you can no more prove that God exists or that Jesus Christ is the son of God than Mary could prove to Joseph who was the father of her child. It is a matter of faith. I find it refreshing and helpful, to be able to say that a person who has integrity, a person who is honest, a person who is upright can also be a person of faith. We can be honest and upright and at the same time believe and have faith.

The last thing: Joseph was RESPONSIBLE. I have said this repeatedly though I haven't used that word. Joseph was responsible. He was betrothed to a woman and he wouldn't run away from the awkwardness of it. He had children to raise, not just Jesus. Jesus had brothers and sisters. He had a home to take care of. He was a husband and a father and a member of the community and in all those capacities, he was responsible.

Well, I said earlier, this man is one of my heroes. And he is. Jesus was blessed by having Joseph as his earthly father. We – each of us needs to be a blessing to those about us as we are people of integrity, compassion, faith and responsibility.

Preached at Austin Heights Baptist Church, Nacogdoches, TX 12/15/1974

YOU HAVE SEEN MY FATHER
Whoever who has seen me has seen the father.
John 14.9

If you have seen Me you have seen my father . . . and my fathers. I can't remember the first time I was called "Little Fuller" but it was a long time before I learned to appreciate what people meant when they tagged me with my father's name. I'm sure some people called me that because I was Fuller's son, that's all – no thought to it. But usually it meant they saw something of Fuller Self in me. I never knew quite what, or, for that matter, didn't care too much.

Later, though, little by little, I have seen it. Sitting with my chin on my thumb and my forefinger at my temple, I suddenly invoke a vision of another man in my place. I am writing a check when the handwriting shows the style of a familiar hand. It's time to meet Peggy for lunch. The door of the McGee building allows me to see the reflection of myself striding toward the building and, at the same, time I can see into the hall of the building. For a moment then, the two images join and from the swing of the arms and the motion of the legs, the carriage of the body, I could swear that my father is walking up the hall of the building toward me. If you have seen me, you have seen my father. You have heard him laugh. You are listening to his vocal inflections.

If you have seen me, you have seen my fathers. At the Baptist General Convention of Texas, I listened to speeches by Robert Naylor on two different occasions. It has been several years since I was part of a congregation for the president of my seminary. It brought a flood of memories. I began to see how he had marked my preaching style -- not my speech patterns. Others had marked me long before. But something subtle about sermon craft was learned, not by listening to professors tell me how, but by listening to this preacher do it. He gave me a sermonic posture or silhouette. He repeated a story from someone else at the seminary. He told of Peter denying Jesus by the fire in the courtyard and than later swimming to shore, where Jesus had fixed breakfast. Smelling the fire, Peter was guilty all over again. Like the fire triggered Peter's past, Naylor's presence spoke to me of my being.

If you have seen me, you have seen my fathers. I taught Dad's Sunday school class in Wichita Falls the Sunday that it was announced that Bill Pinson would be their new pastor. In the class, I referred to my major professor, Dr. Pinson. "Yes," they nodded their heads, "We can see a little of Pinson in you."

But it goes on in the other direction. I know the joy, the seriousness, the fear of seeing my self reflected in another personality. "Where does he get that obstinacy!" Hmmm, I know where. And I take great delight in believing that I have had at least a glimpse of five-year-old Peggy.

Marked by the past, marking the future, there are no blank pages on any calendar, new or used.

Grandchildren are the crown of the aged,
and the glory of children is their parents.
Proverbs 17:6

Adam was the son of God. Adam was marked by his creator Father. And Adam marked the future for good and for ill. We are the sons and daughters of Adam. We bear the marks of humanity. Our fathers appear in all succeeding generations.

You see it, don't you? How one personality reflects others. I sat through the meeting wondering where have I met him? Afterwards, he asked me how we knew each other. And I puzzled as I listened to him talk to someone who walked up to us. Who was I listening to? And then it was clear! "You're Jere Jackson's brother!" "Yes."

I wonder, if, when you see me, you see a Sunday school teacher, J. E. Winfrey. The main thing he taught me was how to put up wall-paper. Or my pastor F. B. Thorn who gave me theology in his humor. Or psychology professor Hoyt Ford, a warm introvert. Or Lindell Harris, Bible teacher, dry but dear, who takes credit for a romance that blossomed in Baptist Doctrine. Or Jesse Northcutt, dean. Or Robert Baker, history professor, graduate dean, and dry wit. Or John Campbell, or Carlyle Marney.

I am marked by personalities who invested themselves in my personality. Seeds are sown in the hopes of finding fertile soil. It is not always, however, the intended seed that takes root.

Jesus was marked by father and fathers. The young man makes an attempt at preaching. It is an impossible task even for him. Well, for one thing there are too many sensory images for anyone to pay attention to the content of his message. "Who does he think he is talking like that!" "Well, he is Joe's boy for sure. Look at the way he uses his right hand to gesture. You'd think he was sawing two by fours." The set of his mouth while he thinks. You expect him to take a nail from the corner of his mouth and drive it home. The shoulder action as he planes, the sure stroke of the hammer on chisel. The Galilean accent, the laughter, the contemplative look. It's Joseph's son.

I'm talking about heritage. We are dependent on the past. How can can we say who we are if we ignore history? The Bicentennial is vital because it gives us a challenge to explain who we are. How have you become this personality?

I am talking about integrity. Who are you at present? Although you are a composite of blood lines, neighbors, you are yourself unique. No one else has gained – or suffered – the impact which defines you. How well or poorly has it been put together?

I am talking about influence. We are responsible for the future. They say, "Our future is in the hands of our youth." Not entirely. What my children do with the world they inherit is their responsibility; but the world they will inherit is my responsibility ... and Dad's ... and Daddy Joe's – he was Dad's step father ... and J. W. Brunner, Sr.'s – he was pastor of their church.

I am talking about redemption. The question past, present, or future is always a moral question and as such requires a moral answer. Each new generation is greeted with new hope. Maybe they will have some answers.

What child is this
Who laid to rest
On Mary's lap is sleeping?
This, this is ...

Has there ever been a great personality whose impact on society could be prophesied even before birth? Oh, we always predict great things for the new-born, but it is mostly wishful thinking. We never know for sure.

But then one day Philip asks Jesus, "Show us the Father." And Jesus replies, as anyone might reply about parents, "If you have seen me, you have seen my Father." Joseph? No, not this time. And now I am talking about revelation, as I have been all along, but a deeper kind. Jesus was marked by the Father. Where? How? In what sense? How can we see it? Perhaps his keen insight that saw into the motivations of those who would trap him. Perhaps the courage to expose base motives for the tenderness with pain. Maybe the compassion for the multitude, grief for the bereaved, indignation when people hurt themselves and others, or his sacrificial attitude, or his sense of authority. Somehow, the Father appears in His Son.

I am still talking about heritage, the heritage of a God who acts in history. A God who visits his people. A God who came to his people in a specific historical personality – the babe Jesus born in Bethlehem. I am still talking about integrity, the man Jesus, who was true to the personality that was his. Jesus lived out all the potential of his unique personality. I am still talking about influence, there has never been such a life changing, world changing personality. But primarily I am talking about redemption. Yes, there was one baby for whom great things were prophesied even before he was born. And he made good on the promises.

This, this is Christ the Lord!

Adam was marked by his Creator Father and he in turn marked those who follow with humanity – its potential and its perversity.

The Second Adam – born in Bethlehem, the city of David – marked by the Redeemer Father. In turn, he marks those who follow him as redeemed.

And so you bear the marks of others in your life just as I do. And you have known my experience. The puzzled look. That man seems to be watching me. Do I know him? He approaches. "Yes, can I help you?" "You wouldn't be Fuller Self's boy, would you?" "Sure am. How did you know?"

But what really puzzled me. She was standing off to the side. The focus of attention was actually someone else but her whisper seemed to cut through the chatter. "God's child," she said. What did she mean? Is God also reflected in other people? How much does the light dim if it is Twice Reflected? Can the Father be reflected in the Son and reflected from the Son through other children?

That is a Christmas question.

Preached at Austin Heights Baptist Church, Nacogdoches, TX 12/21/1975

FRESH GROUND SILENCE

[The Lord was not in the wind, the earthquake, or the fire] and after the fire a sound of sheer silence.
I Kings 19.10-13

It is hard to believe that just verses earlier we read about Elijah's contest with the prophets of Baal and the successful prophecy of the rain which ends an extended drought. But following Elijah's victory over the prophets of Baal, Jezebel warns him, "As sure as I am Jezebel and you are Elijah, I'm going to get you!"

This is a northern story. That is, it is about the northern kingdom and it is a story that circulated in the north—in the kingdom of Israel. But when Jezebel threatens Elijah he runs south to Beer-Sheba which is the southern-most city of the southern kingdom of Judah. And he only stops there long enough to leave his servant. He then goes further south into the wilderness to moan and complain. After food and rest he travels further to Mount Horeb which is in the northern stories, the place where Moses met God. The statement that Elijah was to travel forty days and forty nights is a stylistic way of identifying Elijah's experience with Moses' meeting of God.

This is a classic story of one man's depression which is conquered in a gentle silence. Because it speaks forcefully to me, I want to share with you Elijah's sources of depression, his responses, and the results.

The Sources of Depression

1. Fatigue. The contest on Mt. Carmel called for a lot of adrenaline. It was exciting. And the anticipation of the life-giving rains was exhilarating. But when the excitement was over, Elijah was depleted. Big events in life have a way of doing that to us. Whether they are happy events or tragedies, the big events of life sap us of energy. When that happens even a dog yipping, like Jezebel, can defeat you.

2. A sense of failure. Elijah had humiliated the worshipers of Baal and had dealt a strategic blow to Baal worship, but Jezebel could still taunt him and he felt himself a failure. He declares himself to be no better than those who have gone before him. This is a type of class-pity – an enlargement on self-pity. In his case it amounts to: Prophets make a lot of noise but it never amounts to anything. And I am just like the rest of them.

3. A sense of powerlessness. No matter what I do, thinks Elijah, Jezebel is still there. I can't fight city hall! Along with this goes a feeling of being overwhelmed. Either the forces opposing me are too powerful or the task I have to do is too large. Haven't you ever said, "Nobody could ever get all the weeds out of a yard this big?"

4. A sense of loneliness. Isolation can be destructive. Sometimes we are lonely because others desert us. Sometimes, as in Elijah's case, it is the result of running from others. It is heard in the cry of self-pity: "I have worked my heart out but nothing has been accomplished and nobody knows or even cares."

5. A sense of having been drained by the task. Sustaining others, being the leader, providing

strength, having to come up with the answers. In Elijah's circumstance it was being the charismatic center of attention. This is a drain on your ego energy.

Any of these experiences is sufficient to cause someone to be in state of depression as was Elijah.

The Responses

1. Receive the ministry of others. I know well the need and the value of having angels bring you food. There are those places and circumstances in life when you cannot do for yourself and there is great value in receiving from other hands what you cannot do for yourself.

Another ministry is given when sensitive people allow time for rest and recuperation. Ministry comes in many forms. I am impressed with the courage of those fifty prominent individuals who announced publicly that they are alcoholics. Thousands of people must have been helped to know they are not alone and without understanding.

2. Exercise what initiative you can. Elijah gets up and goes to the sanctuary—the holy mountain. Probably, it is not apparent what good it will do him but he goes. He is in motion, active. Simple exercise, any movement which requires the pumping of blood and oxygen, is an effective antidote for most of the things which ail you.

3. Take one step at a time. Elijah is given piece-meal instructions, not an overload.

4. Release pent-up feelings. Elijah does this by his complaints. Perhaps there is a scribal duplication in the chapter or perhaps it was necessary for Elijah to repeat himself to get it all out. Either way we have an accounting of what was bothering him.

Repressed emotions can cripple or fatigue. Depression is often anger turned inward. It can become self-hatred. This is the unhealthy direction suggested when Elijah complains of his identification with his predecessors. You have seen this kind of self-hatred blown into class-hatred. The exclamation "Black is Beautiful!" is an attempt to answer racial self-hatred. The struggles which I have experienced with my "ministerial image" are typical professional self-hatred. And you hear sexual self-hatred every time someone says, "I'm just a housewife."

Swallowing emotion is a source of depression; so it follows that releasing pent-up feelings are an appropriate response. Of course, there are appropriate and inappropriate means of release. To counter a destructive force with destructive means, like fighting fire with fire, doesn't really gain anything.

Experience the transcendent. Elijah witnesses the hurricane, the earthquake, the inferno — but God is not in them. Then comes the silence. Literally, he hears the sound of a finely ground silence. The adjective refers to something threshed or crushed, something thin, fine, or gentle. It is light, soft. It is a quiet which we seldom experience. No traffic in the distance, no children's noises, no machinery hums, no whispering, no animal chatter, no bird songs, no crickets, no breeze rustling, no earth moving, no fire crackling. Nothing. A gentle quiet, silence.

Elijah covers his face with his mantle. He knows God!

Elijah is a whole man again! He is redeemed!

There are two great therapies: work and worship. We know quite well that it sometimes helps to be busy, but have we forgotten the healing to be found in worship?

The Results

1. Elijah recognizes the value of investing his life in others. In his depression, he was turned inward excessively. Now he has the renewed ability to see how his life can touch others.

2. To extend that point: he sees that his investment of his life can go beyond his reach, his life, his vision. He is given a renewed sense of transcendence. This is one of the characteristics of humanity which distinguishes us from the animals. We can see beyond ourselves. This point and the first one speak of an expanding of his life.

3. The final point speaks of a creative limiting of life. Elijah remembers that God does not need our protection. How can you protect God? It is always depressing to take on an impossible or an unnecessary task. Protecting God is both. God is always capable of a remnant. This northern tale anticipates that great word which the later southern prophet will enlarge upon. God's remnant—God can always find friends. He is capable of 7,000 prophets—a perfect number raised to absolute proportions.

Find the healing stillness of God. Or, as the psalmist would have it:

Be still/and know God!

Preached at Austin Heights Baptist Church, Nacogdoches, TX 5/16/1976

COMING UNRAVELED

Life seems to continually unravel on me. "This isn't the way I had it planned," could be on my family crest. Did you ever ask yourself, "How did I get here from there?"

Next week, we are going to the Southern Baptist Convention in Kansas City and then to visit family in Kansas and on to Colorado Springs to visit more family. I was born in Colorado Springs—the hospital isn't there anymore, or has changed names or something. Maybe it is hiding from me. By the time I was two, we were living in Omaha, Nebraska, where my brother was born. Before I started to school, we moved to Wichita, Kansas. I finished high school in Wichita and went elsewhere for college, coming back occasionally. My final visits were for ordination in 1959, and my brother's ordination in '61.

Between my ordination and my brother Linn's ordination, the church in Wichita had a monumental row that went to court. It finally resulted in the majority of the church being disenfranchised. And they, in turn began a new church. In 1964, I wrote a Master's thesis on the legal implications of the fight. I planned to spend some time in Wichita researching but instead went to Houston because a preacher there had most of the material I needed.

To get to Kansas City, we will go to Granbury and leave our kids with my sister and then Peggy and I will head for Wichita, Kansas. I am anxious to see it. What do you suppose they have been doing for sixteen years? Keeping everything in its place for the time that I would come back? It won't be the same—but neither am I. I hope they can accept that.

I remember an argument—well, a disagreement—between my brother and myself just before he was ordained. I think that we have since changed sides, that is, if we discussed it which is no longer likely.

Change, change, change! I hear someone complaining, "It's just not the same." But it never is! We are constantly changing and can never retrieve the way things use to be. As Will Rogers said about congress, "They ain't what they used to be. But then, they never was." Someone has written something to the effect that with respect to war and travel, the great things men remember never happened.

It wasn't that way at all and it won't be this way long. We change. Some changes are imperceptible. The stalactite drips and the stalagmite grows. We cannot see the change but as we look on one side at a fused column and on the other side at two barely discernible knobs in the ceiling and floor of the cave, we know clearly that the tentacles reaching vertically toward one another are changing.

Other changes are more dramatic. We are sometimes wrenched about. Life suddenly bounces through a jump-shift bid. Like the mountain climber who meticulously picks his way for hours over a short span of precarious rock only to slip a thousand feet in a few seconds, down a mud slide, life can make some abrupt changes.

No, life isn't going to be the same. Why not welcome some changes which are capable of keeping us all awake? The growth of the stalagmite toward stalactite is fascinating to contemplate. But who wants to sit and take notes? An occasional long, quick mud slide makes life interesting. It certainly gives you more to talk about at parties.

If you are concerned about the way life changes, consider the conclusion to the letter to the Colossians. Paul sends greetings to and from a variety of people who are enjoying the flux of life.

Just think about a few of them. **Onesimus** was a slave who ran away from Philemon and got captured in a new sense by Paul. Paul sends him back to Philemon with a view to receiving him back from Philemon and tradition tells us that Onesimus is the bishop of Ephesus at the turn of the first century.

Mark is with Paul. Earlier Paul and Barnabus had argued so strongly over Mark, with Paul vociferously denying Mark a place on their team, that Paul and Barnabus split up.

And **Dr. Luke** is there, too. "The Beloved Physician" has always been a fascinating personality. And here together with Paul are two of the four men who will write the gospels.

Aristarchus is there. This man deserves more consideration than we have given him. He is always with Paul in the tight places. He was so close to Paul in Ephesus at the riot of the Temple of Diana that Aristarchus was arrested. My, how his life did an about face by joining with Paul!

In Paul's letter to Philemon, he calls **Demus** a fellow laborer. In this letter to the Colossians, he simply mentions his name. Later, he will write to Timothy that Demus had forsaken him.

Life is a kaleidoscope. Always changing colors. Always losing old patterns and finding new ones.

How could Paul and the others cope with that? Well, look at Paul's prescription: [Headings taken from the <u>Cottonpatch</u> version of the Bible]:

Keep saying your prayers.

Whatever the changes are, we are on a Pilgrim's journey through God's world. The most significant dimension of life is the spiritual; so keep saying your prayers.

Swift to its close ebbs out life's little day;
Earth's joys grow dim, its glories pass away;
Change and decay in all around I see:
O Thou who changest not, abide with me!
"Abide With Me" Audrey Assad

As Paul says, according to the <u>Cottonpatch</u> style, "Keep saying your prayers and when you do, stay awake on the thanksgiving."

Don't forget to stay awake on the thanksgiving side when you are praying about change. "Oh, they grow up so fast!" you say. What if they didn't grow at all? What if Wichita were exactly the way it was sixteen years ago? What if we all just stayed the same, frozen into the summer of '42 or June the year you married? Thank God for the changes!

Walk sensibly before outsiders.

People are watching. Sure, they watch Charles Colson and Billy Graham and Roger Staubach. But do you know who they really watch? You and me. So what example are you giving them? Paul Hauck has a little book on Anger and Frustration. In it he says that inappropriate behavior when you are frustrated or angry is a poor example of good mental health. Now, that really hits home with me. My identification with mental health structures in East Texas makes me concerned about what people might think about my mental health.

People are watching. So what is the best example we can give to outsiders about how to cope with change?

Use your time as though you had to buy it.

People have puzzled for centuries over what Paul meant by "redeeming the time." Well, I think this translation says it about as clearly as it can be put: "Use your time as though you had to buy it."

"I've got more time than money," I hear. As though time were as plentiful as . . . oh, water. Hmmm, you know we can run out of anything.

Time is valuable. Use it as though you had had to pay for it. And the meaning is that we only have enough time to take advantage of the opportunities which change brings. We don't have time to fuss about the inconvenience, or cry about the injustice, or curse the gods.

Let your conversation be gracefully and properly seasoned.

C.F.D. Moule comments on this verse: "This verse is a plea to Christians not to confuse loyal godliness with a dull, graceless insipidity. If a Christian is ever difficult company, it ought to be because he demands too much, not too little from his fellows' responsiveness and wit."

Paul is saying put some salt in your talk. Now, salty language quite often means profanity or vulgarity and that is not what I mean. Put some salt in your talk. I mean by that zest, life, vitality.

After all, Christianity is preeminently a living religion; so our conversations ought to show life.

So,

Keep saying your prayers.
Walk sensibly before outsiders.
Use your time as though you had to buy it.
Let your conversation be gracefully and prop
erly seasoned.
These four suggestions are good social rules,
they are good business advice, and they are good
Christian directions.

Preached at Austin Heights Baptist Church,
Nacogdoches, TX 6/12/1977

GOD'S STARSHIP

As I looked, a stormy wind came out of the
north: a great cloud with brightness around it and fire
flashing forth continually, and in the middle of the fire,
something like gleaming amber....

Ezekiel 1: 1-28

Ezekiel would have enjoyed STAR WARS. The movie Star Wars is a romantic, idealistic space science fiction movie. In it, good and evil are joined in battle. An old soldier, Obi-Wan Kenobi trains young Luke Skywalker how to do battle with evil. In particular, he teaches him to get in touch with the Force—some mystical, spiritual power. Ezekiel's famous description of the heavenly chariot with its multi-faced angels and wheels within wheels is reminiscent of some of the science fiction space chariots of Star Wars.

Ezekiel was concerned about the neglect of God's Spirit, the ultimate spiritual force. He was concerned about the dark reality of evil. In Star Wars, Darth Vader is a former good soldier who has become something of a prince of evil. Ezekiel is severe in pointing out that the cause of evil is often due to the defection of supposed good guys. Although he harshly denounces those people who trounce on Judah when she is down, he is most caustic when he turns toward his own people to say that they have brought their troubles on themselves.

Several themes could be compared between Ezekiel and Star Wars. The movie is popular because of its outstanding visual effects, because it is a story well told, and because it rather simplistically partitions good and evil with good winning in the end.

The movie has special merit as an illustration for Ezekiel because of the brilliant use of imagination, for this distinguishes Ezekiel from much of the rest of the Bible. Ezekiel used an inventive mind to make his points.

The first great image from Ezekiel is the spaceship of God. This magnificent vision is an awesome description of the presence of God. It describes God as majestic, powerful, imposing, but most of all mobile. Before we get into this any further, it is necessary that we learn about some other imagery.

The Temple in Jerusalem was on Mount Zion on the eastern edge of the city. It faced toward the Mount of Olives which is across the Kidron valley to the east of the city. The Temple was meticulously built and situated according to precise orders.

One of the features of the Temple has to do with the precise positions of the opening of the Temple and the opening of the Holy of Holies. At the time of the equinox—that is when the sun is crossing the equator half-way between the heat of Summer and the dead of Winter—the sun would rise over the Mount of Olives and shine directly through the door of the Temple into the deepest recesses of that building. There are indications in the Old Testament that the people treated that as a symbol of God's residence in that holy place.

Especially important to Ezekiel was the idolatrous practice of sun worshiping. Instead of the sun being the creation of God, it was worshiped as a god. This was one of the sins punished by the captivity.

Now consider what Ezekiel describes as he first pictures for us this awesome chariot. The splendor of the vehicle carries a majestic presence whose being is a blinding light. In chapter nine, this dazzling presence of God moves to the entrance of the Temple. In chapter ten, that presence moves to the East Gate and then in chapter eleven, Ezekiel describes the departure across Kidron to the Mount of Olives.

In other words, what he has given us is the exact opposite of what the people—and distinctly the sun-worshipers—had seen in the autumnal equinox. They had used the shining of the sun as a symbol to say God is in this place and from this thesis, they had developed the corollary: because God is here, it shall never suffer harm. But as Jerusalem and the Temple was falling down around their ears, the prophetic imagination gave them a new picture of God departing the Temple.

Where was God going?

Well, the first thing to be said is that the imagery suggests that God is on the move.

He is going. The Temple cult had grown comfortable with a false mythology that had God confined to that little room deep in the Temple which they called the Holy of Holies. But God, as Ezekiel describes him, rides a well-oiled Starship. It had wheels within wheels so that it could go in any direction without even turning around.

At one point in the movie Star Wars, the good guys are being pursued by the empirical battle wagons, but Han Solo, the pilot, puts the ship into high gear and zap! It simply disappears from view. Ezekiel describes the movements of God's Starship as being quick like lightening . . . maybe even faster. Wherever the four angels willed the chariot to go, there it was. Luke Skywalker in Star Wars is impatient with the pilot Han Solo because he will not put the ship into hyper galactic flight or high gear fast enough to suit Luke. But Solo responds they can't get into high gear until the computer is locked in. No telling what you would run into traveling at the speed of light without a computer! The Starship which Ezekiel describes is better equipped. The computer is always locked in. The wheels have eyes all around the rims.

Do you understand that Ezekiel was using the hyperbolic language of a vivid imagination to illustrate some fundamental truths of reality?

The picture is of God on the move. But where is he going? Ezekiel uses another picture to make his point. The other picture must have had more appeal to Jesus because he seems to have gotten at least three parables from it. In Ezekiel 34, there is a renunciation of the false leaders of Israel who were poor shepherds of God's people. In response to their dereliction of duty, Ezekiel tells us that God will be the shepherd of his people. He is the Good Shepherd who will search for the lost sheep and will separate the sheep from the goats.

So the pastoral description of God as the Good Shepherd helps answer the question from the description of God on a cosmic skateboard. Where is God going? He is going after his people! And with this statement about God and his active search for his people, Ezekiel joins forces with so much of the scripture following the Exodus motif.

Wherever God's people suffer, are deprived, have been victimized or vandalized, God is moving there at hyper galactic speed. This is the repeated biblical message. It strikes a resonant chord within us. We need God's presence!

In the movie, Obi-Wan Kenobi tells young Luke Skywalker to trust the force. And Han Solo scoffs at his archaic religion. Han Solo commands a spaceship – one of those technological marvels with lights and bells and computers and weapons with awesome power. And Solo lives in an era of the Death Star—a weapon that can obliterate a whole planet. Surely if you have all of those things, you are too sophisticated to believe in God!

A little too easily, in my opinion, Solo comes to the point where he sees Luke off to battle the Death Star with the wish: "May the Force be with you."

I have an idea that many in the audience identify with Solo's scoffing and yet are uneasy with it. Maybe we know too well, as a culture, the moving of God. But we have experienced only the dark side of it. Do you suppose that Star Wars is just an escape, a playful fantasy? Is it true that there is a world where clear good is gone? Although the movie sounds like something from the 21st century, the movie begins with the prologue: "A long time ago, in a galaxy far, far away."

Is that where idealism is? Has God left us? If so, where has he gone? Haven't I answered that already? He moves faster than the lightening. He moves fast as the mind of an angel can think to where his people are in captivity. To the refugees, the bereaved, the starved, the abused, the poor, the abandoned. Where is that? I don't remember seeing any of those people around here. Hmmmm.

But who knows, perhaps God's Starship can move to your hurts as easily as elsewhere. After all, he doesn't even need the room it takes to turn around. But it is important to ask, if we are not the victims in this world, are we the victimizers? I wonder if the evil done by malicious princes of evil like Darth Vader or Hitler is much greater than the evil we ordinary people accomplish through apathy, ignorance, and neglect.

The slipshod morality of this present age may lead some to believe that good and evil are but the materials for science fiction but that just is not so. No matter if 100% of our leadership have committed crimes worthy of impeachment, there still is such a thing as right or wrong. And if we separate ourselves from the holy presence and purposes of God, we consign ourselves to the emptiness of the experience of God's absence.

There is sternness in the early half of Ezekiel's book which attempts to warn people that God moves quickly to the side of his hurt children. So, it isn't wise to be the one doing the hurting.

Later in chapter 43 of the Book of Ezekiel, there is a description of a better time. It is a picture full of hope. Oppression is ended and God's children are coming home. The city and the Temple are rebuilt and Ezekiel again has a vision of God's Starship. The glory of the dazzling light comes from the east, through the eastern gate and into the Temple.

So here is Ezekiel's picture of God at a time when his nation knew great distress, turmoil, and helplessness. His vision tells the awesomeness of God. It tells of the swiftness of God. It tells of the grace of God who moves to the side of his hurting people. And it tells of the judgment of the experience of the departure of God for those whose lives and attitudes have shut themselves off from the purposes of God.

And how do we respond? With worship,
praise, thanksgiving, confession and rejoicing.

**Preached at Austin Heights Baptist Church,
Nacogdoches, TX 8/7/1977**

WHAT MUST I DO TO BE SAFE?

When the jailer woke up and saw the prison doors wide open, he drew his sword and was about to kill himself, since he supposed that the prisoners had escaped. But Paul shouted in a loud voice, 'Do not harm yourself, for we are all here.' The jailer called for lights, and rushing in, he fell down trembling before Paul and Silas. Then he brought them outside and said, 'Sirs, what must I do to be saved?'
Acts 16:25-34

On April 10, 1979, massive tornadoes struck Wichita Falls, Texas. Because my parents live there, we took a very serious interest in that experience. I've seen pictures of the storm, which show three or four funnels coming together to make a massive force cutting a path, at times, a mile wide. I grew up in tornado alley and have seen pictures of these storms and been very near tornadoes all of my life. I have never seen any destruction that compares with this storm or any tornado funnel to compare with this one. I watched a 20-minute TV program in Wichita Falls, which was a rerun of a documentary of the storm as it swept through the southwest part of town.

An overriding question of all the questions that have to do with the storm was the question, how can I be safe? Numerous stories from the storm illustrate the panic effort to find security. A housing contractor left the safety of his home to flee in his car. As was evidenced by numerous other stories, a car is no place to be in a tornado. The man was injured, his wife was killed, but the house that they had left remained untouched. Some homes were completely untouched, almost miraculously so, while others were nothing but rubbish. Many were destroyed with the exception of one closet or one bathroom in the middle of the house. With the sky still black from the storm, litter still flying in the air, the looters came out and began their devious work. Even after the storm was gone, its destructiveness could be seen in the fact that clean up had to begin immediately because of rats and other vermin.

The third week of June following the Southern Baptist Convention, we drove home to visit family for the first time since the storm. Driving on Southwest Parkway toward my parent's home, we were struck by the destructiveness of the storm and inability to find the most basic landmarks. We were bewildered as to where the turn toward their house was.

I'm reminded of Psalm 33:17: "A man cannot trust his horse to save him, nor can it deliver him for all its strength." (NEB) Or to paraphrase the question of the Psalmist in 139:

> Where can I gain safety and flee from destruction? If I climb up to heaven, it is not secure; if I make my bed in hell, it is certainly destructive. If I take my flight to the frontiers of the morning or dwell at the limit of the western sea, even there I find no safety and there is no release from my fear. If I say, 'Surely the light will protect me, and a massive street light program will make me safe.' I find that darkness invades even the light that I thought was my security.

So, here is the story of a prison guard who lives through a natural disaster, perhaps, first surprised to find himself alive, but then, second, surprised to discover his prisoners had not escaped which spares him an internal affairs investigation. And he asked, "How can I find safety? How can I find security? What is the secret that will rescue me from the uncertainties of life?" We have taken the plea from the question and the power from the answer.

From the story, one might, as an immediate response, say that safety is to be found in dealing with Christians. And if you have to arrest someone, arrest Christians. They make model prisoners.

But another earlier story in the book of Acts shows that this is not the case, because Peter escapes from jail, and the result of that escape is the death of the jailers. (Acts 12:19) This jailer is very aware that he is responsible for his prisoner, and therefore, with the apparent loss of the prisoners, he is about to take his own life.

A later story in Acts tells of a shipwreck. The result of the shipwreck is that the guards want to kill the prisoners before they have an opportunity to escape, but the guard who is responsible for Paul recognizes that his prisoner is too valuable for that, and so, their lives are spared. (Acts 27:43)

The story is full of the risk of life.

Paul and Silas are at risk by proclaiming simple good news. They bring a cure to a young lady who serves as a medium under the possession of evil forces that are both spiritual and material. *She* is controlled by some evil spiritual force that gives her a certain kind of gift, which in turn is exploited by the maliciousness of people who will make use of the adversities of others to bring profit for themselves. Paul and Silas enter her life in a curative way. They do a good deed, and the result of that is they are attacked, beaten, and jailed; in fact, their feet are put in stocks in the deepest part of a jail. *The jailer* has done all within his power apparently to secure his prisoners, but natural forces intervene in his measures of security, and his life is at risk. When the powers that be come to their senses and realize that it is not necessary to jail these men, they order Paul and Silas to be set free. But when Paul and Silas are set free, they announced the fact that they are Roman citizens! And now *those who are in authority* are at risk for they have ordered the beating of Roman citizens: an offense punishable by death. In fear and quaking, they request that Paul and Silas leave town. And they do —asking for no more revenge than merely a public apology.

At the heart of the story is everyone's question which is voiced by the jailer: **"How can I be rescued?"** It is not the question of a junior or primary child, "How do I go about joining the church? I want to be baptized like Johnny and Mary were last week." It is a question that comes out of a deep sense of terror. It may be a child's question, but it certainly comes from the adult, as well. It is a question that comes from having seen the fragility of our brief candle flame and having honestly exclaimed with T. S. Eliot, "In short, I was afraid!"

We each ask the question in our concern for protection from madness that we see all about us in life.

Robert Jay Lifton in his <u>Home From the War</u> details his work in therapy groups with Vietnam veterans. He explains that a good deal of their anguish is seen in the exploration that they make of the reasons why others died and they lived. As a matter of fact, there are no reasons, and what they end up with is the absurdity of life. When Robert Kennedy was shot, Lyndon Johnson called it senseless violence and Hubert Humphrey said it was the result of the forces of irrational hate. W.A. Criswell commented, "America is not like that." But what if America is like that? Let's throw that thought away. We would rather not even think about it. But it is a possibility that really the crazies are in the majority. Perhaps Friedrich Nietzche needs to be heard: stare not too deeply into the abyss, lest the abyss stare back at you.

Out of World War II, the war correspondent Ernie Pyle lamented, "There is no sense to the struggle, but there is no choice to struggle." And later he wrote, "It seems to me that living is futile, and death the final indignity." And still later he spoke of his wholly hopeless feeling about everything and cried out, "I wish you would shine any of your light in my direction, God knows I've run out of light." Is it true, as someone has suggested, that earth is the insane asylum of the universe?

Quite often our concern is to find safety and protection from the forces of authority.

Certainly, that was the case here with this jailer. The Roman power had control over his life. And you well know that at the propitious moment a madman masking himself as messiah can turn this world into a hellish Armageddon. Whether or not you have ever asked yourself about the possibility of your boss being crazy, you have been aware of the power he or she holds over you—if not the boss in the sense of employment, the boss in the sense of big brother government. God save us from the board of trustees, study committees, executives or anyone who is out to help me "for my own good."

How do we cope with the power of authority?

Sometimes we can hide in the rules. Until the rules are changed—which frequently happens in the middle of the game. At least, we can hide in *the security of orthodoxy.* Surely, one of us as representative of all who hurt can write a foolproof confession of faith that is incapable of misinterpretation. But would it be so simple that it is no more than a statement that God is, or would it be so complex as to tell us to alternate Sundays to use trespasses or debtors in the Lord's Prayer? Maybe there is no security even in inerrancy.

Maybe the truth is it isn't the madness of the universe or the malevolence of the authorities that concerns me most. **Perhaps, most of all, I need protection from myself.** Is it true that I'm under attack by my own body which picks just the wrong time for headaches and backaches and sniffles? Caesar Borgia had great plans to take over Italy, but at just the precise moment for his action, he was sick and in bed, unable to move. Or maybe it's my mind that plays tricks on me. Portuguese sailors sailed west from Portugal 100 miles and turned around to go back home to announce that they had proven that there was no land to the west.

But these are all threats of the world. And though they are real, they may not be the direst threats. Even in his day, the jailer might have heard of the Jewish implications of the meaning of salvation. And he may have been praying as others around him would have, that he be delivered from the penalties of the messianic deliverance. **Could that be it? The**

protection we need most of all is protection from God? All of us have old tapes that run constantly in the backs of our minds which shout at us at the slightest trespass of ancient moral boundary lines: God will get you!

There can be no doubt that somewhere, sometime, if not constantly, each of us has cried out, "What can I do to be safe?"

The answer is the same no matter what the source of that question: believe.

I do not like simplistic answers. This is not one of those. Belief is foundational. The despair Nixon has bequeathed us, and Carter cannot seem to elude, is not do we believe what the president says to us, but do the American people any longer believe in presidents?

We need to profess a belief that can go into dark cells and create light. Our belief need not flee into segregated enclaves that promise to eliminate discipline problems in a monochromatic, mono-economic, mono-valued world. Rearing children in such a greenhouse atmosphere will surely produce falsely superior individuals who will wilt without the protected environment in which they were nurtured.

What we believe about Jesus, who He is, where He goes, what He teaches, and how He dies,–this is profound and life's only security.

What we believe is always as important as what happens to us or what we do. "What does it mean?" is one of the greater questions of humanity. *Believe in the Lord Jesus Christ, and you will find salvation, safety, rescue. The same goes for everybody in your house.* **Believe in Jesus, not in nature.** Or a more modern corollary of nature worship might be to believe in being natural. The return to nature and to the natural has its value, but it is not a source of rescue. To paraphrase Satchel Paige, while jogging, don't look back, the demons may be gaining on you.

Believe in Jesus and not the authorities.

It may not be a bad idea to accommodate the authorities, but there is an authority beyond which requires the greater accommodation.

Believe in Jesus and not in a self-help reassessment of yourself.

I can be assertive. I no longer feel guilty when I say "No." I know I'm okay, and you're okay, too. But for all that wonderful self-help, security is not found in my loss of timidity. Have I indeed lost it, or am I simply more skilled in hiding it?

So, okay. I believe in Jesus Christ. What has changed? Well, not much.

The outer circumstances of life have remained unaltered. Paul and Silas, Christians for some time, were singing hymns in the midst of trouble. Was that idiot optimism or inner serenity? Whatever it was, it was still trouble. Eric Rust was in London during the blitz of World War II. His neighbors had a better bomb shelter than he did, but they would come stay with him because they thought it was safer to be with a preacher. Now, that is idiot optimism because a Christian is in as much danger as anyone else.

So nothing is really changed, **yet everything is changed**, because the inner being is changed. A hospital can house birth or death. A chapel can be the scene of marriage or funeral. The exterior is always the same; what happens inside makes the difference.

So, what happens with the jailer? Maybe a week or a month or a year later there was a jailbreak and with the loss of prisoners came also the loss of the jailer's life. He was a Christian but still vulnerable. The difference can be seen in what little we know of his life after his conversion. He takes Paul and Silas out and cleans and gives first aid to their backs.

His is a new life because he has declared allegiance to a man who faced death with a prayer (roughly translated), "Hey, God, I don't want to die." But he did die and was a person experiencing life to the fullest extent as we experience it with all of its threats and risks.

There is no safety in this world except that security that derives from a commitment to Jesus Christ.

> My faith has found a resting place
> Not in device or creed.
> I trust the Ever Living One
> His wounds for me shall plead.
> I need no other argument,
> I need no other plea.
> It is enough that Jesus died—
> And that He died for me.
>
> Eliza Edmunds Hewitt

Preached at a chapel service at the Baptist Sunday School Board, Nashville, TN 8/24/1979

SAY YES TO GOD'S MOMENT
... Who knows? Perhaps you have come to
royal dignity for just such a time as this?
Esther 4:13, 14

Almost every morning, at least every morning
of the week, I take Angela to school and we drive
down Concord Road. Because of the way our little
town on the south end of Nashville has grown, and it
has grown very rapidly (the fastest growing county in
Tennessee), most of the people who are going any-
where on the south end of Nashville are on either
Concord Road or Franklin Road, the road we run into.
And so as we move down Concord toward Franklin,
almost every morning I say to her, "It looks like the
whole world got to this intersection at the same time
we did." I guess it's my memory; I'm not sure what it
is. She is getting tired of hearing it and every morn-
ing, I think it's a fresh idea. But it does feel that way:
that we all got here at the same time.

One morning, I caught somebody's face out of
the corner of my eye in one of the cars going by as
we sat there waiting for our turn. Later in the day, a
friend of mine named Cynthia said to me, "Didn't I see
you at Concord and Franklin?" I remembered and
said, "Oh, yes, I thought I saw you." And sure
enough! We had seen one another at that intersec-
tion.

I began to pay more attention as to who was at
that corner in the mornings and realized that the po-
liceman at the corner, directing traffic, is the husband
of a woman who works for my wife. I had never no-
ticed him before! They call him Shorty. He is six foot
four. How I missed noticing him, I don't know. This

made me realize maybe the whole world wasn't meeting at that corner, but a lot of people were and I knew many of them; much of my world was passing before me and with me through that intersection. I began to pay attention. The intersection took on some meaning for me.

Sometime back, I sat in my kitchen preparing a sermon. I was going to preach to some people I had never seen before. The television was on in the other room and I suddenly recognized a familiar cadence and the words of a sermon and I remembered that very familiar voice speaking those so familiar words about having a dream. And I thought, "What in the world is he doing on now? I don't remember Martin Luther King doing anything special today." I got up to go into the other room to see what was on television and I got there just in time to see the picture of this man and underneath it dates . . . a birthday and another date. There was something about that that didn't connect right. You only have two dates under a picture when someone has died and I thought, "I don't understand this," and there was no explanation. The only sound I heard was the sigh of Walter Cronkite. I began to switch channels to see what was going on and landed on another station that was still in the midst of the announcement about the death of Martin Luther King.

That weekend, I drove to Nacogdoches, Texas, for the first time in my life and had a sense at that time that a strange intersection was occurring to me in my life. I've discovered from that occasion and from others that there are those crossroads in life where we meet and we meet as though the whole world has come to this place, for this occasion, for this intersection and you can turn the corner go down the block, make another turn, go away from that intersection, but never leave the impact of having been at that cross-roads.

Let me tell you just briefly some of the features of an intersection that comes out of the Old Testament, just such a crossroads. It seems that there was a king who had a queen named Vashti and there was a special occasion. It was a big party and all of the men who were with the king were having a big time. All the women at the party were with the queen. The men got pretty drunk and at some point in the party the king said, "We need some diversion. We need some entertainment. Send in the queen. She's the most beautiful person in the entire kingdom; let her entertain us." The message they got back from the queen was, "No thanks. I don't do that sort of thing." The king got pretty upset about it and said, "Well, then you are just not queen anymore." So the king holds sort of a beauty contest to see who would replace her as queen. A man in the kingdom named Mordecai had a younger cousin who had become his ward and had taken a good bit of pride and considerable care in raising the young girl named Esther. He thought this girl probably had as much promise as anybody in the kingdom, so he enters her in the contest or whatever it was and she becomes queen.

But there's another character in the story, a man named Haman. A man who's selfishness knew no bounds, a man who became the enemy of every-one including, eventually, himself. In his desire to place himself above all others and being offended by the actions of Mordecai, he sets in place a plan that would destroy the Jews. Mordecai comes to Esther to give her a message telling her she must go to the king and intercede in behalf of her people. Esther sends back a message to Mordecai saying, "It cannot be done. I cannot go into the king. Anybody who goes into the king without invitation will suffer death unless the king happens to be gracious about the intrusion."

My text, reading from Esther the fourth chapter. The message has come back to Mordecai and we read in verse thirteen that Mordecai says to Esther, "Do not imagine that you alone of all the Jews will escape because you are in the royal palace. If you remain silent at such a time as this, relief and deliverance for the Jews will appear from another quarter, but you and your father's family will perish. Who knows whether it is not for such a time as this that you have come to royal estate." Esther gave this answer in return to Mordecai: "Go and assemble all the Jews to be found in Sousa and fast for me. Take neither food nor drink for three days, night or day, and I and my maids will fast as you do. After that I will go to the king although it is against the law and if I perish, I perish."

Well, you know the rest of the story. Bravely she goes into the king. She is received. She invites him to a banquet and into a succession of banquets in which Haman's plot was exposed and Haman, who in the meantime had built a gallows to hang Mordecai becomes victim of his own plot and ends up on the gallows himself. But the key to the whole story is this exchange between Mordeai and Esther. The challenge: someway or another God is going to rescue us but unless you act you're liable to perish, and it may just be that God has brought you here for this very moment. It may just be that this is that crossroads in your life when you need to act and Esther's response is, "I see the wisdom of what you have to say and I'll do what's right even if I perish."

What I want to say to you this evening is to challenge you to say "yes" to the gift of God's moment, whatever that is in your life. In this crossroads event, this experience of life where you come to some kind of movement left or right, forward or backward, whatever the opportunities are presented before you, say "yes" to the gift of God's moment.

I. One way to say yes to God's gift is to keep faith with the witness you have received.

Let me speak for just a moment about the witness that Esther had received. Part of the witness, that heritage which was hers, was the heroic action of Vashti. Vashti saw that she was in a position of being a role model. Do you get the picture here? All the men are over here getting drunk and all the women are over here with Vashti and she is in a position to be the example **courageously**. She acts so as to say, I have respect for myself whether the king does or anybody else does and out of a sense of self-respect and in an attempt to be an example for these who are around me, I'm going to do what's best for me and for us. Now, this is not lost on the other men. This message comes to the king and the king is not sure what to do about it and his advisors say to him, I'm sure it was in some kind of words like this: "If you don't put a stop to this, you're going to have more uppity women around here than you can handle."

The example will not be lost on everybody else in the kingdom. So part of the witness that is received by Esther is the example of this sterling woman who has acted sacrificially before her. Another part of the witness received by Esther is the deep sensitivity to tragedy that Mordecai has. Mordecai sees the awfulness that is before him. He is deeply sensitive to what's going on around him and he issues a challenge to Esther, a clear call: there can be no question, Esther, what is right in this situation. So, another part of the witness she has received is the clear call that comes from the conscience of this deeply sensitive man. Where are the witnesses in your life? A father, a mother who had a deep faith, a teacher somewhere along the way who presented to you such clear information about the way life ought to progress for you. Perhaps someone of Brother Berry's stature who has somewhere in your life said to you, "This is what God has to say to you. This is the clear blueprint that the Lord would present to your life." Where are the witnesses in your Life? The way to say yes to God's gift of the moment right now is to keep faith with those stalwarts who are your heritage.

II. Another way to say yes to God's gift of the moment is to oppose the destructiveness that is among us.

You realize, of course, that Haman, who is the very evil figure in this story, is destructive to no one more so than he is to himself. That's characteristic of the evil forces of life. Evil is always self-destructive. He is blind to what's going on around him. He is blind to the forces that are coming out of himself, and Haman hurts no one more than he hurts himself. It is appropriate. It is right. It is the place for us to be. It is the thing for us to do to oppose those forces that are destructive around us. Now, in the story of Esther, things are pretty clear cut. We know who the good guys are and we know who the bad guys are. It isn't always that clear in life and sometimes the struggle of good and evil is a struggle that is within each one of us. It is often true that my most difficult enemies are found within me, but it is always the way to say yes to God, to oppose that which is destructive.

In Tennessee, we're still talking about Jake Butcher. A few years ago, Jake Butcher was the head of a banking empire in east Tennessee and Kentucky and in that place of power that he had, he engineered almost single-handedly the bringing of the World's Fair to Knoxville, Tennessee. In the pathway to getting to that point, he ran for the Democratic nomination for governor in Tennessee. He ran a very close race against our current governor and almost was elected governor of the state of Tennessee. At the height of his power – a good looking, powerful, well-educated, well-endowed man in terms of heritage, a man with everything . . . things began to fall apart. It turns out that much of the building that was going on around Knoxville to prepare for the World's Fair was done because of some very forceful arm twisting. A lot of motels were built with the understanding that money would be only loaned if motels were built and there were subtle business hints and not so subtle business hints that were put out that if you did build the motels, then your other businesses would survive. Illegal loans, hidden ownerships throughout east Tennessee and Kentucky turned out to hurt Jake Butcher more than anyone else. Oppose those destructive forces of life in an effort to say yes to God's moment.

III. Another way to say yes to God's moment is to reach for the best that is within you.

Reach for the most that you have the capacity to do. Reach for the best that you have as God's gift to you in your own personality, in your own being, in your own talent, in who you are . . .reach for the best that is within you. Here is a girl, and when we start out with this story of Esther, that is the best way to describe her. Here is a girl who has not much going for her, lost all of her family except an older cousin who takes her in. Here is a girl who has been put into a school to learn only one task in life and that is to entertain others. Here is a girl who has been put into a school so that she will have a limited capacity in life, so that she will simply be the tool of other people's pleasures. Here is a girl who becomes a woman who is inspired by the example of someone who has gone before her in the same capacity. Here is a girl who becomes a woman who is instructed by the clear teaching of her mentor, her preacher, her prophet, her cousin, Mordecai. Here is a woman who with the gifts that are given to her, takes initiative and acts not as anybody has given an example to her, not as anybody who has given instruction, but out of her own wisdom, out of her own cleverness, she leads the king down a path that allows him to see for himself the evil that is threatening him as well as those who are his subjects. Here is a woman who says yes to God's gift of the moment and makes a dramatic difference in the lives of her people. Reach for the best that is within you.

A little story out of the life of Pearl Buck reminds me of this reaching for all you've got. Pearl Buck, a woman who was born in the United States but lived a good bit of her life in China, growing up as a missionary's child, has written some very inspiring and informative stories of China. She became the first woman to receive a Nobel Prize for Literature in 1938. A few years before that, she left her beloved

China, came back to the United States to live, and at one point, decided she would like to have the rugs that were in the house she left behind in China. However, these rugs were in a house that had been taken over by the enemy and she was sure they were no longer available to her. Despite this, she wrote and asked if the rugs could be sent to her. Sure enough, they were. They were rolled up, packaged, sent out of enemy territory, brought across the Pacific Ocean, shipped across the United States to New York City, sent through customs inspection and then put on a train to her farm in Pennsylvania where they got lost. She wrote to the railroad, asking, "Where are my rugs?" The railroad wrote back and told her they were sorry, but they were lost. "How much were they worth? We will pay for them" she was asked. That did not satisfy her. She wrote the supervisor of the person from the railroad who had sent her the letter admitting that they were lost explaining that she wanted her rugs. She got a similar letter back that said, "We are very sorry we lost your rugs. How much are they worth? We will pay you for them." She decided this was no way to get done what she wanted done. So, she wrote the president of the railroad company saying, "Somehow my rugs got out of enemy hands, across an ocean, across a continent to New York City and you lost them in a few brief miles. I want my rugs." And guess what? She got them.

Sometimes that is the way to get something done. Go to the top, and why not? Reach for the best, go for the most. To reach for the best is to bring out the best that we can possibly be. Corrie Ten Boom, I know you've seen the movie of her life or read her books or are familiar with her name . . .the

Dutch lady who hid Jews during World War II and suffered through her own imprisonment at the hands of Nazis. Corrie Ten Boom says that out of all of the ills that she experienced in life, one of the most difficult moments for her was after the war was over and she was released and healthy again and was preaching and speaking at meetings. After one meeting was over, she recognized a man by the door who was an SS officer and had been one of the supervisors in the prison where she had been held captive. The man walked up to her and said to her, "Praise God, you're right. Jesus has washed away my sins, too," and he reached out his hand and she couldn't move her arm. She looked at him and said, "This isn't right. I have told people over and over again that we must forgive and live new lives and go on with our lives and I've got to forgive you." Her arm was like lead. Finally she said, "God forgive me, too." She was able to extend her hand and shake hands with that man and face the fact that no matter how much she told other people about forgiveness, that on first sight, she hated that man and she had plenty of reason to. She found the best in her, she found the ability to reach out and say yes to God because that's exactly how she did it. She said yes to God.

 We're at a crossroads. They happen every day. Some of them are little corners that don't need a stop sign or traffic lights . . . turtles can cross without fear. Some of them are heavily trafficked intersections and they are dangerous, they are busy, they are exciting and they are alive. Esther faced her crossroads and said yes to God's moment. I pray that each of us will learn with grace as well, to say yes to whatever it is that God presents to us in life.

First preached at Zion Hill Baptist Church, Nacogdoches, TX on Sunday evening 4/21/1985. Austin Heights Baptist Church was organized with the intention of being open to all races. Rev. T. W. Berry, pastor of Zion Hill became my mentor on this issue. His church was the closest black Baptist church to Austin Heights. He led me to understand that the black community had lost a large part of their community through integration. Yes, there was a strong moral gain to integrating the schools but there was a loss of black teams, clubs and other features. He helped me see the value of alternating joint services where one of our churches would host a worship service where the visiting minister would preach and the host church would provide a pot-luck meal. A month later we would reverse roles. That relationship between the two churches made an important impact on the Nacogdoches community. On April 21, 1985, I was invited to return to AHBC for the morning service and followed that evening with a visit to Zion Hill's pulpit.

GRACE IS A HAZEL-EYED BRUNETTE

No one has ever seen God; if we love one an-
other, God lives in us, and his love is perfected in us.
I John 4:12

Grace is a hazel-eyed brunette who rubs my
head and teases me about my loss of hair even while
I take her to pass her driver's test. But her name isn't
really Grace.

Grace is a twenty-year-old with mischievous
brown eyes and a day-old-beard who tells me "Dad,
you're OK." And he goes by another name other than
Grace as well.

Maybe I better explain. Some years ago
Lofton Hudson wrote a book entitled <u>Grace is not a
Blue-Eyed Blond</u>. His point: When we hear words
that speak of great biblical themes, we no longer think
of those themes. Grace no longer refers to God's un-
merited favor; it is the name of a blue-eyed blond.
Redemption does not bring to mind Christ's work on
the cross, it makes us think of green stamps. So,
Hudson found it necessary to say, "Grace is not a
blue-eyed blond." The trouble with trying to say
something important is that we usually say more than
we intend. I find it necessary to say something en-
tirely different about grace. Grace is a blue-eyed
blond - Grace has hazel or brown or green eyes - or
else we cannot know grace at all.

Lofton Hudson made my point for me himself a
couple of years ago. He and I were at a dinner of the
Southern Baptist Association of Family Ministers
when I flippantly told him about a dream. I dreamed
of climbing from a plain room into an elaborate attic. I
told him something about what I discovered in that

attic. He pointed to his temple and said, "You escape into your head." Suddenly there were tears in my eyes. We had a brief, graceful conversation and for the moment, Grace was a white-haired gentleman.

You see, the problem is this: no one has ever seen God. And nobody really knows what unmerited favor means. I've never seen God. Adrian Rogers has never seen God. Even Richard Smith has never seen God. We need a picture, a metaphor an analogy. What does God look like? We need a story, something that would begin . . . A man had two sons. One ran away from home, the other pouted a lot. Have you ever run away from someone and then returned to a warm hug? Have you ever stuck out your lower lip so far you could trip over it but then were found out by someone who really understood you? Have you ever been scared by a storm and run to a friendly lap? Have you ever been so angry you could kill and then had the one with whom you were angry say, "How can I fix things between us?" If you have, then do I have a sermon for you. If you haven't been kissed by grace. . . well the gospel is for you, too, but I don't know what to tell you.

I've never seen God but I have seen Lovis Owens. Both of my children believe that Lovis was their third grandmother. When Lovis invited them to spend the night with her, it never occurred to me that white kids might be out of place in a black neighborhood. Lovis was, a brown-eyed black-haired Grace.

I've never heard God speak, but I have heard Bobbie Durham talk to her son on the phone in the office next to mine—Bobbie was a blue-eyed blond Grace.

Unless you have met someone whose name is Grace, there's not much point in discussing God's unmerited favor.

Let me illustrate. Have you heard of the Quaker questions? There are four questions which can be used as a group process. For some reason they have been called the Quaker questions:

1. Where did you live between the ages of 7 and 12 and how did you heat your house?
2. How many brothers and sisters were at home then?
3. Who was the warmest person in your life?
4. When did God become more than a word to you?

The group answers the questions one at a time taking sometimes twenty minutes or more to process each question.

In a small church during a conference, I led a group in discussing these questions. An older lady, charter member, celebrated grandmother sat near me. She had almost nothing to say during the whole process. When I finally asked, "When did God become more than a word to you?" I heard her whisper, "Never has." I was shocked. But I know personally that there is an important natural progression at work here. If no person has shown you warmth, God is only a word.

What if you know somebody whose living name is Grace, what difference does that make?

Grace identifies us. Grace helps tell us who we are.

For seven and a half years my picture appeared nearly every week in the <u>Baptist and Reflector</u>.

[The newsletter of the Tennessee Baptist Convention]
Frequently people say to me, "Don't I know you? Are
you the editor of the B&R? Do you write Sunday
School lessons? You work for the Sunday School
Board, don't you?" They never get it right but they
have a general idea who I am. And that is the primary
way we learn our own identities. Other people tell us
who we are.

A decade ago, I spent three weeks at Marney's
Interpreter's House. When I first saw Carlyle Marney, I
rushed up to him and sputtered, "HiDr.MarneyI'mJer-
rySelffromNacogdochesTexas!" He put a hand on my
shoulder and said, "Yes, I know who you are. I know
who you are." I spent the next three weeks trying to
plumb the depths of what he was saying to me.
Among other things, he had told me that his own
name was Grace.

A few weeks ago, I went to Danville, Virginia for
the inauguration of Frank Campbell as president of
Averette College. At a dinner in his honor, I moved
through a crowd to shake his hand and said, "Dr.
Campbell, I'm Jerry Self from the Education Commis-
sion." He said "Yes, Jerry, I know who you are." I
don't know whether Frank knows it, but that was a
word of grace. I wanted to shout, "I'm still me and can
be recognized!"

We need a story, an analogy, a metaphor. We
need to hear I John 3:1: "How great is the love that
the Father has shown to us! We were called God's
children, and such we are."

I don't know what we are becoming. I need an
analogy, a "like something," and I need a personal
metaphor, one that will give me identity.

In the hotel next to the Southern Baptist convention in Atlanta was a display describing the shroud of Turin. This shroud could very well be the burial cloth of Jesus. If it is, I know what size man Jesus was. Remember when my parents visited here a few weeks back? Jesus and my father are about the same size. About 5'8". Someone life-size. Not larger than life. Someone of whom John could say, "our hands touched him, our eyes saw him."

The book <u>A Day No Pigs Would Die</u> is the story of a boy whose father was a pig farmer. He raised pigs, bred pigs, fed pigs, slaughtered pigs. The son says no matter how his father washed, he always smelled of pigs. The day his father died was a day in which no pigs would die. One of the things he missed about his father was the smell of pigs.

I wonder what God smells like? I know how rain smells or dirt. I know what work, and fear, and even death smells like. I know what cats and dogs smell like. And people. Ever get into a station wagon with a soccer team after the game? What we really need are scratch and sniff Bibles. We could smell Bathsheba's perfume. Daniel's lions. The wind off the sea of Galilee. The precious oil Mary spilled on Jesus' feet. We would find new meaning to Noah's rejoicing in being off the ark. What does God smell like?

Frenchie's cooking. Grandmother's rose water. An uncle's perspiration. An old leather Bible. (I'm going to respond to the next Mooney who attempts ts sell me a flower, "I can't go to your church. Your god makes me sneeze.")

Now wait a minute. Surely we are too sophisticated for all this. All this stuff about what God looks like or sounds like. God is above and beyond all this. And this silliness about whether God is he or she! We certainly know that God is greater than gender, don't we? God is ... well, what is above and beyond gender? If you don't say "he" and you don't say "she" ... you say "it." But *it* has no personality. Well, sometimes we think an *it* has personality. Ask John, any John, about his boat and John will say, "My boat has personality! Why, she flies with the wind." Strange— as soon as it has personality, *it* becomes *she.*

As acts of grace identify us to ourselves and to one another, they also etch an outline of who God is. Toward the end of the convention in Atlanta, I was walking with Father Bob Dalton, a Catholic priest, designated Baptist watcher, who attends more Baptist functions than Dan Martin [a reporter for Baptist Press]. I made a pessimistic, depressed comment about the convention. Bob made some remark that suggested to me that Baptists do a lot of manipulating but they cannot manipulate God. It was a hope-filled, graceful word. I heard from a Catholic priest that God is certainly larger and loftier than a Baptist convention in Atlanta. But how did I hear that? I heard grace from a small, Jesus-sized friend.

Side thought for extra credit. Maybe God is larger than the Southern Baptist Convention and Jesus is a huggable size.

Grace values us. Grace helps tell us what we are worth.

This is how we know what love is, according to I John 3:16, Christ laid down his life for us. Now wouldn't that say to you that you are worth something if another person were to die for you?

Sounds terribly dramatic! But it does happen. Remember the plane that crashed into the Potomac and the man who helped others climb into a helicopter sling? He kept helping others escape until he had no more energy and slipped beneath the icy waters. People do die for other people.

But laying down life for another in an act of grace is usually done on a daily basis. We seldom notice its importance. If I stick my head in the door and say, "Busy?" and you turn away from a pile of demands and give me your attention, what are you doing? In a small piece, you are laying down your life. When a mother stoops and puts her face nose to nose to a child and squints and listens with all her might to hear just exactly what the problem is, what is she doing but giving up life? Maybe not her whole life, but all of it that she has available at that moment.

What is the most valuable possession of the American species? Saturday. Yes, Saturday is more valuable than silver or gold. So, what are you doing when you take a four hour chunk of prime Saturday and help some poor soul move? That my friends is laying down a block of life in an act of grace.

When it happens to me, something in me says, "Hey, I must be worth something to receive a gift like this."

Grace heals us. Grace is good for what ails us.

John Claypool tells us just that in a personal experience out of his book <u>Opening Blind Eyes</u>.

Between my ears I knew all about grace, and justification by faith, and mercy, and forgiveness, but, to quote the great black preacher Howard Thurman, "the other parts of me had not yet heard the word." Grace was a *concept* to me at that time - not an event in which I participated to the depths of my being ...

[A friend showed him they knew the same agonies.]

As he spoke those words, I felt something akin to fire flow from the top of my head to the depths of my heart, and for the first time in my life I experienced grace - it was not thought about or understood conceptually, but happened to me in the way events do sometimes happen to one. It was like being drenched to the skin by a rain shower and knowing it has made one genuinely and vastly different.

As John, the biblical John, put it in I John 3:18, "Love must not be a matter of words or talk; it must be genuine, and show itself in action."

Grace heals us. It isn't just talk. There is an end result. Again, John tells us a chapter later [I John 4:18] "Love banishes fear." There isn't room for both. Or, as that old story has it, when the child complained of being afraid of the dark and was told, "Don"t be afraid because God is with you." The child responded, "I wanted someone with a face."

Grace is the face and the hands and heart we demand. That could be a commercial jingle. But it is more important than that.

Let me try to say it one more way. Sometimes a hazel-eyed brunette graces me by sharing with me her music. One of her tapes has a song I like very much. The chorus states:

People don't care how much you know
Until they know how much you care.

Preached at Glendale Baptist Church, Nash-
ville, TN 6/29/1986

THE GIFT

What's <u>in</u> the gift? We usually inquire

As we tear open the box like a house on fire.

Not paying attention to postures or protocol,

Too busy guessing and ripping, just tearing it

all.

But *"What's" not* the question that fits this occasion.

In fact a question is out of the equation.

The box is a trinket and so's what's inside it.

It's simply to say in symbolic lift –

Not what but *who* – and no questioning rift.

Hey Loved One: **You're the Gift!**

Jerry M. Self

SURVIVING THE RAPIDS
I had heard of you by the
hearing of the ear,
but now my eye sees you;
therefore I despise myself,
and repent in dust and ashes.
Job 42: 1-6

What is your definition of overwhelmed? I'm
sure you have one – maybe a very private one.

This summer, my daughter and I canoed the
Hiwassee River. One of the TVA dams located at Re-
liance, Tennessee controls the flow of water on the
Hiwassee. When both stations are open there is a
good flow through the river. When neither is open the
river is a dry bed. When Angela and I started on the
river only one unit was operating. That meant a rough
flow and a lot of rapids. More fun!

And it was fun! We capsized the canoe four
times and I caught a cold from it; but it was an experi-
ence which neither of us will ever forget. One of the
times we turned over, we were running through a par-
ticularly fast rapid. The canoe flipped over in an
undignified splat and I was underwater. And stayed
underwater. I fought to get my head above water and
wondered, "What has happened to my life preserver?
Why is my head not above water?" Finally, I popped
up so my chin was just barely above the waterline and
I was moving quickly downstream backwards. That' s
not the way you are supposed to do it. Feet first is
the rule. That way you can push off the rocks and you
don't hit the back of your head on something. I had to
work hard to turn around.

Of course, all this time I was worried, "Where is Angela? How is she doing?" She never let go of the canoe, so she did not have much of a problem. Eventually we got the canoe upright and caught up with our Styrofoam cooler half-mile downstream. We survived. And I enjoyed every minute of it. And I learned in a different way what it means to be overwhelmed.

That must have been the word for Job – overwhelmed. In a matter of a few minutes time, four different messengers come to him – perhaps representing the four principal directions – to tell him that everything he holds dear has been taken from him. His property, his livestock, and finally his children and their families are all destroyed. Job responds courageously,

> Naked I came to this world
> Naked I shall leave this world
> The Lord gives; the Lord takes
> Blessed be the name of the Lord.

But that is only the beginning of the story. Job himself is then afflicted with sores all over his body. His wife, the only family left to him, counsels him to curse God and die. Again Job responds with courage.

> If we accept good from God, shall we
> not also accept the bad?

Friends come to Job and give him all their wisdom and then some. Eliphaz, Bildad, and Zophar debate with Job on the reasons for disaster and the workings of God. When they finish a young man named Elihu lets them know how shocked he is that old men don't have more sense than they do and he sets them all straight.

Then the story takes an incredible turn: God begins to question Job.

> Where's the storehouse for snow Job?
> Have you seen the arsenal where hail is stored?
> Do you know the pathway for heat, or how to cut channels for rain?
> Can you rope together the constellation Pleiades or unbuckle Orion's belt?

The questions pile up. They have an overwhelming character all their own. They are impossible questions, awesome questions. And Job can barely whisper a response: But the questions continue.

> Have you an arm like God?
> Can you thunder with a voice like his?

And on the challenge goes until Job answers:

> I know that thou canst do all things and that no purpose is beyond thee.
> But I have spoken of great things which I have not understood, things too wonderful for me to know.
> I knew of thee then only by report, but now I see thee with my own eyes.
> Therefore I melt away;
> I repent in dust and ashes.

How do you survive the rapids? I don't have all the answers any more than Job's friends did. But I have a few clues and I will lay them out for you to see and you can take them with you if you choose. I have a visceral, tactile parable. I give you my story. There are some basic tasks in life and we live better as we learn to do some rudimentary things.

The first task which, I will lay out for you is **Learn the rules**.

One rule of the rapids is "Feet first." If you are in the water, you want to be looking downstream. When we got back on dry land, I told the person who rented the canoe that we had gotten a very unstable canoe. She asked, "Did you sit in the seats or on your knees?" "On the seats, of course." Well, that was a mistake. Another rule of canoeing goes, "Canoe the rapids on your knees." That gives you a lower center of gravity.

Whatever you are doing, it helps to learn the rules. Job thought he knew all the rules. So did his friends. They all knew the wisdom of Psalms and Proverbs – basic, common sense, wisdom of experience as God's people. If you do right, life will go right. But Ecclesiastes challenges that wisdom. In that book, the writer says "So what! I have lived right and done well. I have everything you could want. It is empty, there has to be more." Apparently, all the rules are not in Psalms and Proverbs.

Job challenges the conventional Old Testament wisdom from another direction. His witness is, "What now? I have done right and look what I have gotten: disaster." Ecclesiastes and Job teach us that no one has a corner on all the truth. The best any of us can do is to capture some of reality and be open to learning more as life brings us opportunities to learn.

I'm not talking about memorizing a set of regulations. I certainly am not encouraging some sort of legalistic approach to living.

Learn as you go. Angela wore a military shirt to the canoe. Someone had worn the shirt in Vietnam and then given it to Jay, Angela's brother. He gave it to his sister and she was pleased to have it. I didn't have any pockets in what I was wearing so I gave her the money which I was carrying (most of my money was locked in the car). As we started down the river she took that shirt off because her tee shirt was enough on a warm day. After a few minutes, I said that she probably should tie the shirt to the canoe, just in case. About that time we capsized for the first time. The shirt was lost. One rule of canoeing states, "Tie things down before they float away."

There are people around who know the system's rules. They know how to control appointments and elections and systems. They do not necessarily know how to live with other people.

I am saying to you that we need to learn how to keep learning. Learn as you go.

Another task of life is to **Go with the flow**.

We really don't have much choice here. There are currents stronger than your will or your power which can swamp all your plans. When the winds and fires and earthquakes of life rearrange all the furniture of experience, you can't go back and redo or recapture what was lost. Look downstream.

Now this can be harder than it sounds. It can be difficult to admit that there are some parts of life which I cannot control. This is where I find Reinhold Niebuhr's prayer so helpful.

I know you have heard the first part of it. The prayer reads,

> God grant me the courage to change the things I can. Accept the things I can-
> not.
> And the wisdom to know the difference. Living one day at a time, Enjoying one
> moment at a time,
> Accepting hardship as the pathway to peace.
> Taking, as He did, this sinful world as it is and not as I would have it.
> Trusting He will make all things right If I surrender to his will.
> And that in this world I might be reason- ably happy, and supremely happy with
> Him forever in the next.

Or with Job, naked I came and go, the Lord gives and takes, blessed be the name of the Lord.

Third: **Trust the process.**

Grief is a gift of God. Remembering upstream is not the problem. Job 29 remembers how it was.

Next **find your friends**.

Friends help. All during our trip down river we were followed by two young men. I'm not sure whether it was coincidence they stayed so close or they were following Angela. Every time we capsized they helped us get things right. Here's another rule of life: never pass up a chance to make a friend.

Job's friends are often criticized for being so hard on Job. Maybe they were. But when they first showed up, they didn't recognize Job – he was in such terrible shape. They cried out. Then they sat by him for a solid week without saying a word. Next, they probed with Job to learn what was happening in his life. And they stayed with him until God brought some relief. Find your friends.

A fifth task counter-balances the second. **Give it your best shot**.

In that river, under water and scared about my life, three forces were at work. The current was pushing me down, my life jacket was pushing me up, and I was swimming for all I was worth.

I couldn't go back upstream. The current wouldn't allow that and so, to that extent, I went with the flow. I possibly could not have saved my life. I am not that good a swimmer. That's why I wore a life jacket. There is one of the most basic rules of canoeing: "Always wear a life jacket!" But, I could get my feet first, get closer to the canoe, check on Angela. There were actions which I could contribute. I gave it my best shot.

At the recent Baptist Joint Committee religious liberty conference in Washington, D.C., one speaker told of visiting with Sam Ervin the night before the Watergate hearings were to begin in the United States Senate. The man commented on the enormity of the task before the committee and asked whether Senator Ervin was nervous. Ervin's reply was that he had been preparing for that moment all of his life.

Maybe the conclusion should be: the antidote for drowning in life is being overwhelmed by God.

Preached at Glendale Baptist Church, Nashville, TN 3/1/1987

RESPECT

Before she was in labor she gave birth; before her
pain came upon her she delivered a son.
Who has heard of such a thing? Who has seen such
things?
Isaiah 66:7-14

"Forget the love. What I want is a little re-spect!" declared one mother when asked what I should preach on for Mother's Day. So let's talk about R-E-S-P-E-C-T – respect yo mama!

The text presents a strong maternal picture of Zion or Jerusalem giving birth and nurturing her children, the citizens of Jerusalem. Then, for two verses, the imagery changes and God is the mother figure.

Here we witness the investment of life in gestation, the risk and pain of childbirth, the nurture and nutrition of mother's milk, cradling, cuddling, carrying, and comforting in a mother's arms. The children thrive and the final word is that this is a picture of power – Don't mess with my babies!

One easily thinks of a tigress protecting her cubs. Or a mother bear who places herself between her cubs and a perceived enemy. What do you give that mother? You give her respect!

The first thing I want to say to you is, **Respect your mother's strength**. I'm not sure that I have often thought of my mother as strong. But she is. Considering all she has survived, not the least of which has been bearing five children, it should be obvious that she is strong. Curiosity and willingness to learn and experiment are some of her strengths. I can and will take apart anything. Some things I fix, others I break, and sometimes I say, "Well, it's time to buy a new one." I get that from her.

Everyone knew that mother's mother was strong. Mother's father, Pop Trammell, had many strengths. But he died of a brain tumor when I was about one year old. Mom Trammell got a job as a dorm mother for awhile. She was one of the first I knew who was mother-at-large. A strong woman. We all referred to her as the matriarch.

I haven't thought of my father's mother as particularly strong. She was just a housewife. And Dad's stepfather was such a domineering man. Yet, while thinking about this Mother's Day, the image kept coming to me of Grandmother stepping out her back door and in a few strides and not many more seconds, she had scooped up a chicken and wrung its neck. Until this week, I haven't thought that was much of a trick, she did it so effortlessly. She was a strong woman.

I've always loved them. Now I want to say I respect them.

This is mother's strength: She has the power to make life out of the very substance of herself. Procreation and nurturing means to pluck a piece of your being and feed it to new life. Gestation is the willful acceptance of a parasite for nine months.

Did you see the movie *The Out-of-Towners*? It starred Jack Lemon and Sandy Dennis as a couple who flew to Manhattan for a job interview and every possible thing goes wrong. After spending the night in Central Park she says that she can't go any further. He tells her, "Of course you can. You fought off a German Shepherd and outran a mounted policeman's horse. You're stronger than you think."

Mother's strength represents powers which we assume. Powers which we ignore. Powers we take for granted. And mothers assume they are to be super-moms, all things to all people, mothers-at-large.

How many times has a mother or mother-figure done what was simply her duty and not thought about the valuable bye-products of her work? Dr. Ruth Schmidt, who was provost at Wheaton College, remembers that when she started college, the only thing she knew for certain was that she did not want to be a teacher. She writes,

> What a role model Anne Pederson was for me. Sitting in her Survey of English Literature class, I thought, "If one could teach like Miss Pederson, it wouldn't be so bad to be a teacher."

My guess would be that if you asked Anne Pederson, she would be the last person in the world to recognize herself as a role model for a future generation of teachers.

Preachers' wives are mothers-at-large. Concern for husbands and those who approach the wife rather than the husband. Some churches relish the idea of getting two for the price of three-quarters.

Lareta Halteman Finger, editorial coordinator for Daughters of Sarah, writes,

> I delighted in my children, but many times I felt trapped. I remember the overwhelming feeling of wonder that would come over me holding our children or watching them sleep. On the other hand, the never-ending demands of such little ones can suck discipline and integration out of a woman.

Mothers are like that, yes they are.

Perhaps it is possible to take for granted too much. Mildred Meythaler describes her experiences on the mission field,

> I recall women in girdles and evening dresses accompanied by men in short sleeves and no ties. When I discussed it with the leader of our mission who had traveled the world over, he told me that he found it standard practice. Men, comfortable; women, uncomfortable.

Of course, you will understand that the strength which gives and nurtures life is not limited to mothers. Carolyn Blevins of Carson-Newman tells the story of Charlotte White:

> ... a Philadelphia widow [who] pleaded in 1815 with the Baptist Board of Foreign Missions to allow her to join the George Hough family as a missionary in Burma. A committee was appointed to investigate the case. When Mrs. White informed them she could pay her own expenses for preparation for the mission field and would have about $300 left to contribute to the mission fund, the committee overcame its reservations and appointed her.

Female missionaries, many of them single for life, form one of the larger bodies of mothers-at-large.

And the maternal strength of giving isn't even exclusively female.

Frances Adeney says that she went through the first pregnancy in their family when their older daughter was born to them and her husband, Bernie, went through the second. As she puts it, "his prayers and labor to adopt another little girl were so intense and exciting." Men are capable of this kind of giving. So, I'm not exclusively talking about mothers. But I am primarily asking for respect for mothers.

There are powerful negatives in this text. Discipline forms part of the picture here.

Mother's strengths are not always seen as strengths and they are not always appreciated when they are negatives. The power to defend life is also an important strength. The power to say, "No! my baby's life is at stake," needs our respect and gratitude. Usually mothers have learned to say, "No" with charm but frequently mothers have felt that the "No" may be more important than the charm.

The skill of confrontation remains a mother's strength. Joyce Shutt, another mother-at-large stood up in the midst of an evangelical meeting and shouted ,"You make me sick. You think there is only one kind of person in the world: ordained men! ..." After a few more choice comments she ran from the room in tears. She had exerted the skill of confrontation. A man chased after her and exclaimed, "That was beautiful ... We needed to hear that." And then he added, "Do you know that you have a gift for emotion?"

Like a foundation, strength is often hidden. Think about the hidden powers that shore up your life and respect your mother's strength, her gifts to you.

The other point I want to make is this, **Respect God's analogy**.

What do I mean by that? Isaiah 66:12-13 is one of several passages where God is described as a mother. Respect the power of that imagery. In a letter published in <u>Children's Letters to God</u> a girl writes, "Dear God, Are boys better than girls? I know you are one but try to be fair."

Actually, I assume that God is neither a man or a woman. But God is a person and personal analogies about God help us. Men have never had a problem hearing masculine references to God. Let's learn something from feminine, maternal references to God.

Personal analogies about God always work in two directions. They teach us something about God whose image people bear. They teach us something about humanity made in God's image. So, in the first place, **respect the analogy of God as mother by sensing the image of God we see in our mothers**. We can learn who God is from our experience with our mothers or in the experience of being a mother. (Several maternal images of God come from the latter part of Isaiah which has prompted Letha Scanzoni and Nancy Hardesty to wonder if Second Isaiah was really Mrs. Isaiah.)

Mothers-at-large can tell us much about the character of God. Catherine Kroeger's is a classic mother-at-large story. With three children of their own under the age of five, the Kroegers opened their home to foster children. When people ask her how many children she has, she replies, "I'm not quite sure. I've lost track." In the recovery room after the birth of her fourth child, she heard sobbing in the cubicle next to hers. She insisted the nurse quit worrying about her and see to the woman in the next bed. The nurse answered all her questions – "The baby has come, the doctor is there, so are her parents."

"Isn't she married?"

"I don't think so."

So Catherine Kroeger yelled through the curtain for someone to pull the curtain aside. There was a sixteen-year-old who had delivered a baby girl three months prematurely. A child having a child. And mother-at-large Catherine Kroeger began, "My name is Cathie. What's yours?"

A mother's story which, if we will listen with respect, can tell us, in personal terms, what God is like.

Next, **respect the analogy of God as mother by learning the image of motherhood we find in God**. We can learn who a mother is to be and how she should act from our concepts of God.

One illustration from scripture. Luke 15:4-7 tells the parable of the shepherd looking for one lost sheep which wandered off from a flock of one hundred. Then, in verses 8 to 10, Jesus tells a parable of a woman with a dowry of ten silver pieces who loses one and cleans house until she finds it. The point of the two stories tells us that God loves his/God loves her precious children and will go to great lengths to bring the straying and lost back home. The story of the woman tells us something about God and the point of the story about God tells us something about who we, as God's agents, should be.

Mothers are sweet and sentiment is nice and Mother's Day can be gooey, meringue desert – which we all would love. But I'm talking scrubbing toilets, and fixing pinto beans and cornbread. Let's have a little respect here.

STEP-FATHERS, TOO?

And when your children ask you, "What do you mean by this observance?" you shall say, "It is the passover sacrifice to the Lord, for he passed over the houses of the Israelites in Egypt when he struck down the Egyptians but spared our houses." And the people bowed down and worshiped.

Exodus 12:26, 27

The stars are beautiful at the Great Glendale Getaway. That is one of my favorite reasons for going. At this one, I am herding two boys into the car so we can go to the men's dorm and get set for the evening. In the back seat, ignoring me as if I weren't there, they discuss their fathers. Good men, both of them, but neither of them are in the car. Confused, one of them refers to me and asks, 'Well, who's he?" "Oh," came the reply, "He's just my mother's boyfriend."

Some time ago Mark asked me to be ready to preach for him on Ascension Sunday if he did not return in time from his daughter's graduation. He assured me that my preparations would not be wasted should he happen to get back in time, because I could use the sermon on June 17 when he knew for certain that he would be gone. So, from my file of *Substitute Ascension Sunday/Sunday after convention/Father's Day sermons*, I selected this one. I like it because it addresses the questions: Is there a place for step-fathers on Father's Day?

Almost everywhere I turn these days, I hear voices suggesting a miss-fitness. "Who's he?" I hear. And the answer is seldom as good as "He's just mother's boyfriend."

What to choose for a text for such a multi-purpose sermon? The Biblical materials are full of comments on miss-fits. For instance, the Exodus tells us of the realization of God's gifts of Identity, Liberty, Leadership, Law, Land. And our text explicitly describes the father's role in telling the story.

Maralee mailed out a newsletter this week where she refers to a note I wrote her once:

> Dress bravely, and make sure an eye sees it, and the powers that be will make you live up to your clothes.

Your clothes are an announcement of your identity. The Exodus experience placards this message to us: discover your God-given identity and then live up to it.

The people of Exodus were molded into a fellowship of the redeemed. That is what happened in the wilderness. God made a people. He gave them **identity**. The Book of Numbers says that a mixed multitude left Egypt. Oh, I suppose some of those people had a pedigree that reached back to Joseph. But for the most part, I imagine it was a mongrel group. But that seems true any time you assemble God's people. There seldom is anything that would bring together all of us except that we share God's redemption. Through the experience of grace the mongrel becomes a hybrid.

Remember how the Exodus began? It began when a failed adopted prince, fugitive murderer discovered a bush aflame and a voice that said, "I am." Carlyle Marney said the verb "to be" is powerful because of its primitive nature. The "I am" verb displays its ancientness by its irregularity. Take a newer verb like work: I work, you work, they work, we work. I worked. I have worked. Regular as clockwork. Boring. I am. You are. He is. I was. I will be. You never know where it's going next. God declared his name: I am. And he taught the people who followed to say those same words.

One of my favorite stories comes from Candid Camera: Alan Funt interviewed a young girl who excitedly told him her sister was expecting a baby. She declared that she would be the baby's grandmother. As you might expect, Funt corrected her saying, "You will be your sister's baby's aunt." She corrected him, however, with, "I'll be the grandmother. I'll be what I wanta' be . . .OK?"

That seems to be what God said to Moses. On occasions when Moses tried to influence God to take a different course, God would proclaim his name: I am, and I will be what I will be. In shaping his people, God listens for his name echoing from his people. He both gives us identity and calls for us to shape ourselves in his image.

God released His people from an impossible slavery. With no other hope but what God could do for them, in the Exodus, they found **liberty**. What a profound liberty was theirs! To go into the desert to sacrifice to their God, to worship as their conscience led them, to move freely as they chose pursuing the promised land.

As evidenced throughout the Scripture, God has given his people the gift of **leadership**. The Davidic monarchy represents the chief example of this point. But God also provided the covenant community with judges, priests, prophets, sages, and fathers and mothers.

God's community has also been given His guidance. The Old Testament concept of **law** smacks of richer stuff than what we see enacted by modern legislatures. Indeed, it is the wisdom of relationships and obligations upon which our modern laws are built. Biblical law has been woven into the bedrock of a covenant relation with the Creator teaching us how to worship and how to be neighbors.

Finally, God provided **land** for His people—an indication that there is a place for all God's tribe. The importance of place is reflected in a World War II story. Nazi troops were billeted at a village called Lidici. One of their officers was killed and the Nazis demanded the surrender of the assassins. Either because they would not or could not, the village did not produce anyone. The retribution was severe. All the men were killed. Children were separated from mothers and placed in concentration camps. They didn't stop there. The village was completely torn down and the ground plowed. The surviving mothers reported that as difficult as the loss of husbands and fathers was, as difficult as separation from family and enduring those horrible camps was, the worst blow was climbing the last hill to home and finding nothing but an empty field.

Identity, liberty, leadership, law and land— these are the gifts of the Exodus. They serve well but do not remain in place long.

First came the captivity—bringing removal from the land, a different set of rules, end of Davidic monarchy, loss of liberty, and a threat to identity. With the loss of land, temple, and leadership, the parent's role became even more critical than before.

Then came the return from captivity. Identity was restored, altered, strengthened. Ten tribes were lost to the people of Israel. Theirs was modified liberty, a new leadership, a more rigid and cautious law, a return to the land.

Later came Jesus Christ—identity was more personalized and inward as was true with liberty. Leadership exhibited again was by the Holy Spirit. The rules were internalized. The concept of land was broadened to God's reign whose borders extend to all humanity.

Next the Roman fist came down hard dispersing both the Jews and the Christians. The cycle repeats time and again.

God provides us structures, institutions, and relations to help us shape our lives and find meaning. The Davidic monarchy, patriarchal homes, or the Southern Baptist convention can do this quite well. Or they can fall down around our ears. When this happens, our fault or someone else's, it means the structure has failed, partially or totally. It doesn't mean God is lost or there is no longer meaning to life. In the midst of destruction, small enclaves of believers come together to teach their children, "This is God's name. He is. And we follow him."

What happens when you come to Father's Day and father has died? It hurts to the very core of your being. You grieve. And some child among you or the child within you asks what does this mean? And you pray that some sensitive soul will be able to speak the name of God and tell you that God is there in the process and the reshaping of life.

What happens when you come to any holiday, for all holidays are family events, and the family has shattered—some one has chosen divorce or deserted the family, or been jailed? It hurts to the very core of your being. You grieve. And some child among you or the child within you asks what does this mean? And you pray that some sensitive soul will be able to speak the name of God and tell you that God is there in the process and the reshaping of life.

What happens when a nation stumbles in a war, a recession, with deaths, disabilities, lost jobs, or natural disaster obliterates all the landmarks that tell you this place is home? It hurts to the very core of your being. You grieve. And some child among you or the child within you asks what does this mean? And you pray that some sensitive soul will be able to speak the name of God and tell you that God is there in the process and the reshaping of life.

What happens when a denomination self-destructs, the convention which structured meaning for you ever since you can remember? It hurts to the very core of your being. You grieve. And some child among you or the child within you asks what does this mean? And you pray that some sensitive soul will be able to speak the name of God and tell you that God is there in the process and the reshaping of life.

Because we share an Exodus experience we are a group—a group that is going somewhere. The past speaks of the grace of liberation. The future promises a home. And we, as God's Exodus people, are always somewhere in the middle. Sometimes our in-between-ness causes disillusionment or even rebellion, but at our better moments it gives us meaning, purpose, identity. Individually and collectively our redemptive experience makes us who we are.

The February afternoon shines as a beautiful West Texas day. I am in Abilene for the thirtieth anniversary of my graduation from Hardin-Simmons University. A vacant spot in the schedule surprises me. I had not expected this free hour. I know what I am going to do although I had not expected to do it at this moment, and I am apprehensive. I drive the rental car twenty minutes north through familiar country to visit . . . what do I call them? Ex-mother-in-law? Ex-father-in-law? "Ex" doesn't fit those titles. Fortunately, titles won't be necessary and I am relieved by that. The look of surprise and delight on her face when she answers the door tells me everything I need to know. We talk happily about my children, her grandchildren, and then she sends me out the door to go see Ernest. I drive four blocks and pull up in front of a white frame house with a sign over the door that says "Domino Hall."

In the back of a large room sit a gaggle of old men. The most distinguished of the lot is an eighty-year-old farmer that I have known over thirty years. I put my hand on his shoulder and he says, "Hello, Jerry," as though we had spoken ten minutes earlier. He speaks my name to the group and their names to me and then all turn away from me to the game. First things first. The game finished, he asks Shorty to take his place and stands to go with me off to the side where we can talk. A voice asks, "Is this one of your boys, Ernest?' He doesn't hear. Or chooses not to respond. I cannot ignore the question but neither can I answer it. I change the subject and we walk over by a pool table. We talk of my children, his grandchildren. Then he begins a story. He tells me about his visit to the doctor. He is the butt, the goat in this story and he relishes the telling of it. He laughs so hard, he can barely finish and I laugh with him. It is a gift.

"Is this one of your boys, Ernest?" Neither of us know how to answer. He gives me a gift and says, "I am. You are. We are." We don't know how to finish those phrases with titles. But, nevertheless, we are.

I can't tell you where my institutions are going. Maybe it is enough to speak the name of God and follow after him. I am. You are. We are.

Preached at Glendale Baptist Church, Nashville, TN 6/17/1990

A NEW PARADIGM FOR LIFE

... whoever wishes to become great among
you must be your servant.
Mark 10:32-45

Lord, a new world order is coming and I want a place among the senior management. President Bush and Pat Robinson have both said the new order is coming; how can I doubt it?

More authoritatively, Joel Barker's hot new book on business, <u>Discovering the New Paradigms of Success</u>, tells me that new models are coming for government and business. His lead illustration is the story of the Swiss watchmakers.

In 1968, the Swiss produced 65% of the world's watches and received 80% of the profit from the sale of those watches. That year, a Swiss technician invented the quartz watch. But it didn't fit the way the Swiss made watches. The Swiss did not even protect the invention. At a world technology exhibit, Texas Instruments and Seiko of Japan both saw the value of the quartz invention and began making quartz watches. Ten years later, the Swiss watch industry laid off 50,000 of their 65,000 watch-making employees.

We better be awake to the new paradigm if we want a job. Among the changes coming: our society will shift from encouraging self-sacrifice to maximizing self, from group goals to individual goals, from serving institutions to requiring institutions to serve ourselves. Can you imagine our nation if we become more self-centered than we already are?

Change is coming and it is coming to our churches as well. SBC churches are financed and staffed by pre-baby boomers, people 46 and older. The boomers (ages 28 to 45), who gave up on brand loyalty, and the busters (people 17 to 27) are making us rethink the way we do church.

George Barna, author of <u>The Frog in the Kettle</u>, wrote:

> The local church will have to earn its place in people's hearts. Institutional loyalty, the presumption of their credibility and altruistic support of them will largely disappear. Only if the institution provides high quality benefits to the individual will it stand a chance of gaining attention and support.

In three chapters of Mark, a pattern repeats itself three times. Each time, Jesus attempts to show his followers that he offers them a new paradigm for life. In Mark 8, Jesus tells his listeners that the Son of Man will suffer, die and be raised from the dead. Peter rebukes Jesus and Jesus then calls Peter, Satan, and recites his famous call to take up the cross and follow him. In chapter 9, Jesus reiterates the doom of the son of Man. This time it is followed by an argument among the followers over who is the greatest. Jesus tells them that the one who would be first must be servant to the others. He uses a child as an example of simplicity of motive. Now comes the third story which is our text, Each time the disciples react in a rather insensitive and contrasting manner. Each time Jesus replies in a way calculated to reorient their understanding about how Jesus intends to amount to something.

James and John are ambitious. The other disciples are, also, ambitious. And they are angry because, no doubt, they feel that the Sons of Thunder have forced their way in line, in front of them. Jesus, too, is ambitious. He has a standard for success and is eager to achieve his goal. He is no less ambitious than his disciples but uses a different paradigm to plot his course and measure his progress.

I have my ambitions and goals as I know you have yours. At base, our immediate goals are part of some larger questions: What yard stick do we use to measure a life? How do we know when we have achieved something of value? What is the appropriate paradigm or model for life?

There are two models illustrated in our text. One perspective is found in the question *WHAT DO YOU HAVE THAT I WANT AND HOW CAN I GET IT?*

The ugliest manifestation of the perspective is the thief who murders someone and takes his valuables. But there are countless socially acceptable forms of this philosophy. James and John believed that Jesus held the authority to name the seconds in command in a grand new political messianic kingdom. That power answers the first half of the question—Jesus had something they wanted. They boldly and crassly asked Jesus to exercise that power in their favor. Thus they discharged the second half of the questions.

This is a good general working philosophy for most of the world. For instance, a recent story on National Public Radio explored the possibility of a new Democratic coalition. The Democrats have claimed to be the party of the poor but have to win votes of the middle class to get into office. Previously, the middle class has looked on government as a source of roads and services to suburbia. But they are getting tired of higher taxes which apparently are aimed at homeless people and welfare mothers. They simply don't want to vote for anyone who might be a candidate for the poor. So what does this story tell us? Well, for one thing, that the American voter looks at a candidate with the question, "What's in it for me?" Forget about "Would this candidate be good for the country?"

You have to understand that just because American business has moved from manufacturing products to selling services doesn't mean anyone necessarily wants to "serve" in the same sense Jesus used the term.

In the old order, this philosophy was object oriented. How can I get a car, a home, appliances, and power tools? Today, the philosophy is more feeling oriented—how can I find fulfillment, achieve success, receive adulation—but it's still the same self-centered philosophy.

And maybe this is our philosophy. You control who becomes the new pastor. How can I get that? I could put an end to this committee work. How could you get me to take it?

Maximizing myself, individual goals, the institution serving myself. This doesn't sound completely new, now does it?

Jesus strove to give his disciples a new paradigm for life. His question is radically different. *WHO ARE YOU IN YOUR NEED AND WHO CAN I BE-COME TO SERVE?*

This question focuses more on a whole identity and fits well some of the emphases of baby boomers and busters.

Notice, however, that Jesus voiced a genuinely costly philosophy. The question pledges a sacrifice of the questioner—and at this point boomers and busters will be offended. They don't want to hear about pledges or sacrifices.

Jesus hears the request of James and John and shakes his head. "You don't know what you are asking. Can you drink my drink? Can you be baptized . . .?" No, the ritual has become too benign for us to recognize the devastation of this question. Jesus asks, "Can you be submerged by the forces that will overwhelm me?"

How quickly they say, "Yes."

And they do fall victim of the same forces. The Book of Acts tells us James was the first of the disciples to be martyred, beheaded by Herod's order. The traditions about John are confused. We are more familiar with the story of an old man exiled on an island prison. Other traditions say that both brothers were dead by the time Mark wrote his gospel. Either way, we know they both suffered from the forces that killed Jesus.

All of which reminds me of my original questions: what is my model of success? Criminal execution?

Who are you in your need? Who can I be to serve you?

As you read through this material, you begin to sense the loneliness of Jesus. Walking ahead, the followers apart from him, gossiping about him, furtive whispers seeking some clue into that mysterious being. Those closest to him, misunderstanding. Those remote from him, hostile.

And, of course, you must realize the Man is courageous. He knows the forces that will overwhelm him and yet he continues.

Maybe he is mistaken. Maybe there is another way. Maybe the new world order doesn't require a cross. And maybe I have misread his story, misrepresented your options. Have I oversimplified? How about an intermediate set of questions:

WHAT DO YOU HAVE THAT I NEED?
WHAT DO I HAVE THAT YOU NEED?
HOW CAN WE NEGOTIATE A TRADE?

Probably there are some satisfying ways to re-shape this. But wait a minute. This sophisticated re-statement, satisfying as it is, makes an important research tool used by many negotiators. Successful negotiators discover the self-centered goals of their adversaries and use that information to achieve their own goals. The question becomes, "How can I use your selfishness against you better than you use my selfishness against me?"

Okay, it doesn't have to be that way. But aren't there really just three models for a negotiation. My selfishness against yours—model 1. My selfishness against your unselfish effort to meet my need—model 2. A joint effort from both sides to unselfishly find a win-win solution—model 3.

Yes, I understand that we are human and we get it all mixed up, but unless we recognize the new model which Jesus offers us and are converted to it, we will never get to model 3. We will stay with the what-do-I-get model until we run into some fool who wants to be our servant and our give-it-to-me tanks will run right over his I'm-here-to-serve sandals. We will flat crucify the guy!

So Jesus tells us the new world order which he models is to become a servant. He is not selling a service. He is a servant.

One of the legends I watched as I grew up was a tall, erect, 80 year old man with a full head of snowy hair. His name was W. C. Coleman and he was a member of First Baptist Church, Wichita, Kansas, where my family participated in church. Coleman was a man who succeeded in the old order of his day by bringing in a new order of his own.

The story went that when he invented the Coleman lantern, he was in competition with others who were manufacturing kinds of home lighting. The lanterns Coleman built were excellent when they worked but were subject to springing leaks. Then Coleman hit upon the idea of selling light rather than lamps. Whenever a Coleman lantern sprang a leak, he immediately replaced it with a functioning lantern and would then fix the leak and have that lantern ready as a replacement. Of course, the story describes a man who began to sell a service rather than a product ahead of his time in business America. But in the setting where I first learned of W. C. Coleman and then heard the story, I hear it as the description of a man who became a servant of his community.

Who can we be . . .?

Preached at St Charles Baptist Church, New Orleans, LA 3/28/1992

ROOM IN THE HEART

Twelve cots
Twelve chairs
Twelve towels
Twelve baggies, full of toiletries
Twelve stuffed lunch sacks
Twelve hours
Room-In-the-Inn

Four bumbling, well-intentioned innkeepers
Two van drivers
One Rose Ann, overseer of all
One maker of lunches
One church member on call
Nine disciples
Room-In-the-Heart

Maralee Self 11/8/1997

THE POWER OF JOY
I thank my God every time I remember you, constantly praying with joy in every one of my prayers for all of you.
Philippians 1:3-5, 15, 18-19; 2:17-18; 3:1; 4:4

From Rebecca Bain's interview with Katharine Paterson, we learn that her book, <u>Bridge to Terabithia,</u> came about as a result of the death of her son David's friend Lisa Hill. She stated that the first draft was difficult to write. The rewrite became a joyous experience.

What I am attempting to do is consciousness raising. Have you seen the poster of the ballerina that proclaims: 'If you can imagine it, you can do it'? Recently I listened to a presentation about a program attempting to impact the children in welfare recipient families. In working with women on welfare, the speaker pointed out the inverse of that wisdom: 'If you can't imagine it, you won't attempt to do it.'

Can you imagine joy? I want you to recognize what it looks like, the smell of joy, the feel of joy creeping up behind you, the light of joy in the eyes of those before you. I want you watching for it.

Not the joy of power but the power of joy.

Biblical images of Joy:

Joy experienced when victory found in the face of defeat.

Joy at the birth of Samuel.

The sharing the news of pregnancies between Elizabeth and Mary and at the births of John and Jesus.

Angels in heaven when sinners repent.

Paul and Silas in the Philippian jail.

The disciples at Jerusalem on hearing Peter tell of the conversion of Cornelius.
The Macedonians when they made a contribution for the Christians at Jerusalem.

Joy is one of the Psalmist's words. Joy is a punchline in Jesus' parables. Joy is the angels announcement at Christmas. Joy is a fruit of the Spirit according to Paul's letter to the Galatians: Love, Joy, Peace, Patience, Kindness, Generosity, Faithfulness, Gentleness, and Self-Control. (There is no law against such things.)

Do I know the texture of joy? Twelve years old. On first base. The pitcher looks at me, winds up and pitches. Just as he lets the ball go, I start digging, pumping those legs, sweat running from my hair down my chin, neck straining, swinging my arms, and NOT falling down, stumbling tripping over myself. There's second base. I leap into the air, tuck a leg under me, slide on my hip, stretch the other leg for the base. And AFTER I tag it, I hear the ball hit the glove way high. I am safe. Jump up and rip the cap off my head and beat the dirt off of my pants. And my best friend in the on deck circle is yelling his head off. Joy is hot and sticky and dusty and . . . sure I know the texture of joy.

And joy is the atmosphere of the letter to the Philippians. Paul made lifetime friends in Philippi. He first was there on a mission trip where he exposed a business practice of exploiting a young girl's gifts. The business community didn't want someone challenging their ethics and they had him arrested and then threw Paul out of town. But Paul rejoiced in jail and later in his friendships. Paul's letter swings back and forth from telling about his latest jail sentence to talking about his concerns for the Philippians. He had troubles, they had troubles. But through the entire letter he speaks of rejoicing. Pollyanna? Well not this jail-bird.

Joy is the power of the undefeated. Madeleine L'Engle in <u>A Wrinkle in Time</u> questions whether joy and fear are mutually exclusive? A zero-sum game?

In jail, songs of rejoicing. From jail, a letter of joy. Isn't it something when someone can have a spirit of joy even in hard times? Now I know you understand hard times. Times when everything seems to be working against you. Joy is the ability to lose but not be defeated.

Joy is the power of the commissioned. Rejoice is an imperative, an instruction, a command. (Something like saying 'relax!') If joy is a fruit of the Spirit, isn't there some level of responsibility here? Shouldn't we expect a level of joy in our Christian community? Take love or peace. Consider kindness, or self-control. What if those fruits were absent from our corporate life? Wouldn't you say something was wrong? At some time in your Christian experience you should exhibit one or more of the fruits of the Spirit. And at any time the collective Church community should display most or all of them. So where's the joy?

Joy is the power of the responsible. For a brief while, I had a student in Taekwondo who was completely uncoordinated. He could not get his arms and legs to do what I asked him to do. One day he walked out of class saying, "I'm not having any fun!" I haven't seen him since. I respect his sense of responsibility for his life. Stewardship calls us to find the joy.

Joy is more likely for the greatly inexperienced or the greatly experienced. (What did he say? He said joy is for kids or old folks. What does that mean? He's just guessing.)

Joy is more likely for those who have known sorrow, pain, and fatigue.

It is not just an item in a self-centered, narrow-focused, 'My God and I' religion. Joy can be corporate and can be a corporate responsibility. We have a responsibility to teach joy. It is not wrong to experience joy – even in times of stress and difficulty.

Katharine Paterson sought to help herself and her son David by writing <u>Bridge to Terabithia</u>. In her story we find Jesse Aarons training in the cow field to be the fastest kid in the fifth grade. But when school started a newcomer, a girl named Leslie Burke, outran everybody. She was the fastest kid in the fifth grade. Surprisingly, Jesse and Leslie become best friends. The two of them create the kingdom of Terabithia which is only reached by swinging on a rope across a dry stream bed. They declare themselves the king and queen of that secret kingdom. Later in the story spring rains fill the stream and Jesse, afraid of the water, considers suggesting they not swing across to Terabithia. He is rescued from his embarrassment by an invitation to spend the day in nearby Washington, D.C. at the Smithsonian. Upon returning home he discovers that Leslie has drowned in the stream. Mrs. Paterson movingly describes his prolonged shock and disbelief and then his anger.

With the death of their daughter, Leslie's parents decide to leave the community and return to their former residence, but they allow Jesse to have some lumber they were using to remodel their house. Jesse takes some of the boards and builds a bridge over the stream to Terabithia. Finally, he invites The Pest – his younger sister May Belle – across the bridge with him into the secret country of Terabithia. He puts flowers in her hair and leads her across the bridge ... the great bridge into Terabithia – which might look to someone with no magic in him like a few planks across a nearly dry gully.

> "Shhh," he said. "Look."
> "Where?"
> "Can't you see 'urn?" he whispered. "All the Terabithians standing on tip toe to see you."
> "Me?"
> "Shhh, yes. There's a rumor going around that the beautiful girl arriving today might be the queen they've been waiting for."

What would be the ultimate joy? To bring joy to another person?

And if you experience joy because you have lit up another life with joy – now listen to this. Here is my one opinion for the day. Who knows, you might agree with me. If you experience joy because you have lit up another life with joy, isn't that when you are nearest the image of God?

Preached at Glendale Baptist Church, Nashville, TN 7/23/1995

BEGINNING TO LEARN

Peter began to speak to them: 'I truly understand that God shows no partiality, but that in every nation anyone who fears him and does what is right is acceptable to him.'
Acts 10.34 [Acts 11.1-18]

Cornelius was a Centurion. The military force at Joppa was a cohort, that is, six thousand men. A cohort was divided into Centuries – obviously one hundred men. A centurion was the one in charge of a Century. That meant Cornelius was something of a Sergeant-Major, a highly significant role in the Roman army.

Cornelius was a God-fearer. That meant he had accepted the mono-theism of the Jewish religion but not the circumcision nor much of the ritual law of the Jews.

Cornelius was a generous and charitable man. He was known throughout the local Jewish community as such according to what his friends told Peter.

Cornelius was a man of prayer.

But Cornelius was a Gentile.

Simon Peter was an Apostle, a Jewish follower of the Messiah, Jesus Christ. But Peter was staying with another Simon – Simon the Tanner. Now tanning was an unclean profession. It involves working with dead animals. For Jews this was ritually unclean. So unclean that there was no way a tanner could purge himself of his uncleanliness. The reason, possibly, that Simon lived by the sea was to keep him away from the proper people. And Peter is staying with Simon. That tells us something about Peter.

Peter goes up on the roof top. A sleepy day perhaps. There he can see men unloading ships. They use their sails as sheets to lower animals off of their ships. And Peter watches . . . and dozes. The sights, the sounds, the smells of the docks and the animals mix and morph in his subconscious and suddenly, God creates a film clip for him. God invites Peter to an unclean dinner. No way, Lord. I don't do unclean. Whoa, there trooper. Where are we having this nap? Huh? Whose roof-top is this? Well, I don't eat unclean.

Peter learns something from his doze and dream. And then he meets some fellows at the door. And they have a funny conversation. I'm the guy you're looking for. Yeah, we know because we are looking for you. Yeah, I know I'm the one you're looking for. Sure we know that because God told us to look for you. Yeah, right, I know, because God told me you were looking for me.

So they go to Cornelius' house and, hey, look at this, Peter goes in. And Peter preaches a basic, straight to the point sermon: Jesus was anointed by God. He did good. He was crucified and rose again. We have been commissioned to tell this news.

Notice this, and this makes preaching valid, Peter began with a statement of where he was in his life of following Jesus. Peter said, I truly understand that God shows no partiality. His expression describes the seizing of an idea. He had a flash of insight. We could say, by George, I think he's got it! He said, in effect, I am a work in progress. God is fine tuning me.

There were some Jewish Christians with Peter who were quite surprised to see Gentiles respond positively to the gospel. Peter asks the Jewish Christians, "How can we withhold baptism from them?" It's not really a question. And baptize them they do.

What a great learning experience for everyone! The gospel is a simple story. Peter's sermons in early Acts give us the salient points. Yet people are constantly learning new things from the gospel. Even Peter learned something from his own sermon.

The gospel is clear but the response is unpredictable.

All through the Bible there are surprises about who responds to God's good news. Jesus set the tone with a parable about two sons. Both were given a task by their father. One said, "Not me," but later he did as he was told. The other said, "Yes Sir," but did not do what he was told. You never know ahead of time how the gospel will touch lives. Cumberland Presbyterian history begins with the premise that we cannot predict who will or will not be saved. Our task is to preach the gospel. Once we have done so, we best be prepared to be astonished with the result.

The Holy Spirit calls forth leaders but anyone may be our teacher.

Peter was the Apostle. Cornelius was a seeker. So who will be the teacher here? Don't answer too quickly. Eventually, Peter will become the teacher but not consistently, as we will see in a moment. God gives us leaders. It is important for the growth and order of the community that certain people be gifted and selected to be administrators and preachers and teachers. We all need to stay awake to the fact, though, that anyone of us might be the teacher of the moment. As Samuel taught Eli or David soothed Saul, children have often been the leaders of their elders. A woman touched the hem of Jesus' garment and taught the disciples a lesson in faith.

Repentance is the way to salvation but it is also a continual means of growth.

When will we arrive? When will we have it all? When will we no longer need to reevaluate, reassess, or repent? Not in this lifetime.

Have you tracked the growth through the book of Acts? Watch closely:

Philip teaches the Ethiopian in Acts 8.

Peter preaches to Cornelius the God-fearer in Act 10.

The disciples witness to some Greeks in Antioch in Acts 11.

Paul and Barnabus reach Gentiles on their first missionary journey in Acts 13.

A debate takes place in Antioch: should Gentiles become Jews first, then Christians in Acts 14.

A council is called in Jerusalem to consider the place of Gentiles in Acts 15.

But then Paul's letter to the Galatians reminds us what a slow learner Peter is.

Ten things you can learn after age 50
1. There is more power in celebrating things done right than criticizing things done wrong.
2. Don't fight grief. Give in to it. Grief heals itself.
3. Revenge is a waste of life. Forget about the aphorisms *Revenge is best served cold* or *The best revenge is living well*. Forget any form of revenge.

4. Learn to redefine and move on. For instance *loss* equals *freedom*. There are some things I cannot do anymore. That means I am freer to do something else.

5. Why not let someone help you? God knows I've done my share of helping others. I know. You want to maintain your independence. Okay. Decide, independently, to allow someone to help you.

6. Enthusiasm trumps precision. Get help from someone who really wants to help you before asking someone who merely can help.

7. Listening is a skill anyone can hone. Just because no one else does it is no excuse.

8. Eye contact says love. If you can see the face, you can guess where the eyes are.

9. Different is not a moral judgment. "What a mess this world would be if everyone were just like me!"

10. Don't grumble if someone asks you to repeat yourself. At least you are not being ignored.

This sermon progressed through several versions. The places it was preached also show movement from Baptist to Cumberland Presbyterian and then Presbyterian pulpits. The dates and churches are:

Zion Hill Baptist Church, Nacogdoches, TX 12/3/1995

Donelson Cumberland Presbyterian, Nashville, TN 5/4/1997

Mt. Denson Cumberland Presbyterian, Spring-
field, TN 5/13/2001
Wimberley Presbyterian, Wimberley, TX
5/2/2010
First Presbyterian, Socorro, NM 4/24/2016

JACOB: LOVE, ESAU: THPPPT

… Esau said, 'I have enough, my brother; keep what you have for yourself."…
Genesis 33: 1-11

Three stories. They are possibly three stories of confusion; but actually, I believe they each tell us something about grace.

First: I am still trying to check the details on this story. But it begins when a man with the same heritage prevailed on Isaac Stern to teach his son the violin. The young man had no particular talent but the father insisted that Stern teach the boy for the sake of the "Old Country." After many fruitless lessons, the father decided the son surely had learned enough to present a recital. Stern tried to dissuade him, but it was no use. So, the father rented a hall and scheduled the recital. Stern, in the meantime, not willing to impose on anyone else, decided to accompany the boy on the piano himself. So Stern attempted to put together a program that the young man could attempt to play and that Stern could also play as the piano accompanist. The program was a challenge for both of them. Isaac Stern is a world-class violinist rather than a pianist. The teacher realized, as time for the recital approached, that he needed help. So he asked an older friend to sit on the bench with him and turn the pages. He asked Arthur Rubinstein, the great Polish pianist to come to the aid of a young man from the "old Country" and his struggling teacher. Rubinstein agreed. So the time for the recital came and the young man sawed on the violin. Stern pounded on the piano. And Rubinstein turned the pages. It so happened that a music critic attended the recital and chose to comment on it in the next day's paper. His comments:

> The one turning the pages should have played the piano.
> The one playing the piano should have played the violin.
> The one playing the violin should have turned the pages.

Have you ever felt you were participant in a story like this? Has life shuffled you to the wrong part of the stage?

We all know the arrogance of the youth who knows all and can do all and feels it only fitting that world class performers be in the background. This usually starts about thirteen and lasts until the youth hits the real world, often after graduation. For me it lasted about thirty-five years, until my divorce led to a different home, a different job, and a different church.

Then there is the mode of playing one instrument acceptably when you could be doing something else much better. You've had that happen some afternoon or maybe for a long summer. I did it for a decade working for a Southern Baptist agency.

And maybe some of you have sat there turning pages when you could have been making a contribution elsewhere but . . . well.

Story two: consider Esau. You know all about Esau, don't you? The dumb jock of the Old Testament who sold his birthright for a bowl of bean soup. His younger twin brother conned him out of his inheritance and his father's blessing. Esau was the jerk who wandered off of center stage in history and we don't really know anything about his latter years.

Genesis 25 relates the birth of the twins Esau and Jacob. Esau—red and hairy.   Jacob grasped his heel. Esau was a hunter, Jacob a tenter. Isaac favored Esau and Rebecca favored Jacob. Jacob prepared a red broth and for it Esau sold him his birthright. Somewhere along the way, Esau picked up the name Edom which apparently means red. When Esau was forty years old, he married Judith and Basemath. They were Hittites. The writer tells us, "this was a bitter grief to Isaac and Rebecca." Isaac commissioned Esau to kill some game and prepare a meal for the reception of his blessing.

Rebecca heard and plotted against them. Jacob put on goat's skins and pretended to be Esau and received Esau's blessing. Esau flew into a rage and vowed to kill Jacob. Rebecca sent Jacob away under the guise of finding a wife. Esau belatedly realizes Hittite women are not the thing and marries his cousin. After some time, Jacob wanted to come home and sent his wives, children, servants, herds and possessions in front of him. After a wrestling match with an angel, Jacob limped toward Esau and his 400 men. Jacob, frightened out of his wits, met Esau who greeted him with, "Hey, bro', 'sup?" and a big bear hug.

And that's about it. Some years later Isaac dies and we read that Jacob and Esau buried him. We know nothing more about Esau.

We do know that his descendants were the Edomites. We know the Edomites had a monarchy 150 years before Israel. We also know that the book of Obadiah is a harsh polemic against Edom. And book of Malachi almost is. It begins with God being quoted as having said, "I love Jacob but I hate Esau."

His argument is that God loves Israelites better than Edomites because they have suffered a worse fate. And we know that Paul used this quote as a taking off point to speak of grace. It seems to me that Esau got a bum rap. He was quick to temper. Made unwise judgments but apparently was an honest hard working man. What little we know of him suggests that he, his wives and five sons flourished as a background for the conniving treachery of his twin.

Story three: Margie asked about my sermon and then suggested the anthem *Immortal Love, Forever Full*," a hymn setting for a poem by John Greenleaf Whittier. [Margie Halbert, choir director at Glendale Baptist Church] I thought it a good choice and then wondered to myself, "What do I know about Whittier?" Actually, it turns out, nothing. I checked my two poetry text books which I have kept from college and realized neither of them had a single reference to Whittier or his poems.

Why!? This is the poet who celebrated childhood in his poem *The Barefoot Boy.* Everybody knows those first two lines:

> Blessings on thee, little man,
> Barefoot boy, with cheek of tan!

You may not realize it but you know many of his poems. He was a great story teller. In his poem *Maud Muller*, he tells of:

> Maud Muller on a summer's day
> Raked the meadow sweet with hay.

A few lines later he introduces:

> The judge rode slowly down the lane,
> Smoothing his horse's chestnut mane.

The two have a pleasant conversation and then part. But Maud imagines herself the judge's wife and he entertains similar fantasies of a happy life with someone different than the cold women of his own caste. They marry people whom one would expect them to marry but throughout their lives, they day-dream of other possibilities. Then comes the lines that you can all say with me:

> For of all sad words of tongue or pen,
> The saddest are these: 'It might have
> been!'

Whittier tells stories of strong women. One such was *Barbara Frietchie*. Whittier tells of Rebel troops marching through Maryland and imposing their Confederate flags everywhere:

> Forty flags with their silver stars,
> Forty flags with their crimson bars.

But Barbara Frietchie took the stars and stripes and flew the colors from her attic window.

> Up the street came the rebel tread,
> Stonewall Jackson riding ahead.
> Under his slouched hat left and right
> He glanced; the old flag met his sight.
> 'Halt!'—the dust-brown ranks stood fast.
> 'Fire!'—out blazed the rifle-blast.

The volley shredded the flag but then Barbara Frietchie leaned out the window, shaking the rem-nants of the flag at the rebels. Listen, you know this poet's work:

> 'Shoot, if you must, this old gray head

But spare your country's flag,' she said.

Ashamed, Jackson turned to his troops to command:

'Who touches a hair of yon gray head
Dies like a dog! March on!' he said.

What a strong woman!

John Greenleaf Whittier lived the nineteenth century. He was born in 1807 and three months before his 85th birthday, he died within eight years of this century. Born on a farm to Quakers, he became a student of poets, particularly John Milton. He wanted to be a poet but his father convinced him poetry was impractical so he turned to journalism. He was editor of the *New England Weekly Review*. In his mid-twenties, need for him at home following his father's death, discouragement because of his lack of literary recognition, a failed romance and ill health caused him to resign and return home. He wrote abolitionist tracts, was elected to the Massachusetts legislature and later was a lobbyist. He began writing poetry again. The Civil War brought national tragedy and the deaths of three of his greatest loves: his mother, his sister, and with the union victory, came the death of his cause. Slavery was ended. The changes brought a maturity to his writing.

His poems include nearly one hundred hymns. Three are in our hymnal. Two are favorites of mine: *Immortal Love, Forever Full* and *Dear Lord and Father of Mankind*. Now you will immediately notice this great hymn has a problem with non-inclusive language. You must weigh that with Whittier's life which included a robust advocacy for women's suffrage.

Oh, yes, our hymnal also includes one we will sing in a moment, *I Know Not What the Future.* I've read the poetry before but never sung the hymn that I can remember. All of this is ironic for Whittier was a conservative Quaker who did not believe in singing at all during the Friends Silent Meetings.

I am telling you the story of a man I have come to appreciate quite strongly in just the last two weeks. A man whom I feel has been neglected in this century almost oppositely from the honor and high regard he received in the last years of his life. In his eightieth year, the town of Whittier, California was named for him.

I said these three stories might all suggest confusion. But I believe they are each stories of grace.

First: From the critic's view, all three men on that recital stage were out of place. But were they? The violinist and the pianist were in their proper places many times before and after. Isaac Stern played the violin solo in the filming of "Fiddler on the Roof." But whenever, before or since, did the young man have such a staging? Did he deserve it? Of course not. He was out of place. But that is exactly the definition of grace.

Second: What good was Esau? He was only needed to be the butt of Malachi's phrase. Jacob is loved, Esau . . .Thpppt. Even Paul used Malachi's phrase. But did God ever audibly say "I hate Esau?" I doubt it. Paul's whole point was the point of election and grace. God chooses some of us to bless all of us. Esau wasn't an ancestor of Jesus Christ. Does that mean he was nobody? No way.

Third: So, was John Greenleaf Whittier one of the great poets? Was he unappreciated, forgotten, misunderstood? Not at all. Thousands have been blessed by his poetry. Some knew to credit him. He was a humble man who shunned attention and was content to worship God. And the end of that story leaves us with songs of grace.

Oh, there is a fourth story. It's about a grumpy old goat pouting as he sits in the background turning pages, turning pages. I just wish he would remember how pleased he was years ago by John Claypool's sermon that taught, "Life is a gift." Whatever life you live, it is by God's grace.

John Greenleaf Whittier wrote in *Sunset on the Bearcamp*:

> Beauty seen is never lost,
> God's colors all are fast.

Preached at Glendale Baptist Church, Nashville, TN 2/11/1996

WORK

... we were not idle when we were with you,
and we did not eat anyone's bread without
paying for it; but with toil and labor we worked
night and day, so that we might not burden
any of you ...
II Thessalonians 3:6-13

This week I had the encouraging experience of attending a celebration for twenty years of a working relationship. Carole Farmer has been the nurse for Dr. Thomas Orcutt since July of 1976. A dinner was arranged to celebrate this and it was an occasion for affirming solid values. Integrity, loyalty, character, and applied energy were the expressions of the evening.

I was encouraged by this because I have been researching the subject of work for several weeks now. To explain that let me back up a bit. When I was asked to preach the four Sundays of July, I began to consider some topics that would fit together as a series. I decided to pursue the topics of **Work, Play, Relate, Pray**. In researching the relationship of these four areas of life, I came across a fascinating quotation. In the same year my father was born, 1914, Richard C. Cabot, a Christian medical professor at Harvard University, stated in his book, <u>What Men Live By,</u> that life is made up of four important dimensions: work, play, love, and worship. An overbalance of anyone of these to the exclusion of another results in a distorted Christian personality. [Harold D. Lehman, <u>In Praise of Leisure</u>] I have combined his thinking and mine to come up with four sermons: Work, Play, Love, and Pray.

Some of what I have learned about work is quite disturbing. Both from my experience and from my study I have found that work for many of us is not a happy time. Our four kids have learned from working at fast food places that employers seldom respect their efforts. They can be quickly replaced by someone else and thus their contributions are not valued. I have learned that an organization can profess the highest values and then completely ignore their stated public policy in the way they treated me. I learned that in working for Southern Baptists and for Tandy Corporation. I have heard for years that people should expect to be trained twice, three times, four times, more times, in the course of their careers because today's jobs will disappear and it is not yet clear how to train for the new jobs coming tomorrow. Recently, I have learned that the very concept of a job may be on the way out. Jobs were a creation of the industrial age. Before that people earned a living by farming or learning a skill and basically approached livelihood as entrepreneurs. Now, we are leaving the industrial age for the information age and with that transition, jobs, as such, are disappearing.

In "Evolution of the Knowledge Worker," Peter Drucker [in <u>The Future of Work</u>, Fred Best, ed] tells us good news and bad:

> ... while knowledge eliminates neither work nor skill, its introduction does constitute a real revolution both in the productivity of work and in the life of the worker. Perhaps its greatest impact lies in changing society from one of predetermined occupations into one of choices for the individual.

The good news is we can make choices. The bad news is it is a lot harder to make choices than to simply have to take what is dished out to you.

Well, if we no longer have jobs, where are we going to put all the workaholics?

William Barclay wrote in <u>Christian Ethics for Today</u>, "The Jew held work as essential – the essence of life. Greek and Roman civilizations were based on slavery." While pastoring a parish in Renfrow during the depression of the mid-thirties, Barclay noted that 19 of 27 elders were unemployed. It was then I knew what Sir Henry Arthur Jones meant when he said that the saddest words in all Shakespeare are: "Othello's occupation's gone."

And what happens to our much criticized and seldom understood Protestant work ethic?

So, here I was planning a sermon for today on work and next week on play and celebration and I get to be a bystander at a celebration of work. What a magnificent experience!

Work. This is not a subject I have frequently addressed in sermons. I found that in 1962, I preached a sermon on "The Christian Responsibility to Work" using the passage from II Thessalonians three. In that sermon I said that there is evil in idleness. It is wrong to burden others. And honest work is essential for a complete witness. At the time, I was in my early twenties. I was pastoring a mission chapel sponsored by the First Baptist Church. First Church was in the heart of the high rent district. The mission was on the wrong side of the tracks – literally – in an extremely low rent district. The pastor of First Church had grown up with my parents. When he learned I was in seminary an hour away, he appointed me to the position of mission pastor. Oh, the church voted to call me, but that was pro forma. J. W.

Brunner, pastor of First Baptist Church, Hillsboro, Texas, was a workaholic. He seldom did pastoral, or ministerial duties but he worked hard. I had a real struggle trying to match what I learned at seminary with what I experienced trying to pastor a small congregation I could not understand, while watching a possible mentor I could not bring myself to emulate. I told my people there was an evil in idleness. I saw it daily. I knew it to be so. I said it is wrong to burden others. To burden others is stealing, I told them. Well, that's not the whole gospel. There was much about their state in life I didn't understand. But allowing for some development of thought here, it is true: burdening others when you have the capacity to care for yourself is stealing. I told them honest work is essential for a complete witness. "Six days shalt thou labor," I quoted, "and then on the seventh shalt thou rest from thy labors."

Are those primitive concepts valid?

The Bible speaks strongly of a work ethic. *Any one unwilling to work should not eat.* Can't say it much stronger than that. In I Timothy 5:8 we read, *And whoever does not provide for relatives, and especially for family members, has denied the faith and is worse than an unbeliever.* Pagans. That's what it says here. If you don't take care of your own by providing the necessities of life, you are just like pagans.

Unfortunately, there developed in the church a feeling that there is God's work, which is special, and the work the rest of you do, which is cursed. The Reformation corrected this by emphasizing the call to work. Vocation, your calling, refers to your work or career as something God called you to do. John Wesley expressed it in earthy terms: "Earn all you can. Save all you can. Give all you can."

One thing is clear from what Paul has to say to the Thessalonians: Attitudes about work are a community responsibility. So, what sort of attitude should we affect, what attitude should we model or teach? The Protestant understanding of vocation includes at least these three points.

God calls us to our tasks. There is a religious dimension to work. Your vocation is person centered. Your life is unique. Your contributions are yours alone.

Work is goal oriented. We can be productive. We can create meaning with our lives.

So what does this work ethic have to say to us today?

We can be dismissed from a job for being too young and too well paid to retire soon. We can be let out to pasture for being politically or theologically incorrect. We can be downsized, right sized, reduced in force, early retired, or just let go on a whim. The corporation bottom line dictates who and how many are canned. The kind and quality of product takes second place to – again – the corporate bottom line, dollars.

Actually, that take on current business practices isn't so new. It boils down to greed which is as old as humanity. A conviction that God is interested in us as persons and wants us to live meaningful lives can direct us in any culture.

Tom Chappell, the CEO of Tom's of Maine, has written <u>The Soul of a Business</u>, a book recommended to me by my friend John Halbert. Chappell tells of his own struggle with trying to make his business fit with his values and the reverse. At one point, he talked with his pastor about maybe going to seminary and becoming a minister in order to do something, well, ministerial. Rev. Eckel's wife Connie interrupted him to ask, "How do you know that Tom's of Maine isn't your ministry?" That question became a turning point for Tom Chappell. His experience and his book are testimonies to how one Christian can discover meaning in his vocation.

I return to my third point of a sermon nearly thirty-five years old. Honest work is essential for a complete witness. We need to tell and to hear the kind of witness that I heard earlier in this week. There are employers and employees who go against the 'bottom line only' tide of the day – employers and employees who cherish human values, who cherish and exhibit integrity, loyalty, meaningful productivity, who are not afraid of commitment and industrious effort.

I went to dinner to play and came away enthused about work.

Preached at Glendale Baptist Church 7/7/1996

PLAY

Jesus sent two disciples saying to them, "Go into
the village ahead of you, and immediately you will
find a donkey tied, and a colt with her; untie them,
and bring them to me. ...
Matthew 21:1-11

A conquering general or a king would enter Jerusalem on a stallion; many had. But only a man of peace would enter Jerusalem on a donkey. Jesus came into town as a peaceful Messiah.

Whether or not the people understood what was happening, they were glad to see him and the story we read is the celebration of the coming Messiah. Most sermons speak of Jesus' humility as he rode on the donkey. Well, sure. Humility is one of the attributes that Jesus teaches us. But what about his sense of humor? Yes. Jesus is poking fun – at all the generals who conquered Jerusalem before him and those who would follow. His triumphal entry is on the back of a donkey. In one event, Jesus was both celebrating his role as leader and savior and giving the raspberries to all other militaristic messiahs.

The Bible is a book of celebrations. Why, Jesus first performed a miracle by turning water to wine at a wedding feast. Celebrations we know. But sometimes even our celebrations can get awfully heavy. The Bible celebrates but does it know a sense of humor? Well, most of the biblical themes are serious. So maybe there is not much room for humor. And little room at all for play.

I guess it is time for me to declare myself and say straight out: I am very serious about play. Yes, I believe playfulness and a sense of humor are necessary for good health. And I include spiritual health in that. After all, isn't one of the fruits of the spirit joy?

The Bible says God sits in heaven and laughs. Now that laughter is usually directed at sinners and unbelievers, but it's laughter none the less. There are many plays on language in the Bible that are difficult to appreciate since we don't speak Hebrew, Aramaic, or Greek. One of the most striking puns in Scripture is the name Isaac. Remember both Sarah and Abraham laughed hysterically over the idea they would have a baby at the ages of 100 and 90. But they did have a son whom they named *Yishaq,* Laughter. And there are some clearly funny stories in the Bible. We just haven't noticed them.

Jesus warns us that if we are going to follow him, we have got to stay with it. After all, he cautions, if you put your hand to the plow and look back, you aren't much of a farmer. Now that is a serious warning. But it is made with a funny picture. What happens if you are plowing doesn't matter whether you use a stick, follow an animal hitched to a plow, or drive a tractor— if you look backwards, you plow in circles instead of straight lines.

Here comes Jesus on the foal of an ass. What a topic for Monday morning! But Sunday worship? Indeed it is.

Jesus on a donkey's back reminds us of the creative power of novelty.

We've never done it that way before. That may be the best reason to try it. This is the power of play. Play is where our creative juices flow.

Jesus on a donkey's back reminds us of the consistency of good people doing good.

Have you ever noticed how often the people

we most admire, the people whose contributions we most appreciate – have you ever noticed how often these are people with a twinkle in their eye? People of peace. People who lead. People whose lives are a contribution are often humble people who have a capacity to play. The best players are often the best workers.

Jesus on a donkey's back reminds us of the wonder of excitability.

Today, we are doing something novel, something good. Some of us have been excited about it. Now honestly, does that include you? People got so excited they tore leaves off the trees and spread them on the ground and started singing hallelujah and Good Ol' Rocky Top!

Jesus on a donkey's back reminds us of the mystery of life.

Work and play, love and pray. They all four go together. Harvey Cox writes that the four traditional forms of prayer can be seen as forms of play. Supplication – asking God for what we feel we need – is an exercise in ordered imagination. Intercession – praying for someone else – is pretending to be someone else. Thanksgiving – well, it's not hard to imagine rejoicing as play. And penitence – asking forgiveness for our sins – is seeing ourselves from a fresh perspective and striving consciously to grow – to be a grown-up. Oh, no! See what I've done! Now we don't have to come to church the fourth Sunday. What am I going to do!? Oh well, let's laugh about it.

Jesus on a donkey's back reminds us of the healing nature of laughter.

Oh yeah! Here is the question we all should consider: What does it sound like when God laughs?

Thunder! That's what I believe. And lightening is the flash of God's smile or the glint in God's eye. And when God laughs all heaven has to join in. Like grandparents watching puppies lick a child's face and hearing the giggles, they chuckle too – you have to laugh. Then when all of heaven laughs there is thunder and lightening from horizon to horizon. The angels laugh so hard tears run down their cheeks and soak right through the cloud carpet of heaven and the laughter of God washes over us. Then the sun comes out and the air smells fresh and clean.

Dante wrote that when he finally arrived in Paradise after his arduous climb from the Inferno, he heard the choirs of angels singing praises to the Trinity and he says, it seemed like the laughter of the universe.

* * *

The Benediction. What is a benediction? The word refers to good being spoken. It names that time at the end of worship when the priest, minister, or rabbi says *GOOD* on the people. So that is our benediction today. Hear these words:

Good on you

And good on yours.

May good be what from here endures.

Now let's go catch folks unawares

By saying, Good on them

And good on theirs.

Amen.

Now give someone a hug.

Preached at Glendale Baptist Church, Nashville, TN 7/14/1996

LOVE

Beloved, let us love one another, because love is
from God.
I John 4:7-12, 16-21

Of all the worn smudged, dog's eared words in our vocabulary, "love" is surely the grubbiest, smelliest, slimiest. Bawled from a million pulpits, lasciviously crooned through hundreds of millions of loud speakers, it has become an outrage to good taste and decent feeling, an obscenity which one hesitates to pronounce. And yet it has to be pronounced, for after all, Love is the last word.
Aldous Huxley *Tomorrow and Tomorrow and Tomorrow*

Everything to be said about love has been said. But if that is so, why does it seem that love is so hard to find, so easy to lose?

My larger task is to discover some keys that will help us learn better how to relate. How can we build solid, valuable relationships? Of course, the answer – love one another – is too easy and too difficult. It tells us too much and it tells us nothing at all.

So what can we learn from John about love?

This is God's love: God sent His Son.

Love those whom God loves.

God is love.

Words of one syllable. How simple the language of First John. But how challenging his words. John seems to talk in circles:

God loves us. We are God's children.

We know we have chosen God if we love
those whom God loves.

What is love? Christ gave his life for us.

Love each other because *love comes from
God.*
If you don't love, you do not know God
because *God* is *love.*
God showed love by sending Christ. If this
is how God loves, we should love.
No one can see God but they can see God's
love in us.
We love because *God first loved us.*

A few elemental themes stated in terse terms and then restated. Soon we discover that these are not just simple circles. We are not waddling around a tree like Pooh, finding our own tracks and thinking we are following someone when, in fact, we are just tromping around the same old tree awaiting Piglet, Tigger or Eyore to explain it to us. No, John actually leads us in spirals and every time we come back to a statement of his themes, we are elevated. We have gone higher in our pursuit.

John says at least four pivotal things about God's love:

1. God loves us **first**. We haven't gone looking for God. We have been discovered by God's love.

2. God loves us **sacrificially**. It cost God to send a redeemer. God sent His only Son. Or say it this way:

God sent *Her* only Son. Somehow, there seems to be more pathos in that image.

3. God loves us **creatively**. See how much God has loved us! God's love is so great that we are called God's children – and so, in fact, we are.

4. God loves us **redemptively**. Because of God's action in Jesus Christ, fear is removed from all current and future encounters with God.

This material has a great deal to say to us about our relation to God but I wish to ask a different question of the text. John presents God's love as a model for our relationship with each other. In a short sentence, John tells us "People – love is the fruit of God's love." So my question, John, is this, "In a day of divorce, family violence, hate crimes, church burnings, racism and teenagers, how can we learn to live together?"

Let's see if we can hear John's answer.

Love initiates. Love is proactive. The best answer is always to be ahead of the problem. When I am tired, confused and frustrated, this is not the advice I want to hear – Plan Ahead. But it is what I need to hear. Decide what you are going to wear tomorrow tonight before you go to bed. That way your day will start happier and easier. This sort of time management advice works very well for love. Anticipate the need. Love first.

Harry Emerson Fosdick tells of his fumbling along in his first pastorate at Montclair, preaching to learn what he believed as much as to help anyone else with their faith. At a deacons' meeting when he was not present two deacons expressed concern over Fosdick's apparent liberalism. The preacher learned about it and with all the confidence of a young man who was being courted by two other churches, he met with the two deacons and asked them whether he should "stay in liberty and peace or leave at once." The two men encouraged Fosdick to stay. In his autobiography <u>The Living of These Days,</u> Fosdick writes that the two deacons often disagreed with him on points of theology after that but they always supported their pastor.

Love risks. Love makes sacrifices. It is costly to care for and about other people. I'm not talking about money, although love can certainly be expensive. I am talking about expended personal energy. Too often money is a substitute for other expressions of love. Love acts when I give me, myself, rather than what is simply mine.

> In one of the first women's suffrage parades in New York it is said that 89 brave men dared to march. After women's suffrage had been adopted, another parade was held in celebration. The original small group of men was invited to march in one section. On the day of the festivities all 520 of the original 89 appeared.
>
> Ernest T. Campbell <u>Locked In a Room with Open Doors</u>

Love enhances. Love works to improve. Love fosters growth. One definition of a parent is someone attempting to work themselves out of a job. Our task as parents, or as neighbors, or as brothers and sisters, or as spouses and lovers is to help the other person grow beyond needing that particular help.

> Ernest T. Campbell tells about his church in Ann Arbor, Michigan that a few days after John F. Kennedy was assassinated one of the members suggested a way to partially redeem the tragedy. He suggested they provide Marina Oswald with an opportunity to improve her English. They succeeded in quietly bringing her to Ann Arbor where they ministered to her in a variety of ways. At some point the whole story

became public knowledge and then the church
and the pastor began to hear from all sorts of
people who informed them their actions were
either unwise, unfair, or unpatriotic. Campbell
answered every letter and consistently replied
to their detractors with the statement, "The one
thing you haven't shown us is that what we
have done is unlike Christ."
Ernest T. Campbell <u>Locked In a Room
with Open Doors</u>

Love liberates. Love removes barriers and
attacks fear. Maralee helped me understand and
appreciate this quality of being loved. Love makes it
possible to go new places and have new experiences.
Something like that happened last week when church
became a free-form experience for some of our
children. Church became song, dance, play and Anne
Carrier's story telling – plus a totally ignored and
unnecessary ten minute sermon. Love works to free us to
become creative.

At Pec, Siberia, during a famine, a young man
drove ox carts over robber infested mountains. He
refused a military escort. When robbers stopped
him he asked them to join his cause and help
transport food to starving people. They did.
Pitirim Sorokin <u>The Ways and Power of Love</u>

Carlyle Marney divided the love chapter, I
Corinthians 13, into three stanzas. The first stanza
describes what love is not. The third stanza asks whether
love will work and concludes that it will. Stanza two,
according to Marney speaks of what love does.

Stanza two says that you cannot say Love with either nouns or adjectives. Love can only be done with verbs, which may sometimes become verbal adjectives descriptive of an action – so Love suffers (long), Love is kind, envies not, boasts not, is puffed up not, is seemly, is not self-seeking, not provoked. It keeps no books on evil but rejoices, and covers, and believes, and hopes, and endures, and never fails. And every verb is a verb of relation. There is not a functional verb in the stanza.
Carlyle Marney <u>The Coming Faith</u>

Preached at Glendale Baptist Church, Nashville, TN 7/21/1996

A VALENTINE FOR MARALEE

The young know of energy and passion.
They boast of strength and a smooth
complexion.
(Though they appreciate none of the
above.)

I choose to wear a cap because I must
and sit so long at times I gather dust.
But we – one well mature, the other just
– we know of love.

Jerry M. Self

2/14/1994

PRAY

In the year that King Uzziah died, I saw the
Lord sitting on a throne, high and lofty ...
Isaiah 6:1-8

We have come to a sad point when our society
has to find artificial stimulants to make life exciting or
beautiful. I suggest to you that worship can be a fan-
tastic source of stimulation. Consider Isaiah.

Evidently the prophet had come to a cross-
roads of his life. In 734 B.C., King Ahaz had rejected
the prophet and his messages a final time and was
seeking security in an alliance with Assyria. Perhaps
with a feeling of frustration and futility Isaiah withdrew
from public life. In his solitude he reviewed his past
and wrote down the messages he had preached
against a stubborn pride-filled people. Early in his
writing, he describes the one event that seemed to
fuel his whole ministry. There was that day when he
was at worship when something happened to Isaiah.

Description of that event could almost sound
like a drug experience. But this is not an occasion
when artificial means stimulated Isaiah to a chemical
high. This was an occasion when Isaiah realized
sheer reality.

Think about that worship experience. Appar-
ently Isaiah was participating in worship in an official
capacity. As court prophet, he stood with the priests
in the ceremonies of the cult. But more important
than any official participation, was his thorough per-
sonal involvement in the experience.

Abraham Heschel criticizes modern Jewish
worship as having everything necessary for dignity
but lacking life. Says Heschel, "One knows in ad-

vance what will ensue . . . . Nothing is going to happen to the soul. Nothing unpredictable must happen to the person who prays. He will attain no new perspective for the life he lives. Our motto is monotony." Isaiah conquered monotony with expectancy.

Perhaps what happened to Isaiah was that he saw through the symbolism of worship. Usually we see only the exterior of worship. We hear the words. We feel the rhythm of the music. We smell and taste juice and bread. Occasionally, some know the wetness of baptismal waters. But sometimes, as with Isaiah, there is the Lord, high and exalted. And his presence fills the room, fills the symbols, fills the participants. Sometimes the symbols give way to reality —the Real Being who fills the symbols of his presence. Perhaps then ritual becomes, as Walter Kaufmann describes it, the difference between mind-killing routine and beauty.

The description here is effective. We are told of throne, robe, attendants. All that surrounds the Divine Being is sketched for us but not God himself. The impact on the mind is powerful. Here is testimony that the presence of God is overpowering, it is an experience sensory overload. You cannot take it all in. It is an authentic high. You have to be there to know.

Other sensations manifest themselves. The antiphonal chanting of the Temple ritual fades into angelic choruses. There is the threefold holy. The Hebrew language has no way to express the superlative except by repetition. Once is good. Twice better. Three times best. Somehow the incense and its smoke contributes to a climax of cleansing. Often he would have gone through the act of ceremonial cleansing; but this time Isaiah knew to the very roots of his being that God had cleansed his soul, his whole being, his very self.

In this magnificent experience God's holiness was contrasted with Isaiah's life and also the lives of his fellow worshipers and his countrymen. Indeed, Isaiah must have glimpsed the gulf between God and humanity. But his recognition of unworthiness is followed immediately by the experience of cleansing grace and gracious commission.

What Isaiah describes is the potential of corporate worship. I suppose you might say this is the paradoxical potential of group worship. Isaiah tells us of the ultimate solitude. He found himself alone with his Creator.

Isaiah's testimony is for us. Here was a man of "good breeding," political stature, intellectually stimulating, a poet, a philosopher. Here was a man who looked backward to a worship experience in order to explain the motivation of his life.

Says the aged archbishop in Bruce Marshall's <u>Satan and Cardinal Campbell</u>, "Two things can save the world: prayer and thought. But the trouble is that the people who think, don't pray, and people who pray, don't think."

Perhaps this explains much of the frustration and discontent of our age. So many of us are living half-lives. Well, which half you have left out is necessary. Isaiah's example is that of a man who both thought and prayed. Worship was foundational for his life. **Let's consider for a moment three parts of this experience which so altered his life.**

First, there was the confession of sin. If you want a good argument, you can spend a lot of time debating whether people are basically good or bad. Perhaps the debate is useful. Perhaps it is a waste of time. But Isaiah's experience is not a bull session. Isaiah's testimony is that he sensed the very presence of God and his reaction was I'm in trouble because I am unclean. No matter what philosophy might say, experience has its own weight.

As one writer puts it:

> It was brought home to the prophet with startling clarity that however well he might have purified himself according to cultic requirements, however well he might have kept the customary rules of morality, in the presence of a holiness exalted in righteousness he and all men were unclean.

Sometimes this is a difficult insight to communicate. The term "sin" has all kinds of barnacles and incrustations on it. It means for some people an archaic concept of wrong-doing that doesn't have anything to do with your life or mine. In order to help you appreciate Isaiah's experience let me share with you mine.

This week I reread a portion of Harvey Cox's <u>On Not Leaving It to the Snake</u>. Cox is saying that sloth, or laziness, and apathy are continuously besetting sins. Interpreting Eve's mistake in the Garden of Eden, Cox writes:

> Before she reached for the fruit she had already surrendered her position of power and responsibility over one of the animals, the serpent, and let it tell her what to do . . . . We do not defy the gods by courageously stealing the fire from the celestial hearth,

thus bringing benefit to man. Nothing so heroic. We fritter away our destiny by letting some snake tell us what to do.

Reading that passage struck me in somewhat the same way that Isaiah was smitten by his worship experience. I was identified, spotlighted, humiliated.

The second feature of this experience for Isaiah was the realization of forgiveness. "He who would speak for God must know forgiveness, not as a doctrine, but as an experience." I can think of no word which is spoken more and heard less in worship. I wish that you could have the flash of insight that was Isaiah's and see the reality of forgiveness. Here is the cure that would conquer much of what ails us. You can't forgive one another because you cannot forgive yourselves. You can't forgive yourselves because you have not seen and heard the reality of God's forgiveness.

Finally, there is the commission. This completes the foundational experience of worship. Realization of forgiveness for deeply felt sin needs the direction of a sense of commission. Again, this is something lacking from contemporary society. Beyond our inability to recognize forgiveness is the blight of not finding meaning, purpose, or direction in life.

In worship Isaiah had an experience which carried him all through life. The reality of his esoteric personal experience became validated by the results in the prophet's life and work.

Out of this story and others like it, the image of fire remains in my mind. Remember the burning bush in Moses' story or the tongues of fire at Pentecost.

Here is what we need: In the midst of apathy and laziness we need a vision of fire, a consuming passion to ignite us into life. Maybe worship can be the spark. Maybe, if you come to worship,—there is double meaning there, if you come and if you come with intent to worship—maybe worship can be the spark.

Preached at Glendale Baptist Church, Nashville, TN 7/28/1996

LISTENING TO GOD'S VOICES

Everyone then who hears these words of mine and acts on them will be like a wise man who built his house on rock.

Matthew 7:24-29

In the musical *The Perfect 36*, we are told the story of Tennessee's ratification of the 19th amendment which gave the vote to women. In 1920, Tennessee became the thirty-sixth and deciding state in that question for voting rights for women. The second act begins with all the women in the cast lined up across the stage where they sing about women's voices. "A woman's voice welcomed you into this world. A woman's voice sang you to sleep," they begin, and as the tune repeats, they recount the influence a woman's voice has on each of us. As they sing, four men enter behind them; two on the left, two on the right. The second man in each pair has scarves over his arm. The first takes a scarf, walks up behind a woman and ties the scarf around her mouth, silencing one voice. They move toward the center gradually lessening the voices until only one sings. Then all are silent. To me it was a powerful representation of the ability of those in power to silence those whom they choose not to hear.

Today is a time for hearing voices. Listen for the voices of God. You see, God has many voices. I hope to make this clear this morning. As I talk about listening for God's voices, I am simply trying to tell you what I believe is important for you and me this morning. As I understand it, that is the task of the preacher.

The Master Carpenter tells us a story about building houses on suitable foundations. "Everyone who hears my words and acts on them," Jesus begins. Hearing and doing. Ah! There's the catch. How many times have you said, "I'd be glad to do something, if I just knew what to do."

My friend Charles Petty once told a group of us that we make too much of our confusion about finding God's will in our lives. Too often we know clearly what is right and wrong. We just choose to ignore what we know to be the truth. That was one problem they had with Jesus and his parables. He was too understandable. Boyd Hunt used to say to his seminary classes, "There may be a lot we don't know about God and the Bible, but truth is a lot like day and night. Maybe you can't put a knife blade into the separation between day and night. But the difference is tolerably clear."

"Be doers of the Word and not just hearers," warns James. All right, but first let's shed a little light on the hearing part. The voice of God is heard in other voices. God, as I hope to explain, has many voices.

"Oh," you protest, "I want an active faith. I want to *do* something about what I believe." Good for you. Listen to me, now, first comes the listening. And I'm sorry to tell you this, most of us are not good listeners.

God's voice can be heard from the person, Jesus Christ.

Here is the necessary starting place. We are Christians, the people of Christ. Whatever else can be said about us, what we share in common, what makes us community is Jesus Christ. What would Jesus say to you today? Well, he probably has already said it. We simply need to listen. And, of course, there is not complete agreement on what Jesus would say in any given situation, but I believe the voice of God sounding through Jesus Christ is tolerably clear. Our problem is we too often choose to ignore it or find ways to silence it. Here is where we begin. God's voice is clearest in Jesus Christ.

God's voice can be heard from the people in Scripture.

Most of what God has to say to us has been said in Jesus Christ. And most of what we can learn of Christ can be found published long before we came upon the scene. What is the Bible? God's word as experienced and voiced by God's people. Now, people will complain that Scripture doesn't seem to have precise answers for our modern technological world. I'm sure there are plenty of occasions when confusion is justified. But God's light beams from his Word yet today and its message seems tolerably clear . . . if we choose to hear it. What we learn, what we teach, what we preach are found in God's Word, the Bible.

God's voice can be heard from the people in Church.

Over the centuries, God's people have witnessed to one another and the world as to what they have heard and seen of God's work. Confessions of faith tell us the gospel in human voices. Why all these different denominations? And aren't we an imperfect bunch? Oh, yes, you know all the arguments about what a poor witness the church can sometimes be. But a witness none the less. Oh, you've got the rhythm figured out by now, haven't you? With all its imperfection, the witness of the church is still . . . what is it? Tolerably clear.

God's voice can be heard from the people in Distress.

Oops! Wait a minute. Didn't expect this. *'People in distress.'* Is that in the text? Hmmm. Well, yes, if you will jump from start to finish of Jesus' ministry to the point where he was about to be arrested and leaves his disciples with several parables. There in the parable of the Sheep and Goat Judgment he frames a question in his followers' voice:

> Lord, when was it that we saw you hungry and gave you food, or thirsty and gave you something to drink? And when was it that we saw you a stranger and welcomed you, or naked and gave you clothing? And when was it that we saw you sick or in prison and visited you? [Matthew 25:37 ff]

You have known the answer since childhood when probably you first heard it from a woman's voice.

> Just as you did it to one of the least of these who are members of my family, you did it to me.

This has always been true. Throughout Scripture. Throughout history. God has chosen the weak and powerless, the disadvantaged and needy to confront and chastise those who hold the reins of power in this world. When we see abuse, when we hear the cries of need, the voice of God seems tolerably clear.

God's voice can be heard from your own heart.

The Reformed tradition rediscovered the priestly role of every Christian. You can hear the voice of God in the voice of your brother and sister in Christ. And you can speak the word of God to them in return. Search your heart. Hasn't God already spoken to you?

A feature of Jesus' parables is his confidence in his hearers. Jesus believed that, if he told you the truth, you would recognize and respond. Throughout Scripture, when God's voice is heard, there follows an agitated reaction. Typically, the prophet Isaiah wails, "Woe is me! I am lost, for I am a man of unclean lips, and I live among a people of unclean lips." [Isaiah 6:5] When Jesus concludes the Sermon on the Mount, those who heard him were astounded. The response at Pentecost models for us how to reply to God's voice, "Brothers what should we do?" [Acts 2:37] That's where we are headed. What should we do with the message God has given us? But first, wake up, pay attention, listen carefully to the voices of God.

One of the great cataclysmic events of this century which is rapidly coming to a close is the collapse of Communism and the restructuring of the Soviet Union. Every commentator and political pundit has had an opinion as to why and how this came about. I like best the explanation of my friend Glen Hinson, Dr. Hinson's explanation tells us that the Russian grandmothers prayed for their country and sang hymns to their children for most of this century and what finally turned that nation was not political rhetoric or armed force but the voices of a nation of grandmothers in prayer.

I heard that.

One thing in particular I want you to hear. As a minister, I have made a commitment to making worship and my sermons an occasion where people have the opportunity to listen to what God has to say about their lives. Not so much that I know more than anyone else what God has to say. But I see it as my responsibility to give others the opportunity, the encouragement, that challenge to listen for God's voice.

Jesus Christ, the Bible, the Church, hurting people, your own spiritual sensitivity all resonate with the tones of God's voice. Before we come to the doing part: Listen.

Preached at Donelson Cumberland Presbyterian Church, Nashville, TN 1/9/1997

WITH THIS MUCH MOPPING TO DO, IT'S NICE TO SEE A RAINBOW

I have set my bow in the clouds,
and it shall be a sign of the covenant
between me and the earth.
When I bring clouds over the earth
and the bow is seen in the clouds,
I will remember my covenant ...
Genesis 9:8-17

Today is a beginning. A beginning of a new ministry together but also the first Sunday in Lent. The one is an opportunity to celebrate and make visionary Statements about what we hope to accomplish. The other is a time to consider the approach to the cross by Jesus with a somber evaluation of what his sacrifice means to us. Beginning with Ash Wednesday, many Christians spend six weeks – 40 days plus six Sundays – in fasting and prayer during the week and feasting on Sundays. Lent seems quite a contrast to any mood of celebration we might feel about a new start at Donelson Cumberland Presbyterian Church. But there is a common thread. That thread is found in one of the lectionary verses for this Sunday, the story of the rainbow. The common thread which comes from Genesis 9 is hope. The rainbow creates in us, calls forth from us, establishes for us: hope.

The flood and rainbow story stands out as one of our favorites. The boat, the water, the animals— what a story! But I don't believe we really have paid much attention to the gargantuan realities of this story. This is a really big story. Perhaps Noah was the mayor of a large city. He is described as an unusually righteous man in a time when character was not much in evidence. At some point Noah is impressed that God wants him to build a huge structure. So Noah begins to collect the necessary timber to build something on the order of Nashville's new arena. And then he builds a boat that is slightly taller and wider than this building and three times longer. He puts three decks in his ship. At the same time he collects timber, he also collects animals and birds. Two each of some but seven each of others. And he also collects enough grain and supplies to feed everybody for a long time. Consider this picture. This crazy old man is building a zoo the size of the Queen Mary in the Sahara desert. There is no place to float his boat and what a boat it is!

Ah, but one bright, dry, sunny day, Noah herds all the menagerie into the Ark and takes Mrs. Noah, their three sons and three daughters-in-law and they close the door and set up housekeeping inside their sailing zoo. Then it starts to rain and rains hard. For a month-and-a-half it rains. The rains bring a flood that finally lifts that huge boat and sets it moving. For five months they float. (Someone has said the church is a lot like the Ark. The only reason we tolerate the stench inside is because the storm outside is worse. I don't know how accurate that is as a description of the church, but it sure describes the Ark pungently.) All right . . . after five months, the Ark hits land and stops floating. But the world is still flooded. So no one can leave the Ark for another seven months. One year and ten days after entering their floating zoo, they all disembark. Wow! This is a big story. And rightly so.

This is a classic story of disaster. Part of the story has to do with the evil in the lives of some people. Part of the story has to do with innocent people caught up in a disaster. Part of the story is just about the destructive power of natural events. All of the story focuses on the rainbow. Whether disaster comes from our guilt, assaults our innocence, or just is—we need hope. Hope for forgiveness, hope for rescue, hope for tomorrow.

What does the rainbow say to us? Think about this:

Rainbows stay consistent.

Every time you have light reflecting off of raindrops, you see a rainbow. God has crafted this world so there are always rainbows. And the order of colors is exactly the same in every rainbow. The arch has the same curve.

Rainbows splash us with variety.

They may all be the same colors, but they are every color.

Rainbows mark our transitions.

Another way to consider the elements of a rainbow would be to consider the passing of the storm. Or the movement from dark to light. Rainbows always come on the edges of life.

According to the story in Genesis, the Ark rested on the mountain on the 17th day of the seventh month. The Israelites crossed the Red Sea on the 17th day of the seventh month. The resurrection occurred on the 17th day of the seventh month. Transitions which give us hope.

Now, if you are right in the middle of a mess, if you have a lot of mopping to do to get life clean again, I want you visualize Noah stepping off the Ark. Behind him is the mooing, braying, cackling, growling, grunting, barking, cawing, bellowing and hissing. Behind him is a family that has feared and argued and loved and fought. And in front of him is green of new growth; but beyond that is slime, sludge and mud. So much mopping to do. But then he turns and stretched across the sky from one end to the other is a bow with deep indigo, violet, blue, green, yellow, orange and red.

Have you ever seen a full rainbow? Usually we don't. We see maybe ten or twenty degrees, but not the full 180 degrees from earth back to earth. Forty years ago I had a summer job to earn school money. I was on top of Old Baldy mountain in Washington just outside the Idaho border. We could see across the "chimney of Idaho" almost to Montana and could nearly see Canada to the North of us. It had been a damp, drizzly night and the trip up the mountain from camp had been foggy. Later in the morning, we could see a good distance in any direction. There were still clouds to the East and toward noon we could see the most beautiful rainbow. I'll never forget that scene. It was is if I were observing the most magnificent landscape imaginable and across the sky was the signature of the artist.

By the way, the mountain was well below the timberline. The reason it was bald was because it was the heart of the Bluckensdurfer burn. Years before there had been a sizable forest fire. I was told that a ranger named Bluckensdurfer was killed when lightening struck his ranger station setting fire to the forest. I was also told that changes in forest ranger lookout construction would prevent future similar lightening strikes. By now, the forest has reclaimed the mountain. I'm sure the locals no longer call it baldy.

Hope. That's today's story. Find your rainbow. There is hope.

Preached at Donelson Cumberland Presbyterian Church, Nashville, TN 2/16/1997

A CRICKET IN MY HEART

But this is the covenant that I will make with the house of Israel after those days, says the Lord: I will put my law within them, and I will write it on their hearts; ...

Jeremiah 31:31-34

Internalizing values is the secret of maturity. Jiminy Cricket tried hard to be Pinocchio's conscience but he never was too successful. Anytime Jiminy Cricket forgot to watch out for Pinocchio, that wooden headed kid would wander off and get in trouble. Jiminy Cricket was upset by this and said, "If only I could get inside of him!" I guess what we need is a cricket in our hearts to tell us right and wrong. Jeremiah found the cricket for his heart.

Jeremiah began his ministry under King Josiah. Perhaps you remember that Josiah was king when the scroll of Deuteronomy was discovered in the Temple. When the scroll was read, a great revival broke out. Josiah was thought to be the greatest king since David. But spiritual activities take place in a political world. Josiah was the John F. Kennedy of the Old Testament. He was cut down in his prime. Both Assyria and Egypt had dominated Judah. Josiah successfully threw off Assyria's yoke. At a strategic moment, Pharaoh Neco led the Egyptian army North to join forces with the Assyrians to oppose a common enemy to the East. King Josiah saw this as an opportunity. He took after the Egyptians thinking he would win a great victory for Judah but instead got himself killed. Josiah's death is one of the most tragic events of the Old Testament. In many ways, it was the beginning of the end that led Judah toward the Babylonian captivity.

Jeremiah watched while bad leaders were followed by worse. He had the unhappy responsibility to warn his nation about their foolishness and their sins. And he received constant criticism and abuse. When false prophets were saying that God would rescue Jerusalem, Jeremiah told the people Jerusalem would fall. When false prophets were saying that God would bring a quick end to the exile, Jeremiah wrote to the people to settle down and learn to enjoy Babylon because they were going to be there awhile. When the people began to despair because they had been there so long, Jeremiah reminded them he had bought property while soldiers were camped on it. They would go back.

One of the strengths of the book of Jeremiah is the recounting of the prophet's prayer life. His prayers were confessional. He would preach God's message with confidence but then he would retreat to his prayers confessing his lack of understanding. With Jeremiah we can learn that prayer is sharing our life with God. Prayer is also seeking assurance from God about our lives. And prayer is a wonderful opportunity for intercession. Jeremiah's personal communication with God led him, naturally, to the discovery of God's promise of the new covenant. Here is where Jeremiah found God's cricket for his heart.

One of the most significant passages of the Old Testament is Jeremiah's comment in 31:31-34 where he describes the new covenant which will supersede the old and be written on our hearts instead of in our books. This is the high point of Jeremiah's writing and one of the most significant passages of the Old Testament. It is quoted in Hebrews. Jesus used this concept in his words at the Last Supper: "This cup is the new covenant in my blood." This scripture is the source of our distinction between the Old and New Testaments.

It is clear that God cannot reduce his standards and remain God. But we cannot live up to God's standards. So we have a dilemma: how can Holy God remain related to unholy people? By changing the hearts of the people. When God's word is carved on the hearts of his people, they will find God's forgiveness and God's forgetfulness.

Jesus echoed this in a conversation with a Samaritan woman—hardly the person or the place where we would expect great spiritual truth—when he told her that true worship is spiritual, a matter of the heart and not a matter of architecture or geography.

When we have a personal relationship with God, we identify ourselves with God.

God writes his message to us on our hearts. What a personal comfort! There is no need to worry about being lost in the crowd. Do you sometimes think all Christians look alike, so why would anyone notice me? How much more personal could the gospel be? God writes on our hearts! Of course, our hearts are not blank. Maybe some erasing is in order.

You don't have to have a teaching certificate or be ordained or have a military commission to do something creative or redemptive or meaningful. While all these things have their place, the most important thing about each of us is what comes from our hearts.

I recently drove past a blue collar neighborhood. Small five room houses on narrow lots. Ahead there were tables in a yard with toys and tools. A temporary clothes line displayed dresses, shirts, pants. As I came closer, there was a side torn from a cardboard box with El Marko pen capital letters advertising "ESTATE SALE." I sensed someone's sense of humor told me what was in their heart was more important than what was for sale in their yard.

When we have a personal relationship with God, we exhibit God's holiness and integrity.

Early imagery in this passage shows God leading his people by the hand. Just as there is a progressive disclosure of God through the Bible, there is a progressive development in our personal spiritual lives.

When God's word is written on the heart, then our hearts tell us what God wants of us. We don't have to be taught what our hearts know. What would it be like if we did not need teachers? Well, we won't know that anytime soon. Here is a foretaste of heaven. Now wait, before anyone gets too excited, I'm not saying that teachers can't go to heaven. I'm saying we will have no need to teach or be taught in heaven. This passage is not a proof text for doing away with teaching. It is simply an affirmation of the power of knowing God personally.

When we have a personal relationship with God, we are redeemed through God's gracious forgiveness and forgetfulness.

Consider, if you will, the power of Divine Alzheimer's. God forgives us and forgets the evil we have done. If only we could learn to mimic this Divine attribute. A friend told of his colleague's comment, "That's the third time you have disagreed with me." My friend said he could not remember the first two disagreements and did not understand why his colleague was counting.

Rest assured, God does not forget anything more than our sins. God does not forget us. This is the personal message of the gospel. God remembers his children.

In chapter 32, Jeremiah describes the purchase of a plot of ground. This is just before the fall of Jerusalem and Jeremiah is under house arrest or in jail. He buys some property from a cousin and describes in detail the meticulous process of payment and transfer of deed. Why such a concern for petty details when likely there were soldiers of the occupation forces camped on that ground? And besides, Jeremiah ended up in Babylon himself and probably did not see that property for seventy years—if he ever did see it! Jeremiah is giving witness of his faith. He says graphically, "I am not dead yet. You have not succeeded in killing me!"

Boethius, accused of treason and imprisoned without a trial in the time of Kind Theodoric, wrote his <u>Consolation of Philosophy</u>. John Bunyan wrote <u>Pilgrim's Progress</u> in Charles II's jail cell in 1660. And how many letters did Paul write from prison! Jeremiah had written a "Book of Doom" during the reign of Jehoiakim which is part of the first part of our book of Jeremiah. Now as Jerusalem falls about his ears and he is a prisoner in a besieged city, he writes his "Book of Consolation."

Carlyle Marney was preaching a revival in a southern city. During that meeting, he stood on the front steps of the church with a church member who noticed how the front steps of the church had been worn down through the years. Marney observed that the steps had not been worn down by the church members carrying their woes and their sins into the church. The steps were worn by the church members carrying their woes and sins back out of the church and taking them home with them for another week.

We don't have to do that. Bring your heart to God and let him tattoo it with grace.

Preached at Donelson Cumberland Presbyterian Church 3/16/1997

TWO WRONGS MAKE AN *"AI CHIHUAHUA"*

… let it be known to all of you, and to all the people of Israel, that this man is standing before you in good health by the name of Jesus Christ of Nazareth, whom you crucified, whom God raised from the dead.

Acts 4:5-12

If two wrongs don't make a right, what do they make? A few years ago we discovered a film named *The Milagro Beanfield War.* It is a story of Jose Mandragon and his village of Milagro. This is a small town somewhere in the Southwest which is drying up. Some law was passed in 1935 which restricted the use of water in order to conserve a natural resource. A large corporation is buying up land and has a plan to create a great resort center built around a dam and lake. When the project is finished, there will be plenty of water but for now, no one can irrigate their fields. But one day, Joe Mandragon starts irrigating a field and begins to grow beans.

Everyone goes into a panic. We've got a good thing going here, some people thought.

He might mess up the works. What does this upstart think he is doing?

The sheriff tries to talk sense into Joe. He asks the state police for help. They contact the governor's office. The governor sends a special investigator. They begin to follow Joe around hoping he will make a mistake. No one wants to do anything publicly which will draw attention to their actions. No one wants to bring bad publicity on the resort project. And everyone stumbles over the others making mistake after mistake.

Recently, I have discovered a copy of the book on which the film story is based. In the book, there are wonderful details missing from the movie. For instance, throughout the story, as mistake compounds mistake, someone will cry out, "*Ai chihuahua!*" As when the sheriff Bernabe Montoya drives his old battered pickup by Amarante Cordova and sees he is carrying a pistol. Cordova is an ancient man, nearly blind, who simply never has learned how to die. Sheriff Montoya asks him why he is carrying his Colt Peacemaker and learns it is loaded with bullets Cordova has bought with food stamps. All the sheriff can do is cry, "*Ai chihuahua!*"

In part, the story is about three or four different political bodies. All of them dislike and distrust the other. None of them want to be responsible for acknowledging their past mistakes. None of them want the responsibility of making the next mistake. And in the end, they all look like fools. Joe Mandragon's experience must have felt something like being tried by the Sanhedrin.

Last week, we read the story of Peter and John who had healed a lame man. The turmoil this caused led to a sermon by Peter. That sermon got Peter and John arrested and brought before the court of the Sanhedrin. This is the same official body which succeeded in having Jesus crucified only a short time earlier.

Who are these people? It might be helpful to understand the court in which Peter and John find themselves. The Romans had conquered Israel. They had their political appointees in place. But, for the most part, they let the Jews run their country according to their own laws. The Sanhedrin was a Jewish court. It was made up of priests and elders—something of a Jewish Presbyterian General Assembly. The people with the most authority were those who were of the High Priest party. There was only one High Priest at a time. But former High Priests stuck around, retained their title and some of their power. As a matter of fact, Annas had been High Priest and had succeeded in getting five of his sons and his son-in-law Caiaphas named as his successors. So, the family of Annas was quite powerful. This man owned the Bazaars of Annas. To understand his position, imagine the Temple area as a shopping mall full of stores and ATMs where you could buy birds, animals and anything else you needed to make a sacrifice or get the right change to give an offering, and then imagine one man controlled them all. That was Annas. As the major religious leader of Jerusalem, he was aware of Jesus and his disciples. As the mall manager whose table Jesus had upset, Annas was keenly aware of Jesus and his followers.

Now, think about the immediate background for Peter and John. It hasn't been that long since someone reported to the Sanhedrin that Jesus apparently brought some guy named Lazarus back to life. And Jesus was attracting quite a following. This could generate a lot of Messiah talk, which could upset the Romans if it got out of hand.

Everyone goes into a panic. We've got a good thing going here, some people thought.

He might mess up the works. What does this upstart think he is doing?

The Sanhedrin meet. Caiaphas listens to the debate and then says, "It is expedient that one person die on behalf of the people so that whole nation not perish." If you're going to make an omelet, you have to break some eggs. From that moment, members of the Sanhedrin attend Jesus' classes and attempt to snare him with his own words.

During Passover, they meet and debate some more when suddenly in comes one of Jesus' own followers, a man named Judas, with an offer. They agree to pay him the price of a slave to betray his teacher.

In the middle of the night, the sheriff and the state troopers led by the governor's special investigator bring Jesus to the High Priest's palace. There they find Annas who questions Jesus about his disciples and what he teaches. The time and place of this interview is entirely illegal, but the night is young and you ain't seen nothin' yet. Everyone is sent to Caiaphas' house where the Sanhedrin quickly gather. Paid witnesses attempt to make a case against Jesus but mostly they contradict each other. In exasperation, Caiaphas demands, "Are you the Messiah?" "You said it," Jesus replies. And then Jesus continues, "That means there will be a time when you will appear in my court." That does it. Jesus is condemned to death on a charge of <u>blasphemy</u>. But there's just a small problem. I mean, besides the fact this is an illegal meeting in an inappropriate place. They don't have the authority to convict a fellow Jew of a capital offense. *"Ai chihuahua!"*

At dawn, they go to the Temple and officially convene and again convict Jesus of blasphemy. Now, how do they get someone else to carry out the sentence? They tromp off to Pilate's court. They won't go to the Gentile court because their ethical sensibilities will not allow them to be ceremonially polluted at Passover. So, they ask Pilate outside. They say, "This is a bad dude. Have him executed." Now, Pilate was a cruel and somewhat bumbling political outcast. He had been sent to Israel, the Roman equivalent of Siberia, because the Romans didn't much like him. And the Jews learned not to like him just as well. Pilate was not necessarily big on ethics and conscience. But he wasn't going to be dictated to either. So he asks, "What are the charges?" "You don't need to know," is the response. "Okay, then you judge him in your own courts," retorts Pilate. "All right," they say, "He is guilty of treason. He doesn't pay his taxes. And he is trying to take over the country as a king." Whatever happened to the charge of blasphemy?

Pilate takes Jesus inside to talk with him and comes back out to say. "This guy hasn't done anything wrong. He may be crazy but he isn't a criminal." Oh, the noise that created! Including some comment about the wild Galilean. Galilee! Well, that's Herod's area. Send him over to the man in charge of the Galilee department. And off they go to Herod. You remember Herod – the sadist Tetrach who had John the Baptist beheaded. Jesus will not so much as say a word to Herod. Herod dresses him as a clown prince and sends him back. "Well," Pilate reasons, "if I find no fault and Herod finds no fault, let him go." "No!" they shout. So Pilate attempts to make them an offer they cannot refuse. He says, "I'll give you a choice. At Passover, we traditionally let some prisoner go free. You can either have your King of the Jews or you can have the notorious bandit-murderer

Lee Harvey Barabbas. Either peaceful Jesus or psychopathetic serial killer and federal building bomber Barabbas." And they chose Barabbas. "*Ai chihuahua!*"

Now, Peter is before the same court of clowns. He quotes Psalm 118:22: "The stone the builders rejected has becomes the chief stone." You threw away Jesus as trash. But God declares he is the greatest treasure.

Mistake after mistake after mistake. You know, if you are off course by two or three degrees, it won't make much difference in the next block. But if you continue following mistakes, you could eventually miss a whole continent. Mistakes happen. Life is full of our blunders. The cross was a cruel and a criminal mistake. But here is the lesson: From the trash heap of humanity, God took the stone that was thrown out and fashioned the keystone. God took what was called useless and made it more than useful, made it necessary.

You don't have to compound mistake upon mistake. There is a way to turn life around.

Why are you stumbling over yourself piling mistake on mistake?

Is it <u>physical?</u> Are you taking your medicine? Do you need a diet or an exercise program? Do you need to see a doctor?

Is it <u>mental</u>? Do you need to learn to read directions? Do you need further training? Are you attempting a task for which you are not well suited?

Is it <u>psychological</u>? Are you grieving? Are you dealing with unpleasant memories? Do you need to talk to someone? I take Thursdays off, but I am here most other days. My number is in the book.

Is it <u>social</u>? Are you running with the wrong crowd? Did you have a bad day, week, or year at work? Do you need a mother's-day-out program?

Is it <u>spiritual</u>? Huh? Is it spiritual? Do you mean prayer can cure a klutz? Maybe, if it's spiritual. That's what this story is all about. What pushes these people's buttons? Arrogance, greed, jealousy, selfishness—this is a spiritual story. And so is yours—a spiritual story.

So, tell me pastor, does the story have a happy ending? Did Peter's sermon prompt a revival in the Sanhedrin? No, it didn't. Well, of course, Nicodemus and Joseph of Arimathia were already followers. Others among the priests and elders joined them. Gamaliel, a highly respected teacher, spoke well of the Christians. But, no, basically the larger group continued to harass and arrest the disciples. They blundered along piling mistake on mistake.

But that doesn't have to be your story. God can take remnants from the recycle bin and create a treasure. Let God take your *"Ai chihuahua!"* and redeem it into **Hallelujah!**

Preached at Donelson Cumberland Presbyterian Church 4/20/1997

GOOD NEWS IS GOOD NEWS (THIS AIN'T NO THINKING THING)

The eunuch asked Philip, "About whom, may I ask you, does the prophet say this, about himself or about someone else?" Then Philip began to speak, and starting with this scripture, he proclaimed to him the good news about Jesus.
Acts 8:26-40

Such an upbeat Good News, Good News story! Now, chapter 8 doesn't start with good news. The 7th chapter of Acts is the story of Stephen preaching and being stoned. He is killed! Chapter 8 begins, then, with fear in the church. People scatter away from Jerusalem leaving just the apostles and a few others in Jerusalem. Then as the story develops a fellow named Simon the Magician comes along and sees and hears some wonderful things and wants to buy the Holy Spirit. Peter isn't too excited with that and deals with him in some very harsh language. I am not sure you want to know what the original Greek says. So, the story doesn't start with good news and then we come to this passage. Phillip comes upon an Ethiopian, the treasurer of some Egyptian country, who has come to Jerusalem to worship. Now, who is this guy? He might be Jewish—he could be a Jew from Ethiopia who has come to Jerusalem to worship. More likely he is a proselyte, that is he is someone who has converted to Judaism or possibly he is what they called in those days a *God fearer,* that is, somebody who goes to the Jewish synagogue, believes in one God and worships with them but hasn't gone through the Jewish rituals to actually become Jewish.

Well, we don't know. Anyway, here he is reading Isaiah and asking questions about it. He gets enough instruction from Phillip that when they see water, he wants to be baptized. After that happens, he goes on home rejoicing and Phillip who was on the way to the coast anyway, goes up and down the coast preaching until he comes to Caesaria which is home for him. There he spends his career. Later in Acts, we find him with daughters that have grown up and become evangelists. This is a <u>GOOD</u> <u>NEWS</u> story. Now I mean that in both senses—the Good News we understand biblically, is the gospel—the story of Jesus Christ. And more broadly we understand good news as good news! There isn't any way we can pare that down to the nub. It just says what it is. Good News. I think this is a Sunday when we need to talk about some good news.

Good news is good news. As simple as that really is, it is not something most of us understand. I think most of us, I am almost willing to bet, that about two-thirds of this congregation has grown up with the attitude that really good news is bad news. Now what do I mean by that? What I mean by that is that most of us have grown up with the attitude that things are going TOO good, that means that things are about to go south or turn sour. If everything is going too good, uh oh, something is around the corner that I don't want to hear about. We have the attitude that if we live in sealed off boxes—and right now, I am in a good news box which really has me scared because I have to leave this box and I will go down hill. The next step is bad news. I don't like here and what happens from here? Well, it could get worse. I could go from bad news to good news and you know what that means?

It means bad news is coming up again. And so bad news is good news is bad news. That is not a very comfortable way to live life if you are always worrying about how things are going to get worse. Yet somehow that is the attitude many of us have grown up with, lived with. Good news is bad news because good news means things are going to turn bad.

Well, let me tell you a little secret about life. First, the bad news and then the good news. The bad news is there is always bad news. It isn't waiting around the corner. It's here. There is ALWAYS bad news. Anyone of us can testify to that. But let me tell you the good news. The good news is there is ALWAYS good news. Sometimes it is just a matter which one you want to pay attention to. The bad news is they killed Stephen and drove the Christians out of Jerusalem. If that is the way you want to look at it, that is definitely the truth. The good news is, that things got so hot in Jerusalem, they had to leave, and by leaving Jerusalem, the rest of the book of Acts and the rest of the story of Christianity is freer from Jewish restrictions.

One of the good things in the early part of Acts was when the Christians had to leave Jerusalem and got in a freer Jewish and certainly Gentile atmosphere. The bad news is, this guy Saul is persecuting the Christians. Yes, but the good news is one of the world's great geniuses, Saul, so intensely looked at Christianity that eventually he was converted and became our greatest theologian and writer. Good news/Bad news. Which do you want to call it?

The good news is GOOD NEWS. As simple as that. This last week at The Academy of Country Music, Trace Adkins received some award—I think

maybe the newcomers award—and in the show, he
sang his popular current hit:

"I've been thinkin' about a love situation.
All this attraction in the present tense.
And I've come to a logical conclusion,
Love's not supposed to make sense."
This ain't no thinkin' thing—right brain, left
brain.
It goes much deeper than that.
It's a chemical, emotional, physical devotion—
a passion that we can't hold back.
There is no need to analyze
There is no rhyme or reason why.
This ain't no thinkin' thing!

Well, this, in a sense, is what I want to say to
you. This is Good News and it ain't no thinkin' thing.
It is a no-brainer. We can just celebrate and say,
"We've got Good News, hooray!" We don't have to
have some commission to analyze it to see if it is re-
ally good. We have Good News.

I have been reading and in the process trying
to learn something from Lyle Shaler's new book <u>Inno-
vations in Ministry</u>. It is a fascinating study of what is
happening in the church today. Early in the book he
tells about a friend of his who is a reporter. This friend
has a sign over his desk, this man who writes stories
for newspapers, that says, "Bad news is better news
than good news." The point is, bad news sells news-
papers. Good news doesn't. So for a reporter, bad
news is better news than good news. But for the rest
of us, good news is better for us. One of the things
Lyle Shaler says in his book is, "The church has lots

of good news." –meaning both the Gospel and all the good news that is happening in the church.

Let me tell you some good news. It is good news that there are people in our world and right around us that want to study the Bible. The Ethiopian is not the only person that has his Bible open today. There are people around us who WANT to study the Bible, who are eager to learn what the Bible has to say to them. Lyle Shaler says that one of the things that has come out of the emphasis in the business world on excellence is that there has been an emphasis on excellence in the church as well. Demming's emphasis on quality in business practices, has carried over into the religious area, too, and there are people who want to see quality Bible teaching in the church. The good news is that we have Sunday School here every Sunday at 10 o'clock with growing attendance and good Sunday School teachers. The good news is that there are people who want to study the Bible and the good news is, we teach the Bible.

Let me tell you some good news. The good news is there are people in our world and in our community right here who want to learn about Jesus Christ. "Of whom does he speak," says the Ethiopian, "Of himself, or of another?" And Phillip begins at that point to speak to him and teach him about Jesus. The good news is there are plenty of people around us who want to know about Jesus. Lyle Shaler says that a lot of people predicted that by the end of this century, the church would wither, and be composed only of very old people and very old women. First, let me say to you, if old people and women go to church, that is good news. But one of the things Shaler has discovered is, the number of young men who are going to church is on the increase. Young men are coming to church; all kinds of people are coming to church. People want to know about Jesus Christ. In every worship service of this church, the central theme of our prayers, of our singing, or our preaching—of ALL that we do—the central theme here is the Gospel of Jesus Christ. That is good news.

Let me tell you some good news. The good news is there are people in our world and in our community that want to join the church. The Ethiopian's study with Phillip leads him into the process that makes him a Christian and a part of the first century church. There are people around us that want to join the church. For sometime now, people who study the church have been discouraged about Baby Boomers and the x-generation. X-gens and Baby Boomers do not have brand loyalty. They don't buy their dad's Oldsmobile. They are not brand loyal and they are not likely to go to Dad and Mom's church. But the interesting thing is, Baby Boomers and X-Gens do go to church. Lyle Shaler tells us there are 7 different kinds of churches that they attend:

They go to new congregations—well, that is not us.

They go to big mega churches—huge churches—well, that is not us.

They go to downtown churches—well, that is not us.

They go to non-denominational and independent churches—well, that is not us.

They go to churches that emphasize people more than institution. AH-HA

They go to churches that have an emphasis on preaching, teaching and fast-paced worship—maybe.

They go to churches that welcome seekers and pilgrims and people that are looking for meaning.

Well, no one church can be all seven of those things, but we can at least be two or three! There is good news there. We can be a congregation who attracts people who are looking for church.

Let me tell you some good news. The good news is this world is populated and this community has people in it who will come to us. Now, if you've studied anything about church growth today, that sounds like exactly the opposite of what I need to say, because most people who have analyzed church growth today say you have to go to them and you have to fashion the schedule for them and you have to do what they want you to do to attract them—you have to go to them. Well, let's think about that in its scope for a moment. Philip went to the Ethiopian. But he didn't go to Ethiopia. He didn't go to Africa. He went out of town a ways. The story says the Ethiopian came to Jerusalem and he is on his way home, just barely outside of town. And Philip finds him on a preaching route that is going to take him to his own home. Yes, Philip went out to him, but essentially, the Ethiopian came to him. We can have a religious, evangelistic ministry and we don't have to go to Japan, or South Africa, or South America or Asia. We don't even have to go to Kentucky. We can stay at home and find people who want to come to us. We may have to step outside the door and find them, but we don't have to go to Ethiopia.

We have good news. Somebody is probably thinking, you don't know my story: I don't have good news; you don't know about living in my family; you don't know about my job; you don't know about my health. You are right! I don't understand the bad news that you have lived or are living with.

For my 25th wedding anniversary, I got a divorce. After 30+ years of service to a church and a denomination, I went into the boss of the agency to talk to him about how we could do things better, and before I could say a word, he told me his plan for making things better was for me to leave—to get a job someplace else. I went in for an annual physical, just routine stuff, and I found out I had cancer of the thyroid and I had to have surgery. And my kids—well, none of them are in jail and we have decided not to kill any of them, they are really good kids. But you are quite right. I probably don't understand the kind of bad news you've experienced. But my point is not that we don't have bad news. We do. My point is, we ALWAYS have good news. We ALWAYs have GREAT news. What I read in Acts is: if two people get together and read the Bible, they can help each other find the good news for themselves. And you know what the good news here is? We always have at least two people. We've got good news!

Preached at Donelson Cumberland Presbyterian Church 4/27/1997

ONE'S ENOUGH

To speak of forgiveness, how can I
with more feelings than can fit this place in time,
but with no enthusiasm for talk or even mime?
to speak of forgiveness now, can I?

In a perfect world forgiveness poses no problem.
Offenses, quickly recognized bring forth apology.
Apologies once heard are easily forgiven.
Poor me, devoid of such sensibility.

Seldom do I sense hurt's causes in a run.
Rarer still I recognize the damage that I've done.
How quickly apologize to someone gone: dead or
moving?
How quickly easily forgive someone absent: divorced
or daydreaming?

Life's not fair we tell the kids.
Not that they needed the telling.
But a life without making amends?
A life where there's no reconciling?

Life means jagged edges:
a bump or nick, a little white lie.
'Don't worry about it.'
But it collects in my lower GI.

Some people should carry a sign,
'Irreconcilable by design.'
If we can't make up with evaporated kin,
can we make do with a reachable friend?

On occasion my quiet 'I'm sorry'
cannonades with booming admission.
My simple 'It's OK. Forget it,'
voices more than an easy remission.

David cries 'Against God only have I sinned.'
'Nonsense!' buried Uriah calls, 'Count again!'
But when did death's voice carry under the sun?
In grieving repentance David stands alone save One.

So, if there is One to taste the brine of my apology,
One to flourish when my forgiving's through,
whether either or neither's offended/offender -
One's enough. One will do.

Jerry Self
February, 1994

BULLETPROOF VESTS FOR THE SOUL

... Put on the whole armor of God, so that you
may be able to stand against the wiles of the devil.
Ephesians 6:10-20

From these final verses of Ephesians we get
the picture of Paul in prison. He is possibly chained
to a Roman soldier or sees soldiers on a daily basis.
No doubt he has befriended them and told them about
Jesus Christ. His experience may have been close to
what John Steinbeck described. Steinbeck's share-
cropper has had his farm foreclosed but not by the
local banker. No, the banker was responsible to the
home office, and the home office was responsible to a
board of directors; and the board of directors had to
explain their actions to thousands of stockholders.
Even so, Paul knew the man with the keys couldn't
unlock the door because he reported to someone who
reported to someone who reported to someone. The
adversary was large and invisible. But if Paul couldn't
see the powers that be which controlled his freedom,
he could see the soldiers and the way they were
clothed and equipped. Their armor set him to think-
ing. I have gone through three stages of development
concerning this sermon and I want to tell you about
them. Rather than give you three points from the text,
I want to tell you my three separate thoughts about
the text.

**My first thought was: This is not a contem-
porary or politically correct text.**

This is a text about militia uniforms and
weapons. It is a masculine text. It smacks of boys
who want to play soldier. It doesn't seem to speak to
women's issues. It doesn't seem to recognize social

pluralism. It is triumphal and militaristic. This is an aggressive, combative gospel. All the arguments about why we should not sing Onward Christian Soldiers can be marshaled against reading this text.

In some way or other I face this problem with every sermon. Perhaps you have had a similar experience with scripture. The text may be fascinating, intriguing, curious, mysterious, or puzzling. The foundational question always comes, no matter what the text, what does God have to tell us here? Sometimes the answer is so blue sky clear there is no escaping it. At other times it takes time, prayer, and serious commitment to discover the message.

My second thought was: These are violent times.

Read the newspapers.

We are pulling out of Afghanistan. Will Americans be evacuated in time? Will women who spoke out in behalf of other women escape with their lives?

Four police officers were shot this last week in Albuquerque, less than a mile from where we live. Fortunately, the Kevlar vest of one officer stopped the bullet.

Only a few days earlier, a 13 year old shot and killed another 13 year old at a school just South of Old Town in Albuquerque.

Gallup, New Mexico, has one of the worst crime rates in the state.

Our news broadcasts are full of stories about victims. All about us people are being assaulted. And the frightening thing is these victims are our neighbors. The assaults are happening close by. More frightening still is the realization that the attackers are our neighbors as well.

When you realize that women and children are more often the victims but sometimes also the abusers, then violence becomes a woman's issue, too. We're not talking about boys' macho games. We are talking about life as it really happens.

My third thought was: I missed the radical message in the scripture.

Both sensitivity and violence are addressed in resurrection power. The biblical message usually turns us inside out.

Look at the text again and maybe this time I will not miss the radical message here. In summary, this is what the passage says.

1. The problem is deeper than physical violence or abuse. The problem is spiritual.

2. Defending yourself against spiritual violence and abuse cannot be done with Kevlar vests and assault rifles. You need God's armor which is truth, righteousness, peace, faith, God's salvation. Our only offensive weapon is the word of God.

3. Rather than fear, our continual posture should be one of prayer.

Yeah, right. An invisible armor for invisible enemies. What is this, an X-Files sermon? Paul was in prison. A lot of good it did him!

Jump back there. It did him a lot of good. Paul carried God's protection for his person which defended him better than anything his guards wore.

The expression "put on the armor of God" is a little vague. Does it mean that we are given a bullet-proof vest which God fashions for us? Or does it mean that God gives us the armor He himself wears? Probably the latter. Because, you see, when Paul looked at the centurion next to him, the helmet and breastplate, what he saw reminded him of biblical passages like Isaiah 59:17: Justice was the Lord's armor; saving power was his helmet ...

Amazingly, the weapon of God's resurrection power is talk. The word of God has enormous power.

David Buttrick tells a story from the Czech underground. When the Russians overran Czechoslovakia they mounted a huge parade as the conquerors. Tanks and missiles and soldiers stomped through the streets. But suddenly there was a little blue pickup truck weaving through the parade. In the back of the truck was a six-foot sign that read, "For God's sake, why?"

Yes, I suppose ending up in jail means Paul was a failure. Just as Jesus failed when most of his followers got tired of him and left. Just as Jesus failed when he too was imprisoned and executed. Failures until we come to Peter's realization. We don't have any place else to go.

You, Lord, have the words of life.

Preached at Donelson Cumberland Presbyterian Church 8/24/1997

WHO WILL ANSWER YOUR PRAYER?

On the day when Elkanah sacrificed, he would give portions to his wife Peninnah and to all her sons and daughters; but to Hannah, he gave a double portion, because he loved her, though the Lord had closed her womb. ...

I Samuel 1:4-10

The setting for this text finds us following up on the book of Judges. With First and Second Samuel, we are beginning a new set of stories that will usher us into a new era leaving behind the time of the Judges. The two books of Samuel will tell us two basic stories: one is about leadership, the other about the presence of God. The major leaders described are Samuel, Saul and David and their stories are some of the grandest of the Old Testament. You know them all. They are epochal events. Huge stories. Memorable tales which we love to recite to our children. So how do we get into the story telling? Where is our beginning point? Well, the most natural story setting: right in the middle of a family squabble.

We begin with a religious festival. It's a holiday and the family is gathered for a big turkey dinner. Sound familiar? Ever been there? But no one is happy. They don't like to be together because there are family issues. When they get together certain *people* say certain *things* in a certain *way* which always results in *certain responses*. And everybody is miserable. Get the picture?

Let's see what the issues are. You may be surprised because what is happening is not quite what you may have thought. Elkanah has two wives. Han-

nah has no children. Peninnah has several children.
During that period of history, and others as well, chil-
dren were your future. Old age without children would
be a disaster. Children were your heritage and your
security. Polygamy was not greatly practiced. That
would refer to multiple wives. Few could afford that.
But bigamy was common. Two wives, now that was
within the range of possibility for many. Or so they
thought. While bigamy or polygamy could answer the
problem of having sufficient children, both of these
practices created severe marital problems. And we
have an excellent example right here.

One wife bears children. One wife doesn't.
Now it appears that the problem here is that Peninnah
is favored and Hannah is not. There existed then an
erroneous belief that, since God caused or prevented
pregnancy, then having children was a sign of God's
blessing, barrenness was a sign that God had cursed
you. Actually, that is only secondarily the problem
here. We have a complex family dynamic at work.
Elkanah loved Hannah. He used Peninnah to get
children. There is where the problem begins. Penin-
nah understands her husband's feelings all too well.
She is intensely jealous and uses the popular erro-
neous theology to dig at Hannah every chance she
gets.

"I'm sorry, did my children get in front of your
children? Oh, that's right. God hasn't given you any.
Aren't children a blessing? Well, you wouldn't know,
would you? What must you do with your time? You
don't have any children to look after!"

They come to the temple for a religious gather-
ing. On this occasion the family would sacrifice an
animal and part of the festival would involve contribut-

ing half of the meat to the temple and then using the other half for a family meal. Not unlike Thanksgiving at grandma's. A certain amount of food would be provided for Peninnah and her children. A different portion would be given Hannah. Now the text is a bit obscure here. It may say that Hannah gets a single portion, not as much as Peninnah. That would underline the difference between having children and being barren. Or the text may mean that Hannah got a special portion, maybe more than Peninnah and kids. That is the interpretation of the Revised Standard Version. That would underline the difference in Elkanah's feelings toward his two wives. Either way, Elkanah creates a major family crisis—and he doesn't have a clue as to what is going on.

Now, Eli plays a fascinating pivotal role in our story. As I said, there are two major stories in the Samuel literature. One tells about Samuel, Saul and David, the great leaders of Israel. The other story tells about how God is present with his people. Eli, to some extent, represents both of those stories and sets for us the problem both of those stories will answer. Eli was a leader and represented God's presence. Eli was a failed leader and did not adequately represent the presence of God.

In the next chapters we read a prophecy that Eli and his sons will be removed. We read of a battle where Eli's sons bring the ark of the covenant to the battle front to represent God's presence in the battle. The Israelites cheer them and the ark. The Philistines are frightened by the cheers and attack early out of their fear with the result that they win the battle. We read that they kill Eli's sons and capture the ark. We read Eli hears of the defeat and loss of the ark and falls backward, breaks his neck and dies. We read Eli's daughter-in-law goes into early labor and bears a son whom she names Ichabod, which means God's glory departed. Sounds like a *The Grinch Who Stole Christmas* story.

Every time I stand up to carve a holiday turkey, I breathe a silent prayer that no one falls over backward and breaks their neck this time. I know you do, too.

Now, back to Hannah. Hannah runs from the table in tears—oh come on, that never happens in real life—or does it? She runs off to pray. And that gives us an opportunity to meet Eli. Eli is an old preacher who sits by the door of the temple and watches what goes on around him. He thinks, "Here comes another wife in tears. She'll go into the temple and rant about an insensitive husband, or son who never writes, or a daughter or daughter-in-law who doesn't appreciate the way she 'specially basted the roast." But no, this one is trying to pray but the words aren't coming out. "Oh, brother, another drunk. It happens every holiday. Too much wine before, during and after the meal and they can't handle it." But that's not the case here. This woman has a deep heartache and a genuine prayer. Eli returns to pastoral instincts he hasn't used in years. He blesses her with the words, "The God of Israel will hear your prayer." She goes on her way at peace, more from her own prayer than from his words.

Who will answer your prayer?

Ultimately, God will. Eli said the right thing to Hannah. The God of Israel answers our prayers.

Occasionally, a great leader will answer our prayers. Or, if you prefer, God occasionally answers our prayers through great leaders. Maybe you have seen this happen in your lifetime. A Samuel, Saul or David bursts on the scene, larger than life. And something marvelous happens. Goliaths fall, nations unite, temples are built, peace reigns. It happens.

Sometimes a local minister says the right words. Every now and then, it happens. Eli was a bumbling father. He apparently was a mediocre priest. At least once, he said something helpful and appropriate. A pedestrian, we might say. Run of the mill, one might call him. Salt of the earth, if we're kind. Ordinary, could be a fair assessment. Most of us try to do our jobs the best we can. There are days when someone points a finger and announces, "God will get you for that." And we know that's the truth. But sometimes, on the most ordinary day, doing business as usual, I've heard someone say, "Why, you're an answer to prayer." It could happen.

Surprisingly, those closest to us quite frequently answer our prayers. Elkanah has no idea that he has driven Hannah to her prayers. And I expect he has not much more awareness of how he participates in the answer she receives. But it happens.

Maybe one thing that stops up the prayer process is the unacknowledged answers we have received to prayer. Here's an idea you can use at the holiday table. Ask the people there, "Who has answered your prayers?"

Of course, the God of Israel answered your prayers. And maybe someone else . . .

Preached at Donelson Cumberland Presbyterian Church 11/16/1997

TEACHING COWBOYS TO COUNT AND FARMERS TO DANCE

Then Jesus said, "There was a man who had two sons ..."
Luke 15:11-32

He had two boys. For all their differences, and there were many, deep in the inner recesses of their souls they were just alike. Neither one understood or appreciated what they had.

The cowboy wants to ride the free range. He wants to go to the saloon and drink, gamble and dance whenever he feels like it. He wants to sleep under the stars. So one day, he confronts the Old Man and says, "Give me." And off he rides into the sunset. He attacks the world with his cowboy attitude. I'm all by myself out here. I can go and do as I please as long as Daddy's money holds out. One day, the cowboy finds the saddle bag empty and then realizes he isn't really a cowboy. He has just been pretending. A real cowboy could make it on his own. This one cannot. He gets really hungry and would have even eaten the meal that was used to feed cattle but no one would give him any.

The farmer gets up before sunrise to tend to his chores. He works hard outside and in the evening, comes in to figure the accounts. He never considers what he wants. He simply does what he is supposed to do. He's offended that his cowboy brother walks off with part of the family's resources, but he's not really sorry to see him go.

So very different they are. But deep in the inner recesses of their souls, they were just alike. One day the cowboy comes home. Listen to the conversations:

> I'm no longer good enough to be your son.
> *Hurry! Bring better clothes.*
> *This son of mine was lost.*
>
> What's going on here?
> I slaved for you and you don't appreciate me.
> This son of yours wasted valuable family re
>   sources.
> *My son, you are always with me.*
> *We must celebrate!*

What an incredible story! The parable has been called the greatest short story every told. It can be turned about like a precious stone so that it catches different light and sparkles with new colors.

Such a rich story can be read from many perspectives. John Leggett describes the possibilities by imagining the filming of a movie which will go on to win multiple Academy awards. Cameras have been set up in every possible location but only one image will make the final cut. Which one? One person will focus on the younger son. At first telling, he seems to be the story. Another will say the whole reason for the story is to get to the elder brother's reaction. There's the story. "No," says another, "The point of the story is about the party—focus on the celebration." Wait, a minute! You missed the point. It's the story about the Father. This is a story about a loving, waiting Father. "But," says someone else, "There's another possibility. This is really a story Luke is telling. The story is about Jesus, the Master story teller. This is a wonderful story about Jesus telling a wonderful story." Of course, the truth is, all of those opinions are correct.

The Father allows his children their natural personalities.

The two children in this story are like all kids the world over. They are not the same. The Father honors their distinctiveness. The younger son wants to leave home. He wants a different life from what he has experienced so far. Good for him! Let him go. Initiate! Experiment! Travel! Take what we can give you and see what you can make of it. These are not bad things. If the child wants to leave, hold the door.

The elder brother wants to stay home and be responsible for things. All right! Here, you can be in charge of planning, and be responsible for the personnel, and here, take the check book. Write the checks, reconcile the bank statement. Do the shopping, clean the toilets, plan the menu. You want to work? Go for it. These are not bad things. If the child wants to work, hand him the tools.

The Father teaches His children skills which are not natural to them.

The cowboy doesn't know how to count and what counts. He assumed a worthiness and then assumed he had lost it. The farmer had made his life a drudgery. His devotion to duty was laudable but stifling. It may be slow coming, but at some point, most children will approach a parent and say, "Okay. I don't know everything. Can you teach me how to do this?" What an act of love and grace, to patiently teach a skill for which the child has no natural aptitude. If you are fast, anyone can teach you to race. If you inherited the organizing gene, anyone can teach you to file. If you have a bent toward chemistry, anyone can teach you to cook. But what if you need to be able to fix the plumbing and don't know the difference between a ratchet and a sachet? Who will teach you?

The Father speaks to His children where they can hear his affirmations.

It's good to hear someone brag on you. It's good to hear someone say to a third party, "I love this person." Oh, I know it can be embarrassing sometimes to hear a parent describing your exploits. But there are darker days when it will feel good to remember the words.

This boy comes home to say to his father, "Give me . . . " But this time it is not the callous selfish demanding that the world take care of him. This time he begs a slave's position because, he says, "I am not worthy to be your son." He has yet to learn that sonship wasn't something he earned in the first place. He is not a son by virtue of worth and will not lose his sonship by virtue of worthlessness. The father boasts loudly to the others, but it is his son's ears that must hear. "This is my son."

The Father speaks to His children in clear terms.

"My son." How those words needed to penetrate the elder brother's mind and heart. I have a mental picture of Jesus telling this story. As it gets to the last exchange he must have looked deeply into the face of one of the Pharisees and spoken the words of the Father, "My son, you've always been home."

Reading the Greek text, I was stopped short by the twenty-fifth verse. The expression "the elder son" is *ho huio autou ho presbuteros*. The Presbyterian boy. Presbyterians are those church people who organize themselves on the Elder system. I believe the Pharisees were the Jewish equivalent of Presbyterians. Ernest Campbell comments that we have a problem in that we have a Loving Father gospel but an Elder Brother church.

The radio is on at the back of the house blaring a commercial announcing it is ten p.m. and asking if you know where your children are. On the front porch, the father sits in a rocker with another cup of coffee and watches the road. It doesn't have to be ten o'clock at night for him to ask, "Where is my child?"

Preached at Donelson Cumberland Presbyterian Church 3/22/1998

WHAT IS GOD DOING TODAY?

But Judas Iscariot, one of his disciples (the one who was about to betray him), said, "Why was this perfume not sold for three hundred denari and the money given to the poor?" (He said this not because he cared for the poor, but because he was a thief; ...)
John 12:1-8

Sometimes it's hard to pay attention to right now. We are part of a stream of life which reaches back long before our awareness and will stretch forward after we are all gone. We benefit or suffer from what others have done. Those who follow us will benefit or suffer from what we do. The poor will always come knocking at our doors. There are responsibilities in life which are continual. But some opportunities are fleeting. Right now is an opportunity which never happened before and will not be repeated.

Jesus was in the heart of a maelstrom. We know from John 11:57 that he had been virtually declared an outlaw. It must have taken an act of courage for him to approach Jerusalem. This story finds him in Bethany. It is Passover. Jerusalem will be packed. This is Fan Fair, Christmas shopping in the mall, a Home and Garden Expo at the fair grounds or boat and tool show in the arena all rolled into one. At Passover, the crowds pouring into Jerusalem have to find housing in one of the perimeter communities. One of those small towns that ringed Jerusalem was Bethany. The Titanic is about to go down completely. This is *it*, or almost so. We are on the very edge of disaster. Time to focus on the moment. But it is hard to do so. In Isaiah's words,
Do not remember the former things,

or consider the things of old.
I am about to do a new thing;
now it springs forth,
do you not perceive it?
I will make a way in the wilderness
and rivers in the desert,
to give drink to my chosen people.
Isaiah 43:18-19

I remember seeing a picture from the Nagano Winter Olympics. A speed skater in bright colors has arms and legs extended as he leans forward. Obviously, from his posture he is moving rapidly. The skater is in perfect focus but all else is blurred. The photographer had moved the camera with the skater as he took the picture. As we focus on this tableau, let's forget past and future, forget crowds and conditions. Jesus is being prepared for burial. Maybe no one else understands this but he is only days away from a grave. This is the remarkable thing about a funeral; it captures us in a small piece of time. In fact, for a few minutes, time seems to stop and our focus becomes very narrow. Judas certainly doesn't understand. Maybe no one else does, for that matter. Even if none of us are too clear about what all this means, let is look at the figures.

Martha cooks.

Thank God for the angels who cook during our grief. Martha is true to type. We consistently find her doing the household chores. Sometimes she complains that Mary isn't carrying her part of the load but she never complains about her work.

When tragedy comes, when the hard times fall upon us, there are still chores to be done. Preparing a meal or eating what has been prepared can be an overwhelming task. Bread and meat make a sandwich. If you have bread, you can put it somewhere— where do you put the bread? Let's see, if I have bread in this hand and . . . Why am I holding bread? And what was it that goes with—whatever that other thing was? Here, says Martha and her sisters, let me fix that for you. You don't need a sandwich. Here's a casserole. Why do we paint angels wearing wings when everybody should know that angels wear aprons!

Mary emotes.

Mary loves Jesus. That's not to say Martha doesn't love Jesus. I think it is very clear that Martha loves Jesus and expresses her love by cooking. Mary emotes her love. Mary cries easily and often. She laughs just as quickly. Mary is an emotional lightening rod. She immediately absorbs the emotion in the room, feels it deeply and expresses it lavishly. She is one of those people who cries for us when we cannot. On a previous occasion, when Jesus was a guest in this same home, Mary sat at Jesus' feet and simply listened to him teach. This time, she anoints his feet with an expensive perfume. The act lavishly displays her love. It is also an act of humility. She touches his feet, not his head. Selflessly, unselfconsciously she honors him. John tells us the house was filled with the perfume. John has a way of saying things that have rich meaning. He suggests to us that the scent of this act of love reached far beyond where Jesus sat.

Judas stumbles.

Judas was the treasurer of the group. That tells us that Jesus trusted Judas. John informs us that Judas had regularly abused his trust by stealing from the money bag. Judas reminds us that we sometimes stumble over our strengths. Evidently, Judas had a talent for organization or managing money. Jesus recognized his strengths and challenged him to grow personally by working with the band of disciples in a way that he could contribute. Or maybe not. After all, Matthew, the tax collector, probably had more of the skill needed to be the group treasurer. Perhaps Jesus saw some ability in Judas along with a great need to be challenged. Maybe Jesus decided Judas had a weakness here, a need to grow and he gave Judas the opportunity to prove himself. But Judas self-destructed. In modern sports parlance, Judas choked.

Judas is appalled at Mary's lavish action. "This money could have gone to help the poor." Those words set up such a line of lessons.

This money could have gone to help the poor. John uses those words to inform us that Judas didn't care anything for the poor. He simply wanted a large pool of money available from which he could steal.

This money could have gone to help the poor. Jesus finds in those words an opportunity to focus on the present reality. Helping people with needs is something we always can do. Jesus is not saying the disadvantaged are trivial or that they don't have any importance in his kingdom. In fact, he says that should be a continual practice. He says, however, they were at a more basic point in the human drama. Right now, we have something else to do.

This money could have gone to help the poor. Jesus turns to Judas and tells him clearly, **"She is preparing me for my burial."** Here is an explanation no one would have anticipated. There are a world of things we could be doing. Most of them good things. There are some excellent things we could be doing. But here we are with a task at hand. Let's see what it is that Jesus wants done here and now.

We often point to Jesus as our model. He was the sinless one who sought to do the Father's will. He is a model of love, of giving, of sacrificing, of character. You know all this. We point to Jesus often. Here we see him in a different role. Jesus needed these people. He models for us a man in great need.   He gave his friends a wonderful opportunity to minister to him. He drew from them their best and their worst.

Lord God, help us to see what you want from us today.

Preached at Donelson Cumberland Presbyterian Church 3/29/1998

ANGELS

Sunday morning the preacher said,
 "Real angels don't wear wings;
They wear aprons." "Yes," I thought,
 "and they wear other things . . ."
Like a uniform for a policeman
 or maybe for a nurse,
A gown or tux when someone vows,
 "For better or for worse."
They wear chalk dust on a teacher's shirt
 while a student learns to read;
A Cub Scout leader's uniform
 when he's explaining a good deed;
A doctor's white coat while he tries
 to help someone in pain;
A minister's robe when he reminds us
 life is not in vain;
Maybe shorts and tee shirts
 when a helper cuts the grass;
A college professor's coat and tie
 while he's explaining things in class;
Whatever friends and in-laws wear
 when they say, "Come for lunch."
And include me with their family,
 like I'm related to their bunch;
A 5-year-old's bride costume
 that she wore for her birthday;
It was fun when she included me
 to share with her that way.
The sweatshirt that a coach wears
 during drilling with a team;
The poet's old frock when he wrote,
 ". . .Things are not what they seem."

The ink stains on my Mother's hands
     when she wrote me her "earnest prayer"
Was that any time I needed her,
     she would always be there.
(So when she died I wondered
     how on earth I'd ever cope;
She wears a breeze and sunbeams now;
     her spirit gives me hope.)
Do real angels ever have fur coats,
     a tail and four small paws?
Fuzzy, animated affection
     that loves you "just because."
Pro'bly angels don't wear halos,
     since we know they don't wear wings
And we'd be surprised at all the head-gear
     a real angel wears or brings:
There's a hard hat when one's building
     a home, a school, a church,
A miner's hat when buried fuel
     is the object of his search.
Hair-nets for cooks who work all day
     fixing food to feed a crowd,
Soldiers' helmets for the guards
     where an enemy's not allowed.
A ball cap that's worn backwards
     when someone's working with the youth,
Helping them learn rules of play,
     to learn teamwork and truth.
A play dunce hat for comics
     who make us laugh a lot,
'Cause when we laugh we soon forget
     some problems that we've got.
Since there're no earthly wings or halos,
     I bet there're no harps to play.

Real angels will just carry
        what we especially need that day:
Some flowers or a pain pill
        a brownie or book,
A thinking-of-you card, a smile,
        a sympathetic look.
A dust cloth and a vacuum
        to help with cleaning up.
A cup of soup when you are sick—
        and then they wash the cup!
We may just get an e-mail note
        they typed to say "hello."
The sky's the literal limit
        on how "high"-tech angels go.
To sum it up, real angels
        show us someone special cares.
Since they don't wear designer labels,
        we "entertain them unawares."

By Jane Dowden

Jane surprised me with this response to my sermon. Well done, Ms. Dowden!

WONDERING WHAT HAPPENED

Now it was Mary Magdalene, Joanna, Mary the mother of James, and the other women with them who told this to the apostles. But these words seemed to them an idle tale, and they did not believe them.
Luke 24:1-12

Well, indeed, what had happened? Well, what had happened is what we are all about today. Today, we came together for a sunrise service as happened all across this city, all across this country. We met – we use this expression "at the break of dawn" or "at the crack of dawn." The interesting thing about dawn is that dawn doesn't crack, it doesn't break . . .it creeps. We left the house in the dark and we go a few hundred yards and turn north for about a block, and turn east for a block and a half, and then north and then east and every time we turned east, the sky's color changed just slightly . . .dawn creeps.

Which reminds me of a story. A fellow went to a football game and he got so drunk, that his friends had to carry him home and put him to bed. He didn't remember the game, he didn't remember how it came out, he didn't remember being carried home, in fact, the only thing he knew was, he woke up and it was 6:30. But he didn't know which 6:30. So he lay there thinking, is it going to get lighter or darker? Dusk, just like dawn creeps.

Well, you know the expression: there are people who watch things happen, there are people who make things happen, and there are people who wonder what happened. And here we find Peter and his friends, and maybe ourselves as well, wondering, what happened?

I want you to pay particular attention to **three different expressions** in this text from Luke. **First**, the women come to the tomb, they are expecting to find Jesus' body and they brought spices and they are coming concerned about the care of this dead body of this one they love, and he is not there! So here is the first expression I want to bring to your attention: literally, they were without a ford, that's the literal term here, **without transit**. It is like you come up to a river that is swollen, there is no bridge, there is no ford, there is no way to get across. You cannot get from here to there. It is like our expression "up the creek without a paddle" or "painting yourself into a corner." It came to mean, becoming befuddled, perplexed, not knowing what to do. At wit's end. Sometimes the expression is used to suggest a near hysteria. I am in a fix and I don't know how to get out of it. This describes the women. They understand grief; they understand this process. They have come to take care of the body. It is not there and they are without "transit;" they are unable to get from here to there. Mentally, this is too new of a box. How do we get out of it? Expression number one.

Expression number **two**. Somehow it is revealed to them what has happened and they are convinced that Jesus is not dead anymore and they return to the men and they explain it to them. And the men say: **with my light as I see it now, this is nonsense.** Here is the expression, with the light I have, as I see it now, and then you say whatever it is you say. It is a way of saying, "I have looked at this thing from every possible angle and here is what I see." It could be, I have examined this thoroughly, I think you ought to buy this car. I have examined it thoroughly and I think you ought to get out of here as quick as you can. The expression is, I have looked at this with my light, and to my eyes, this is what I see . . .and what did they see? Nonsense. It is a very stylized way of saying I have examined this from every possible direction. It is kind of a high-fallutin' way of saying, "I know what I am talking about." But, Peter goes to the grave.

Expression number **three**. He stoops and looks in and sees only grave clothes, and some versions say, **he was amazed**. Others will say **he was astonished**. I like the contemporary English version: **he wondered what happened**. He wondered or marveled at—he was seeing something different, something new, and it made him wonder, it made him marvel at what he was seeing. A bunch of confused folks that morning. Different kinds of confusion to be sure. But confused.

The earliest testimony we have of the resurrection is the ending of Mark which simply leaves us with an empty tomb: **he wasn't there**. We have to deal with that. Or the witness of Paul which says, he appeared to Peter and he appeared to me. The earliest witnesses of the resurrection were those two and Luke touches on both of them here—the empty tomb. There is a reality you have got to deal with. The tomb was empty. And Peter and Paul, two giants of that first century church, both say, "I saw the living Lord." There is the testimony of the resurrection. If we have done nothing else of value this morning, we have read Luke's account of the empty tomb and testimony of those who saw it. If we have done nothing else of account, we have seen our children become butterflies and portray for us a symbol of the resurrection. Let me add to this just briefly, two minor comments and one major point.

First minor point: appreciate and claim the value of the negative of the dark, of the mysterious. You have had the experience, haven't you? You have heard a child screaming in the other room and you go in and you have no idea what is going on. Or you come upon an accident scene and you don't know what is going on here. Or you are sitting in front of a computer and it is doing strange things, and you have no idea why. You are without a ford, without transit, you're up the creek without a paddle, you have painted yourself into a corner, you are perplexed, you are almost hysterical, you don't know what to do! How do I get from here to there? And you have also had the experience of saying, "I know what I am talking about, I have looked at this from every angle, and it is sheer and utter nonsense and later you find out you didn't know what you were talking about. It wasn't nonsense at the time. You thought it was. And you have come to the closet that holds all your anguish and pain and turmoil and you open it and it wasn't there and you wondered why is it empty and where has it gone and I don't understand this . . .and you were amazed.

What the Bible tells us is, these people were not giddy, impressionable, silly folk. It would be hard to believe any resurrection story that began with Mickey Mouse and Donald Duck saying, "Jesus is risen." These were real, live, flesh and blood people that hurt and have pain and discover the negatives of life and get mystified and confused and THEY are the

ones that tell us, "We didn't believe it. Not at first."
Claim the value of the negative, dark experiences in
your life.

Second minor point: Remember this: **most
of us don't hear what we are not ready to hear.**
You read the gospels and Jesus on every corner is
saying, "I am going to die, they are going to nail me
on a cross, after three days I will rise again and all of
this has some value," and all the time they are talking
about who is more important. Is he more important
than I am or am I more important than he is? They
never were ready to hear. This is an important word
for parents, for teachers or for most of us. You can
talk yourself blue in the face, but if they aren't ready to
hear, they aren't going to hear. That is the case with
the disciples. I guess one of the things that says to us
is, maybe we ought to be a little less critical, a little
less judgmental, because maybe after we have
looked at it from every possible angle, and we have
turned it every way we can, we still don't know every-
thing.

Major point: **The resurrection is revealed to
us; it is not discovered by us**. Everybody that ran
into the empty tomb eventually understood the reality
of it, but not at first. Every one of them discovered the
tomb was empty and made several assumptions:
what did they do with his body? Have you got it?
Where did it go? Somebody stole it. It was not until it
was revealed to them that they understood. Faith is
not a matter of the mind; faith is a matter of the heart.
We do not have to check our minds at the door. We
do not have to say, "Thinking is out of place." But
when it comes down to it, faith is a matter of the heart

and it is revealed to us. It is not something we can discover.

Somebody has pointed out the reason we all go to church on Christmas and Easter is because those are the two events in the church year when we have to understand it is a mystery and we don't understand it all and we can explain away a lot, but we can't explain away the birth of Christ and his death and resurrection.

So one of the things I am saying to you this morning is, "I can't explain this any better than you can." I invite you to come with me and celebrate the mystery of the resurrection.

This morning at the sunrise service, we had the purple garment up at the top of the cross and as part of the process, we took it down and we put the white up there. It is symbolic. The white on the cross at Easter is a symbol that the shroud has been thrown off. It is no longer a shroud. It is a flag of victory. It tells us a whole lot about that cross. On Friday, it was an instrument of torture; the means of execution. But on Sunday morning, it is a hall tree; it is a coat rack, it is a clothes line. It is just a place to throw a used crown and a no longer needed shroud. The flag of victory is hoisted before you. So what time is it? Are things getting lighter or darker? Well, here is the evidence. It is your decision.

Preached at Donelson Cumberland Presbyterian Church 4/24/1998

WAY BEFORE PLAN B

… When they had come opposite Mysia, they attempted to go into Bithynia, but the Spirit of Jesus did not allow them; so, passing by Mysia, they went down to Troas.
Acts 16:6-15

Harry Emerson Fosdick preached a sermon on this chapter titled *Handling Life's Second-Bests.* In it, he speaks of wanting Bithynia and getting Troas. Well, that requires a little explanation. In the first part of this chapter, just before the text we read, Paul diligently wants to enter a part of the world that is now called Turkey. For some reason he was not able to do so. We are told that the Holy Spirit prevented him from going to Bithynia and other places he had hoped to evangelize. Instead, he ends up in the coastal town of Troas. While at Troas, Paul had a dream in which a Macedonian called for him to bring his message over to the European continent. Our text tells us he did exactly that.

The tenor of Acts 16:6-8 suggests that Paul must have been blocked and extremely frustrated. Perhaps he was confused and irritated. Some writers suggest that health problems kept him from traveling. Whatever the explanation, Paul found himself exactly where you and I have often been. He wanted to do something and could not, for all his best efforts, do what he wanted to do. Paul had sketched out a perfectly sound Plan A. He would go to Galatia and preach. When that was not possible he went to Plan B. Bithynia would be a good place to plant a church. But that didn't work either. So now he is in Troas and who knows what other places between Galatia and Bithynia may have frustrated him.

In Fosdick's sermon, he tells us that the artist Whistler wanted to be a soldier. However, Whistler failed a chemistry test at West Point which effectively washed out his military career. According to the artist, "If silicon had been a gas, I should have been a major-general." His original plans fell through and instead he became a renowned artist.

Paul's original plans did not succeed and instead he brought the gospel to Europe and dramatically marked the remainder of world history. What if Christianity had remained hemmed in to a geographical area that almost completely turned Islamic in a later century? Well, that's one of those *what if* questions that can never be answered. But it should be clear to us that Paul's third or worse choice eventually led you and me to Jesus Christ.

Consider, for a moment, what a large story is found in the sixteenth chapter of Acts. The chapter begins with Paul and Silas drafting Timothy to go with them. The three attempt to enter Turkey but are rebuffed. Paul receives the Macedonian call and they immediately seek a way to cross over to Greece. At that point in the story, the narrator begins to say "We" instead of "he" or "they". Maybe that means Doctor Luke had attended Paul in some way and he, too, had been drafted. They cross the Aegean Sea in a quick two days, suggesting that even the wind and the currents were in a hurry to get them to Macedonia. They head for Philippi, one of the most strategic locations and look for a place where people pray. Once there, they reach a broad spectrum of people: Lydia is a successful, affluent business woman. They minister to an abused slave girl. This gets them arrested and provides an opportunity to witness to the Philippian jailer and his family. The whole chapter tells of Paul and his friends coping with the fact that life never quite goes the way we planned.

Frank Sinatra sang:

> I've been a poet, a piper, a pirate, a pauper, a pawn, and a king.
> I've been up and down and in and out, and I've learned one thing.
> Whenever I find myself flat on my back,
> I pick myself up, dust myself off, and get back in the ring.

What can we learn?

Open your spiritual receptors.

Learn to see, hear, feel God's leadership. Our world is too empirical, too factual, too data oriented. If you can't see it, hear it, touch it, or more especially count it, then it doesn't exist. That's the way we live. That's what we believe. Nonsense.

Hone your coping skills.

You don't have to live life as a victim. Your middle name doesn't have to be "Poor Me." One thing I attempted to say earlier – and hope to say in this Easter season series of sermons – the church is a place for us to help each other grow. Here you have a room full of people who can say "I know how you feel."

Lean in a progressive direction.

We fall a lot. Part of moving around on life's journey involves stumbling, tripping, colliding and falling. Well, we can learn to fall in the direction we need to go rather than falling backwards.

At Chad Winsor's funeral the pastor Ted Kitchens talked about how well the two of them worked together as a ministry team. One story Ted told was about the fact that he would sometimes react rather childishly to criticisms. He would go into Chad's office and complain about how he had been mistreated and Chad's response would be, "Snap out of it."

I am not yet the person I hope to be. This is not yet the church we would like it to be.   Why not? For one thing our plans are often frustrated. We meant to do this but couldn't for some reason. So, are we going to put on a giant 'pity party' or will we snap out of it and get on with our lives. As long as we live, we can change and grow.

In early March, Maralee and I rushed a trip to Texas to see her brother and say good-bye. While there, Chad told us that he wanted to finish his life in a way that honored Jesus. That was his final concern. He certainly had not planned to die at the age of 49. Last week, he had gone through all his alternatives. Only one was left. He died in the presence of his family as they sang hymns. He finished life honoring Jesus.

Preached at Donelson Cumberland Presbyterian Church 5/17/1998

THERE MUST BE A POINT TO THIS STORY

Naaman, commander of the army of the king of Aram, was a great man and in high favor with his master … though a mighty warrior, suffered from leprosy …
II Kings 5: 1-14

One of the features of Elisha's ministry was an emphasis on acts of compassion. He was one of the most political of the Old Testament religious figures. He sometimes appeared to be a crotchety old man. There are some curious stories about Elisha, but what I like best about him are the stories like this text where he shows his compassion. The story of Naaman's healing displays a wealth of detail and we can get lost in the story to the point that we miss the point.

Let's look at the pieces and see what they tell us.

Naaman was a great general. He served at the head of an army headquartered in Damascus. Damascus is the capital of Syria, a nation to the North and Northeast of Israel, a nation that often fought with Israel. At the time of this story, the nation is called Aram and is populated with Aramaens. In the story we read that the Aramaen army raided Israel and the King of Aram sent a diplomatic letter to the king of Israel—a little puzzling, but understandable.

Naaman has a skin disease. In the Old Testament the word "leprosy" covered a wide variety of skin diseases. He probably didn't have Hansens' Disease, or modern leprosy, or, if he did, the disease was in the early stages. Obviously, the Aramaens didn't impose the same restrictions on leprosy that the Jews did.

273

A Jewish girl has been captured and assigned to serve Naaman's wife. The girl doesn't appear to be bitter. This probably was a common experience in that world. Who knows, maybe her lot improved, but we really know only one thing about her. She knew that an Israelite prophet could help her new master and she says so.

One of the realities of life seems to be that national leaders never quite know how to communicate with the leaders of a different culture. The King of Aram sends a letter to the King of Israel introducing Naaman and asking for help. All the principles on the Syrian side of the story assume the Israelite girl has told them the truth. Naaman and his wife desperately want a cure and Naaman's king recognizes the value to him and his kingdom in having their foremost military commander healthy. But the letter does not do justice to the king's request. So the King of Israel believes the letter to be a ruse to excuse further Aramaen abuses.

Here's where Elisha enters the story. He sends a message that Naaman should come to see him to prove a point. Naaman goes to the home of Elisha to get his cure. The interchange between Naaman and Elisha has gotten a great deal of attention. It's a funny story with a delicious point of its own. Let me make sure you get the whole picture here.

Naaman is a successful, powerful and wealthy man. He has brought with him nearly a hundred thousand dollars in silver and gold plus ten changes of clothing that didn't come from The Dollar General Store. He has come from his home, the capital city Damascus. Damascus has been labeled the oldest continually inhabited city in the world. It is located northeast of the Sea of Galilee and Mount Hermon in northern Palestine. Three major caravan routes passed through Damascus. Major roads extended from the city to the southwest into Palestine and Egypt, straight south to Egypt and the Red Sea, and west to Babylon. Damascus owed its prosperity to two beautiful rivers, the Abana and the Pharpar. The beauty of Damascus is seen in a story from Moham-mad. As a young prophet he was in a caravan about to enter the city, but when he saw the city, Moham-mad cried out that man may enter only one paradise and his was to be above. Mohammad never did go into the city of Damascus because it was too beauti-ful.

Now that you know all that, consider the pic-ture: Naaman and his escort wait in front of rather ordinary house, by Syrian General-of-the-Army stan-dards. A servant comes out and says, "Go dip your-self in the Jordan seven times." WHAT? At least the prophet should come out and wave his hand over the spot and evoke the name of his God. How would you like to go to Johns Hopkins Hospital for a quadruple by-pass by an internationally known surgeon only to have a nurse hand you a tube of Neosporin with in-structions to rub this on your chest? This just doesn't meet my expectations. Naaman stomps off. But here we see something about Naaman's secret of his suc-cess. He has surrounded himself with intelligent advi-sors who aren't afraid to confront him. And when they do, he listens: "The advice you got won't be difficult to follow. It will not hurt you to take a bath in a muddy river. Who knows, it might help."

Well, you can see, I'm sure, several spin-off points for life. The Israelite slave-girl makes the best of her circumstances. The King of Aram states his wishes but isn't really clear enough in his request. Naaman wants a grandiose treatment and almost misses the cure because he is too proud. And there are a couple of secondary stories that follow that you would enjoy reading on your own.

But I see a problem with this story and a larger point. Unfortunately, they are usually missed when this passage is studied.

The problem is this: Naaman is healed.

Naaman was not a believer. He may have been a believer in miracles but not, the best we can tell from the text, a believer in the true God. How come Naaman was healed but my brother-in-law wasn't?

This week I was in a meeting that included Jack Mras the executive director of the Tennessee Association of Churches. Jack is a retired Methodist minister. He and I talked privately about his son, a forty-two-year-old with lung cancer. Jack reminded me that we consider at some point whether we will outlive our brothers and sisters, maybe whether we will outlive our spouse, but who among us ever considers whether we will outlive our children? He told me that he and God sometimes have arguments. I said, "Good. Go for it."

You see, there is nothing wrong with pointing out the problem. God is certainly larger than whatever problems we have with the story. I would suggest two things. First, if you have a problem with Naaman's healing when others are not, admit it. Face God with it. Second, resolve the problem with God. Find your own resolution in prayer.

I'd like to suggest my resolution here. I do this not so that you have to accept it as yours and not to release you from a homework assignment. My resolution appears simply as testimony.

What happened to Naaman? He was healed once. Maybe God graced him other times, but we only know of this one healing. He was not released from his mortality. He was not swept up in a fiery chariot like Elijah had been. Even Lazarus, whom Jesus called forth from the tomb, had to re-enter that tomb.

I remember driving along a one-way street in Wichita, Kansas. I was making deliveries while working for my uncle. I glanced down to check an address and when I looked back up, I realized that I had narrowly missed a parked car. Who knows how many times God has said, "Yes, I know what he is doing is stupid, but I'm not ready to take him yet?"

Our lives and our deaths, our health and our illnesses are gifts of God. If I choose to play accountant so as to add and subtract what God has given me and compare it to what God has given you, the end result will be for me to say, "God has been gracious to me." I can't speak for anyone else.

For some reason, God had a point to make in healing Naaman. That leads me to the larger point of this story.

The larger point is this: Elisha wanted to demonstrate that God had given a prophet to Israel.

His emphasis was to point to the power, grace and compassion of the true God. Elisha says quite clearly right in the middle of the story, "Why have you torn your clothes? Let him come to me, that he may learn that there is a prophet in Israel." That is the point of this story.

What is the point of your story?

What does your life tell us?

How's it going with you these days and what's the point of that story?

This, my brother-in-law Chad taught us. He faced his own death at the age of forty-nine and said he hoped to die in a manner that would honor Christ. He knew the point of his story.

Ah, me! This is a hard question, is it not? It seems this question goes well with a question we were asking just a moment ago. When you ask God, "Why haven't you healed me or mine?" you should also ask, "What's the point here?"

Preached at Donelson Cumberland Presbyterian Church 7/5/1998

A HATRED ONLY GOD SHOULD HEAR

... O daughter of Babylon, you devastator!
Happy shall they be who pay you back
what you have done to us!
Happy shall they be who takes your little ones
and dash them against the rock!
Psalm 137

How do you handle a Psalm like this one? Usually when we read the Bible, we expect to find some word from God directed to man. This Psalm reminds us that the book of Psalms is quite different. Here we find men's words directed toward God. Sometimes the words are praise and sometimes petition. The Psalms are a combination hymnal and prayer book. But always the words are the expression of men toward God. This Psalm, which begins so beautifully and ends so harshly, is obviously of man. What do you make of it? Let us note that the Psalm is of one piece. You cannot take what you like and throw the rest of it away.

Three things challenge me about this Psalm.

I am embarrassed by my petty angers and anemic forgivenesses.

We might swell up in self-righteous pride and say, "Thank God I am not as that Psalmist. I bless those who curse me. I pay tithes of all I possess. I fast on second, third and fourth Sunday evenings." There is no place here for feeling holier-than-who-ever-it-may concern. The truth is that we have shared the feelings of the Psalmist but without his poetic ability to express our anger and hatred, and more to the point, without nearly the justification.

The Psalm is a statement of hatred, pure, simple and honest hatred. And perhaps this is part of what shocks us about it: we see ourselves reflected in this hatred. The Psalm unmasks us. I don't remember ever using those words to curse anyone but I know the feeling and am ashamed for it.

After reading this Psalm, could we learn to appreciate at least a little of the miracle of grace? Each one of us is capable of such a vitriolic response as we read here. But often we do not respond that way. We sometimes return good for evil. And at other times, we have learned to apologize or forgive even though that may have taken a super-human effort. And there have been occasions in your life when you were thoroughly in the right and you were the victim of nonsensical wrong, yet you conquered natural feelings to catch a glimpse of the other person's problem or perspective and this siphoned off your boiling anger. Oh, maybe it doesn't happen all the time, but it happens. And when it happens it is because of the purification of God's grace. Sometimes we act out Booker T. Washington's comment: "No man is able to force me so low as to make me hate him!"

After the battle of Gettysburg was over, a Union soldier lay badly wounded. General Lee happened to ride by the young man and even though the Yankee was faint from exposure and loss of blood, he raised his hands, looked Lee in the face, and shouted with all the hatred he could, "Hurrah for the Union!" Lee dismounted and came over to the boy—the Yankee thought it was to kill him—and with a sad expression, General Lee said, "My son, I hope you will be well." After Lee left, the boy cried himself to sleep on the battleground.

How long it took him to recover from the wounds which war inflicted upon the soldier's body, I do not know. But that massive wound which wars of all kinds inflict upon men—that wound called hatred was in the process of being healed by that soft word which turned away wrath.

I am shaken by the realization someone may be praying this Psalm about me.

The shock of the conclusion to the Psalm may be partly due to the exposure of our own resentments. But there may be another lesson in the shock. We are repelled by the ugliness of the spirit expressed here. Could we learn from this one of the dangers in bringing harm to another human being? C. S. Lewis makes this point by reminding us that arousing resentment is the natural result of injury to a person. Writes Lewis, "If he dies spiritually because of his hatred for me, how do I, who provoked that hatred stand? For in addition to the original injury, I have done him a far worse one."

In <u>Ambassador's Report</u>, Chester Bowles tells of the European bias which was left in India. Most of the desirable park benches, for instance, bore the placard "For Europeans Only." Indians were excluded from British clubs except as servants. You can imagine the kinds of illustrative material which could be cited. Bowles remarks, "I came to realize that this attitude of white superiority was the aspect of colonialism which is most hated by the colored peoples of Asia and Africa."

I am frightened by the example of yelling at God.

I'm learning how to yell. I'm something of a novice at cussing. Why do we have such curse-filled

Psalms in the Bible but nothing like it in the hymnal?
Sure Psalm 137 starts out, "I can't sin . . ." but it calls
for driving bass, pounding drums, and Whitney Hous-
ton's full-throated voice:

> "Aaaaiiiiih will always hate you-ou-ou."

Or Michael Bolton's passion:
> I said I hate you but I lied.
> Hate can't describe this stuff I feel in
> side!
> I said I hate you. I was wrong.
> Hate could never, ever feel this strong.
> I said I hate you but I lied.

Of course, you would never sing such a song.
Just as you know why we don't have imprecatory*
Psalms in the hymnal. Can you say "imprecatory?"
No, I don't think so. You know we have to intersperse
parental warnings or we could never have read Psalm
137 publicly. We really should not let children or im-
pressionable teenagers read the Bible. So where
does your anger go while you're smiling and saying
"That's nice."? That's why we're all on prozac.
> What do you do with your anger?
> Unnnh.
> Something wrong?
> No, it's just a twinge.
> Ohh.
> What . . .
> S'alright. Cole Slaw. 'Scuse me.
> Are you sure you're . . .
> Some heart burn 'sall.
> Cabbage.

Lot of that goin' around.

Scripture really does help us with anger. Paul tells us to be angry and sin not. Now, how in the world?

Well, the Psalms help. Yell at God. Anger needs expression to be released and drained from us. To whom can we voice anger without the danger of destroying a relationship? "How long, O Lord!" What else could have a better purging effect and would be less destructive?

I would yell at God because then I can pretend thunder is God's answer.

I would yell at God because the potential for revenge is so much greater.

I would yell at God because I won't be put on hold.

I would yell at God because yelling at people can be hazardous.

I would yell at God because the poison has to be released.

I would yell at God because once anger is expressed, other feelings follow.

I would yell at God because God can take it.

I would yell at God because God invites me.

I would yell at God because God knows what to ignore.

I would yell at God because God listens completely.

*imprecatory: to invoke evil or a curse on someone or something, or to contain a prayer for evil to befall someone.

TRINITY WITNESS
… When the Spirit of truth comes, he will guide you into all the truth …
John 16:12-15

This is Trinity Sunday so it would seem reasonable that we should begin with an explanation of the Trinity. After I explain the doctrine of the Trinity, I will explain Einstein's theory of relativity and follow that with an interpretation for husbands of how to understand women and a guide for wives on how to tolerate men. If we have time, I will outline a tax proposal which the Tennessee General Assemble should pass unanimously and all Tennesseans will embrace.

Or I could simply say, "No one can possibly understand any of these things.

We all know that the Trinity is made up of God the Father, Jesus Christ, God's only Son, and the Holy Spirit. So that means we worship three Gods? No, just one God and those three are the one. So then if all of God is one in Jesus, who was in heaven while Jesus was on earth? Aha! This is not going to be easy.

There are at least three things I can say about the Trinity and I find them in this text.

We are not going to understand everything about God in this life.

Jesus plainly told his disciples that they could not bear the whole load of what he would like to tell them. I doubt that we are much ahead of the disciples on that point.

Personally, I feel encouraged by this. I would like to believe that God is bigger, stronger, tougher, more loving and thoughtful, better organized and nicer looking than I am. If God isn't more complicated than I can understand, then we're all in trouble.

I remember a visit to Washington, D. C., for some meeting or other. I had some time to look around the Capitol Mall, one of my favorite neck-craning sites. Up in the Washington Monument, I could look at the White House, the Capitol, Jefferson's and Lincoln's Memorials. Beside me, was a lanky fellow in pressed jeans, boots and a large Stetson. He asked me, "Say, mister, can you tell me what that building is?" "Why, yes," I answered, "That's the White House. That's where the president lives." His eyes bugged and he whipped off his hat. "Golly!" he exclaimed.

That's right where we need to be on Trinity Sunday. As Leann Womack sings:

> I hope you never lose your sense of wonder,
> You get your fill to eat but always keep that
> > hunger
> May you never take one single breath for
> > granted.
> God forbid love ever leave you empty-handed.
> I hope you still feel small when you stand be-
> > side the ocean.
> Whenever one door closes, I hope one more
> > opens.
> Promise me that you'll give faith a fighting
> > chance.
> And when you get the choice to sit it out or
> > dance—
> I hope you dance,
> I hope you dance.

Somehow God has taken care of time and space.

More precisely and more biblically, God has taken care of any part of time and space that we need for him to. We believe and teach that God created all that is. If God put it all together over billions of years and took a long time getting to the people part of creation or if it took him a week with Sunday off, doesn't matter so much to me. The important thing is to affirm that God created and we are his creatures. In Jesus Christ, he recreates us and redeems us. Through the Holy Spirit, he moves and directs us to find the Savior Son and the Loving Creator Father. If you are worried about how we all got here, or what to do with your past sins, or what you need to do about your life today, or where it will all end up, God is there. If you want to know about life in Springfield, Hopkinsville, Texas or Mars and Venus, God is there. The Bible doesn't emphasize so much that God is eternal as it says he is the same yesterday, today, and tomorrow. That's a scale I can understand. He has time and space covered. Some of the explanation for that comes in Trinitarian formulas. If you want a reference from the book <u>The Doctrine of the Trinity for Dummies</u>, it would simply say, wherever you are looking, God got there first.

At the heart of what God is about, is truth.

You've heard it before from Jesus: "I am the way, the truth, and the life;" or "the truth shall set you free." In this passage he calls the Holy Spirit the Spirit of truth. And what is the truth? Well, the Spirit of truth comes into our lives to glorify Jesus. And Jesus wants center stage to point out that all the Father has is his. What does that mean to us?

It means that Father, Son and Spirit share in creating you. That's the truth.

It means that Father, Son and Spirit share in loving you. That's the truth.

It means that Father, Son and Spirit share in redeeming you. That's the truth.

It means that Father, Son and Spirit share in planning the best for you. That's the truth.

When a new child is born, that baby is pretty much like every baby ever born—two eyes, two ears, a consistently similar body temperature. God created us this way and it makes for good parental care, good schooling, and good medicine that we are creatively similar.

But each of us is different and distinctive. Our diversity strengthens us as persons and as a society as each one of us has a different and special contribution to make to our world. God planned that and he liked his plan. But a part of our distinctiveness is found in the unique ways we all rebel against our parents, our society and our God. That's another opportunity for God to show his love and redeem us.

Last Sunday, we celebrated Pentecost and today we are still trying to cope with the implications of God's Spirit moving among us. We can be shaken by the realization that God is a God of the *now*. How often *now* is a vital part of God's word to us! This is the work of the Spirit—to impress upon us the *now*ness of God.

John Leggett told a story from one of his professors. The professor was attempting to explain

Pentecost to three young girls in a catechism class. He told them God moved as a mighty wind and caused great excitement. Tongues of flame appeared and people preached the gospel in languages they had never before known. Two of the girls took his remarks in stride as another preacher story. But one girl stared at him in amazement with a dropped jaw. Finally, she was able to say in a hushed tone, "Golly, Pastor Tom, we must have been absent that Sunday." The richness of this story found by Pastor John is the feeling of the girl that this could happen—*now*.

Maybe if we could find that child, wherever she is, we could invite her here to explain to us the Trinity.

Preached at Mt. Denson Cumberland Presbyterian Church, Springfield, TN 6/10/2001

HOW CAN WE SING THE LORD'S SONG?
… with gratitude in your hearts sing psalms,
hymns and spiritual songs to God.
Colossians 3:16

Song sung blue, ev'rybody knows one;
Song sung blue, ev'ry garden grows one.
Me and you are subject to the blues now and
then,
But, when you take the blues and make a
song,
You sing them out again, sing them out again.

Song sung blue, weeping like a willow:
Song sung blue, sleepin' on my pillow.
Funny thing, but you can sing it
With a cry in your voice,
And before you know it, start to feelin' good
You simply got no choice.
Neil Diamond

Neil Diamond is singing about the Psalms. We
need to learn to appreciate and appropriate the power
of a lament psalm.

Psalm 103 is described as one of the noblest
hymns of the Bible. Such songs of praise are uplifting
and are important aids to worship.

In Colossians, Paul encourages us to sing our
gratitude. This also is a significant means of worship.
But psalms play other roles as well. "When you take
the blues and make a song, you sing them out again,
sing them out again."

Two examples: Psalm 137 is a song that pro-
claims: "we are so distraught that we can't sing; we

are so hurt we pray that our tormentors babies will be murdered." This isn't a war-chant that hopes to lead to the destruction of the enemy. This is simply a classic case of singing out the blues.

Psalm 88 is a lament. A classic lament begins with a complaint, followed with an appeal to God, and concludes with a statement of trust that God hears and answers prayer. Not Psalm 88. This begins with a complaining appeal and never gets beyond an angry, hopeless wail. So why is this in the Bible? Because people often present this same offering to God - an angry, hopeless complaint, accented with "See, God doesn't hear. God doesn't care." The answer to that complaint is simply this. Oh, yes, God knows how you feel. Your complaint is right in the middle of God's songbook. "Funny thing, but you can sing it with a cry in your voice, and before you know it, start to feelin' good, you simply got no choice."

Lent provides us an opportunity to rediscover the importance of the Jewish songbook. When Jesus led his disciples through the last supper, teaching them through symbols and the example of his humility, they interspersed that Passover meal and concluded it with psalms.

Then, in the climax of the cross, Jesus departed this life with Psalm 22 on his lips, in his heart. Listen to this psalm as though hearing it at the foot of the cross.

> My God, my God, why have you forsaken me?
> Why are you so far from helping me, from the
>   words of my groaning?
> O my God, I cry by day, but you do not answer,
>   and by night, but find no rest.

Yet you are holy, enthroned on the praises of
    Israel.
In you our ancestors trusted, they trusted, and
    you delivered them.
To you they cried, and were saved:
    in you they trusted, and were not put to
    shame.
Psalm 22:1-5

**Preached at Wimberley Presbyterian Church,
Wimberley, TX 3/17/2004**

A SIMPLE SUMMER SERMON (MAS OR MENOS)

When the day of Pentecost came, they were all together in one place. And suddenly from heaven a sound like the rush of a violent wind, and it filled the entire house where they were sitting. Divided tongues, as of fire, appeared among them, and a tongue rested on each of them. All of them were filled with the Holy Spirit and began to speak in other languages, as the Spirit gave them ability.
Acts 2:1-4

Summer is the season of hype. The lectionary affords us a series of blockbuster, stupendous, can't miss this whatever you do, texts. The story of Pentecost is bracketed by John's account of the last supper where Jesus promises the Holy Spirit and Paul's reminder in Romans 8 that the Spirit intercedes for us with groanings that cannot be uttered. These are contrasted with Ezekiel's vision of the Valley of Dry Bones: "Oh mortal man, can these bones live?"

Another text should accompany Acts 2, and that is Genesis 11:1-11. There we read the story of the Tower of Babel. That's the ancient explanation for languages. All the earth spoke one language and God, it seems, decided people needed a variety. Actually, that is not quite the point of the story. Genesis 11:1-11 has a chiasmus form. Chiasmus comes from the Greek letter CHI or X which describes the literary form. Many psalms and stories in the Old Testament use this form. The first element matches the last, the second element matches the next to last, and so on. The point of the story is the middle, or keystone element. Here's a home work assignment for you: figure out the Chiastic code of Genesis 11:1-11. The first and last elements are the phrase "all the earth." The central element, and therefore the point of the story is, "God came down." And, you see, that's the point of each one of these texts.

Large scale events. Too big for television, you have to see them on the big screen. Pentecost—the Holy Spirit brings life to the church.

But wait a minute. If summer is the season of hype, it is also the season of disappointment. Blockbusters have a tendency to become bombs, misfires. The Grand Summer of Kyle's Sabbatical will probably be nothing more than a series of aging has-beens. Jerry's bald, Jim Denham is gray, Roger Paynter can't keep a church. Boring! How about having Ben Stein call role in "*Ferris Beuller's Day Off?* Beuller, Beuller, Beuller.

How big an event was the Christian Pentecost? Do you suppose they read about it in the *Roman Daily Sentinel*? If you were at Starbucks in downtown Jerusalem and looked out the window, could you tell that Pentecost was happening? I remember a phone call to check and see if we were all right. "Sure," I answered, "We're fine." Well, my caller informed me, Paul Harvey just reported that Nacogdoches was flooded. We didn't know. Our house was on relatively high ground. Later, John T. and Helen Faye Lewis discovered that their son, Chuck, had been diving in the flood waters to retrieve possessions from fraternity brothers' cars.

What if the Apocalypse comes and nobody notices? If the reviews aren't good, no one will show up.

I used the term "Christian Pentecost." The story begins with a Jewish Pentecost. Pentecost means something like 'fifty days' and is the feast of weeks, 49 days, seven weeks (a week of weeks) after Passover. Traditionally, it is the anniversary of the giving of the Law—a celebration. It was an excuse to go to the big city. In fact, sometimes Pentecost drew a larger crowd than Passover simply because it was a better time of year for travel. It is one of the annual ceremonies where we do all the same things we did last year at this time. We look forward to it. All the older folks have a story about their favorite event— which someone always claims didn't quite happen the way *you* remembered it. In other words, lots of hype. And the hype usually leads to disappointment. What's the difference between Christmas, Easter, Memorial Day, Independence Day, Thanksgiving . . .and your birthday? Temperature.

Genesis eleven—neglect of God's leadership as politicians spend tax funds on pork barrel building projects.

Ezekiel thirty-seven—neglect of God's leadership leads to an ill-advised war and the destruction of lives and dreams.

John fifteen and sixteen—an idealistic young man faces his coming execution and tries to encourage his supporters.

Acts two—following his execution, his supporters try to reorient themselves into a hostile community.

Romans eight—an aging preacher gives advice about what to do when defeat chokes your throat and you can't even cry for help.

All the hype and nothing to show for it. Boring, routine holidays. Then God steps into the picture.

Do you speak the language? ¿Como estas? ¿Muy bien, y tu? Uhmm, mas or menos. Mas o menos—more or less, so-so. This is it—mas or menos?

Do you *hear* the language? The Gospel is straight-forward, plain talk. God through Jesus Christ, has a claim on our lives. No hype needed.

If you understand the language of the Holy Spirit, then you know that God can enter your life at unexpected moments and rev up your heart. At the last supper: Are you discouraged? I'll send help. At the celebration of the Law: tongues of fire. Paul to Romans: Can't pray? The Spirit will do it. Ezekiel: can these bones live? Up to you God. And God breathes on the bones. The same Hebrew word, *ruach*, means breathe, wind, and spirit.

Do you *see* the symbols? This is an analog, not a digital, world. Personal and spiritual values are preeminent, not technical and scientific values.

I'm not opposed to science and technology. While laying on a table experiencing extracorporeal shock wave lithrotripsy to crush a kidney stone, I very much appreciated science and technology.

But I fear that we have focused on the toys, the balls and the shoes and forgotten the players; we have focused on the tools and forgotten the craftsmen, the artisans, and the cooks; we have focused on the weapons and forgotten that weapons kill people and the wielders of weapons are killed.

Language is a big issue throughout these texts. Traditionally, non-charismatic Christians have interpreted the New Testament as describing two kinds of speaking in tongues. The emotional ecstatic kind that Paul writes about in the Corinthian correspondence and the facility with various languages in Acts two. That may be wrong. It may be that Luke who wasn't an eyewitness misunderstood the story. Almost any Jew who traveled to Jerusalem would understand Aramaic and the universal language of commerce: Greek. So, Peter didn't need to speak a dozen languages. And anyway, that's not what Christian Pentecost is about. Pentecost is about God making himself known. God coming down. The language of Pentecost is not Aramaic or Greek or Egyptian or Libyan. The language of Pentecost is whooping, hugging and dancing and whirling and jumping up and down. Either way, however you explain the tongues, everyone heard something for themselves.

Pentecost is all about experience in the present tense and not about past or future. That leads me to say:

Do you *feel* the mood of worship? God doesn't operate according to clocks and calendars.

An ordinary event may be the occasion for an extraordinary intervention. We can read about Pentecost but that doesn't mean we understand what we have read. You can read a text book on almost any subject and with some degree of accuracy can say, "OK, I understand what this book is teaching." But Pentecost is one of those, "Well, you just had to be there" stories.

God acts and we shape our calendars accordingly. Like the man whose barn was covered with targets, all with an arrow in the middle. He shot the arrows and then painted the targets. *Anno Domine*—God acts and we shape our calendars, not the other way around.

Just as the twentieth century began in August, 1914, and the twenty-first century began September 11, 2001—not at midnight when some human devised calendar changed.

Our biggest mistakes in life usually boil down to ignoring the obvious. Isn't it fascinating that our technology has presented us smaller more convenient devices to carry around our communication connections with the world and somehow we are more divided and cut off from one another than ever before?

In William Faulkner's <u>The Sound and the Fury</u>, Dilsey, the maid, watches the Compson family self-destruct before her eyes. One Sunday, she takes her children and Benjy, the idiot son of the Compson's to church. A guest minister is scheduled to speak. At the time for the service to begin, a side door opens and in marches the children's choir, four girls and two boys. Next follows two men. The second man is large and imposing, dressed in a frock coat, with a magisterial bearing. But he was the regular minister and quite familiar to all. As he passed and took his seat, the entire congregation watched the door through which he had come expecting some guest of equal stature to come through the opening. Gradually, the realization spread that someone else had preceded their pastor and they began to focus on the little man who was now sitting before them. As the music and other pieces of a worship service began to take place, disappointment seeped down the aisles and through the pews. The congregation could tell by looking that the shriveled little man before them could not possibly touch their lives with anything he might cough up that day. But as he began to talk about a recollection of the Lamb of God, Dilsey sat bolt upright. Before the sermon was finished, tears rolled down her cheeks. As they left church and the comments about the power of the message, her children begged her to stop crying. But something had been revealed to Dilsey through that scrawny little man. Something indescribable, but something sufficient.

Ignore the hype. Listen for the breeze, the breath, the Spirit.

Preached at Austin Heights Baptist Church, Nacogdoches, TX 6/4/2006

NOT AN ORPHAN

… I will not leave you orphaned; I am coming
to you.
John 14.15-21

"Are you coming back?"

This question differs in intensity, desperation,
depth, or plaintiveness from any of the other forms it
takes. "Will you be home for supper?" "Can you be
here for the balloon festival?" "You do remember
what time curfew is, don't you?" Well, that last one is
not really a question.

"Are you coming back?" A teacher wants to
know if the pupil will return for the next grade. "Are
you coming back?" The child asks the departing, di-
vorced parent. "Are you coming back?" The loved
one asks the soldier. In other words we ask, "Will I
ever see you again?"

I know this question. You have asked it too.

This question haunts us in every news story
about children separated from their families in the
polygamous compound in Texas.

Howard Hurd, was an Orphan Train Rider. In
1925, he and his brother Fred Swedenberg were re-
moved from their home in Upstate New York because
of neglect. Howard was three and his brother was six.
Eventually they were sent to New York City and
placed on a train with several other children and sent
to the Midwest to live in a foster home. The boys were
separated and went to different homes in Nebraska.
There were around 150,000 to 200,000 children who
were dispersed in this fashion between 1854 and
1926.

"Will I ever see you again?"

The response? "I will not leave you an orphan."

Jesus uses strong family images to make his points. Move back earlier in the fourteenth chapter of John. Jesus tries to teach his disciples about the perils of the next days. He intends to comfort them and warn them by saying that where he is going, they will go. Thomas is confused. "We don't know where you are going," he protests. Jesus uses a metaphor, "I am the way, the truth and the life." Then he continues with the explanation that he, Jesus, is the way to the Father. "Just show us the Father," interrupts Philip. "Have we been together all this time and you haven't caught on?" Jesus says. "If you have seen me, you have seen my Father."

Jesus expands his comments telling them that those who love him will play by his rules. Show *character*. He has to leave them but will send an advocate. He's *committed* to them. He will not leave them orphaned. Have *confidence*. We are family now, he says in effect, and we have our inside stories. We are deeply into one another. This is a *caring* community.

After five plus years of marriage it did not appear I was ever going to be a father so our son was adopted at the age of three and a half weeks. He was not technically orphaned but couldn't be kept or cared for by either mother or father. We began by telling him every day of his childhood, long before he could understand the meaning, "We're so glad we adopted you." Being an adopted child would never be a derogatory term in our household. Now we have a blended set of adopted, born-to, and step-children along with a goodly number of surrogates. The next child along loves it when someone notices that her older brother bears a strong family resemblance to her. Nature or nurture? What people see as a family resemblance, in most cases, amounts to learned be-havior, mannerisms, facial tics, posture, a way of car-rying oneself.

My son, through me, has my father's sense of humor. Probably one of the stronger family character-istics rampaging through my siblings, my children, and nieces and nephews is Dad's sense of humor.

I remember crossing the campus at Stephen F. Austin State University for a lunch appointment. As I approached the McGee building, I saw through the glass door someone walking toward me. I knew in-stantly from the swing of the arms, the carriage of the body, the tilt of the head, I was watching my father come to meet me. What was he doing in Nacog-doches, Texas? It may have taken a full minute for me to realize I was looking at my reflection in the door. If you have seen me, you have seen my father.

Family images provide the power in Jesus' message "I will not leave you an orphan."

Caring, commitment, confidence, character – let's talk about it.

Love empowers. **When you care for some-one that someone grows stronger.**

Some of you remember Dean Martin singing:
> You're nobody 'til somebody loves you
> You're nobody 'til somebody cares.
> You may be king, you may possess the
> world and it's gold,
> But gold won't bring you happiness
> when you're growing old.
> The world still is the same, you never

> change it,
> As sure as the stars shine above;
> You're nobody 'til somebody loves you,
> So find yourself somebody to love..

Love given strengthens both the giver and receiver. When you choose to bring a life into your universe to love – what a rush! Can you imagine the moment when Joseph knew both wife and baby were comfortable and asleep, running to the Innkeeper, he would have gushed, "It's a boy! We have a son!"

Commitment defines your level of love.

According to the *Orphan Foundation of America* each year 25,000 young people "age out" of the foster care system. Without familial support only half finish high school and 2% graduate from college. Family means being there for loved ones.

When you love someone, you show up. When you care, you stick around. When family calls, you come back home. Commitment is a treasure. When commitment is given, return the favor.

Confidence grows from being loved.

Where do we learn self-confidence? Self-confidence is rarely self-started. Your self-confidence probably grew from the awareness that someone important to you showed confidence in you. *The Barium Springs Presbyterian Children's Home* reports Allison's story:

> At the tender age of 14, Allison has already lived through more obstacles than most of us handle in a lifetime. She was raped at age 11 and has no parents to help guide her through the emotional trauma she endures. All alone in the world, Allison

quickly turned to drugs and a dangerous lifestyle.

In trouble for not attending school, Barium Springs' community support workers were asked to help Allison. On drugs and newly pregnant, it became vital that Allison get help with her drug problem so her baby would survive. When one of our staff picked Allison up to take her to the rehabilitation center, it became evident of just how little she had. Her house was empty. No sheets on the bed, no personal hygiene items or clothes to pack and the worst part was her heart had become a reflection of her environment – empty and damaged.

Today, Allison is drug-free and a healthy baby is on the way! She has a long road ahead of her but she is now part of the Barium Springs family. It is through the generosity of many that Allison will get the support she needs to build a better life for herself.

Character blossoms from the confidence of being loved.

Why at this critical moment does Jesus insist on challenging his disciples with "if you love me, keep my commandments?" Maybe at least in part because character, moral behavior is a reflection of your experience in being loved and loving in return. *Hillcrest Family Services* in Eastern Iowa tells David's story:

"I am 17 and the youngest of four brothers and seven sisters. I no longer know where my family is except for my mother – she is dead. I can almost be counted as homeless except for Hillcrest. I would continually beat up people with my friends. I hacked into my school's computer server system and did drugs. I was a total low-life loser who just wanted to fit in. I have been in Residential Treatment at Hillcrest just eight months and already I've changed my thinking totally. Staff members encourage me to make my own positive decisions but they don't punish me when I do wrong. Instead, they try to help me any way they can to see a better way and they care about me. I grew up in the church, but didn't accept Christ until after I came to Hillcrest. I became a Christian on St. Valentine's Day. It wouldn't have happened without Hillcrest. From then on, my attitude towards life is a new one. I have been off drugs for one year, have been calm and I haven't beaten anyone up."

"Will I ever see you again?" The question rumbles in the grief-heavy chest of Mary at the foot of the cross. "Will I ever see you again?" cries out from Mary Magdalene's heart as she approaches the tomb.
Excited by the resurrection and overdosed by forty days of teaching and growing, the disciples gather in Galilee to be commissioned and watch friend and mentor disappear again. "Will I ever see

you again?" A voice challenges, "Why are standing around gawking? He'll be back. You are not orphans."

Preached at Covenant Presbyterian Church, Albuquerque, NM 4/27/2008

I PRAY, THEREFORE I AM

Jacob was left alone; and a man wrestled with
him until daybreak.
Genesis 32: 22-31

Who is Jacob? God is the God of Abraham,
Isaac, and Jacob—Abraham we know well; the
founder of three great religions: Judaism, Christianity
and Islam; the grand example for Paul's teachings—
we know Abraham. Isaac? Well, Isaac was almost
toast until God provided a ram in the bushes. Isaac
was a hen-pecked dupe of his wife and younger son.
We know Isaac, too. But now Jacob was a liar, ma-
nipulator, con-man, arch sibling rival ... whom God
loved more than his bumbling but honest older
brother. Jacob, the deceiver, became Israel, prevailer
with God and man. Him, we don't know so well.

Jacob was a man who knew his own mind. He
knew who he was, what he wanted, and he knew how
to get it. Here we find him on his way home. Having
outsmarted his father-in-law Laban, taken both his
daughters and the best of his herds, he owns his fu-
ture. All belongs to him—unless, of course, his older
brother carries a grudge. The silver-tongued deceiver
who can talk a starving mother out of her child's
breakfast fears the man who suffered his first major
con. Jacob sends his best flocks and his family on
ahead in the hopes that his brother's anger can be
tamed by gifts.

However, before the adversarial twins can
meet, a stranger drops into Jacob's prayer retreat and
they grapple. Jacob, for the first time in his life, limps
away without the gold medal. But instead of bearing
the brand *loser*, he finds himself a new kind of winner.

He is the prevailer. All right, Jacob always thought he was The Prevailer. But now, in one night, he discovers he had never prevailed. His first and greatest deception was on himself. Before he deceived others, he deceived himself. Now then, fearing his brother and conquered by an unknown stranger, exposed to his real nature, he is given the opportunity to become the person God always intended him to be.

What name best fits you? I would choose Granddad, honey, and Jerry long before Reverend. If people did not know you were listening, what would they call you? Carlyle Marney asked his doctor, "Who are you when you're not a doctor?" The doctor replied, "I'm always a doctor!"

Who are you? Consider for a moment how that question changes. Without being able to verbalize it, a child asks, "Am I the good or the bad child?" Children probe the meaning of being eldest, youngest, or middle– or only. Who are you? The question alters some at school age or adolescence. When we first face college or the job market, we must decide on being a Lobo or an Aggie, a teacher, engineer, lawyer or Indian Chief. Single or married? Military or civilian?

One day, all the definitions leave. Who are you when you retire? Who are you when bereaved? Then, hard as it may be for some to consider, one day you may say to yourself, "How much longer will I be John's widow or Jane's ex?"

Play the part of the children for a moment and pick an identity. At times, I knew myself to be the skinny one, the slow one or the fast, the smart one, the funny one. Pick a new name. How about Braveheart? Or here are a few more: Hugs-a-lot, Patriot,

Care-giver, Sturdy Friend, Resilient Companion, Gra-
cious Host, Gourmet Cook.

We moved to New Mexico and changed identi-
ties. We are no longer Tennesseans or Texans. I
have volunteered for Maralee in two different hospice
programs. In both places I underwent criminal back-
ground checks. Last August, I began substitute
teaching in Charter high schools—more criminal
background checks. We moved into an apartment;
then are moving to another now—credit checks and
criminal background checks.

In high school people would call me funny.
Some friends referred to me as the class clown. I've
got quite a sense of humor. One day, in the cafeteria
line, a boy I didn't know, and now that I think about it,
never saw again, said to me, "I've never seen you
smile." I ran into a stranger and he rattled my sense
of self-understanding.

Here is my prayer for each of you: May some-
one throw you off your pedestal and graciously
deepen and broaden your self-understanding even
though it bruises your ego. May you experience an
act of grace that leads you to realize who it is God in-
tends you to be. You see, a major part of how we de-
fine ourselves is by comparing the "I" against the
"You" when we collide. Every time you wave, shake
hands, pat a shoulder, push back, hug or grapple,
something sparks recognition. I'm one like you—or
Not!

I am not a Fundamentalist! On the other hand,
in this godless world, I'm pretty conservative.

I am not a Liberal! On the other hand in this
buttoned-down, anal retentive world, I'm pretty pro-
gressive.

I am not my father—no matter who I saw in the mirror this morning.

I am not my mother—no matter whose voice I heard during the children's time.

When they don't know you are listening, do they call you Son of . . . ? Daughter of . . .? How about Child of God?

Every morning, Francis of Assisi prayed, "Who art thou Lord and who am I?" Perhaps he missed a morning or two with that prayer. But he did not miss a keen understanding of what the basic questions are.

Martin Marty tells us, "Ours is the first attempt in recorded history to build a culture upon the premise that it is not important for the workings of man and society whether or not God is present."

God who alone is self-defining, God the great I AM, God who reveals himself in Jesus Christ—a man who knew most assuredly who he was, God holds the answer to your search for personal identity.

Rene Descartes struggled with philosophy and at a point of despair doubted everything until he came to the realization he could not doubt the fact that he was doubting. At that point, he proclaimed, "*Cogito ergo sum*"—I think, therefore I am. Maybe so.

Jacob was frightened out of his wits by the prospect of meeting his brother. He encountered a spiritual stranger and realized he had been a stranger to himself. With a new understanding of himself, his world, and his life, he might have said, "*Supplicatio ergo sum*"—I pray, therefore I am. Amen.

Preached at Covenant Presbyterian Church, Albuquerque, NM 8/3/2008

BIRTHMARK STORY

… Guided by the Spirit, Simeon came into the temple; and when the parents brought in the child Jesus, to do for him what was customary under the law, Simeon took him in his arms and praised God, saying, "Master, now you are dismissing your servant in peace; …'

Luke 2:22-40

Children's sermon

I have a birthmark on my neck. A birthmark is like a designer label. Your mother puts it there when you are born to identify you and say you are special. Our parents and others mark us in other ways. They teach us our accents and mannerisms. They tell us birth stories too. When I was little, I would stand and make speeches in baby talk. My mother said I was probably going to be a preacher. Now, how do I know that story?

Sermon

Chip Davis, the genius behind Mannheim Steamroller, says that his mother tells the story that at the age of six months, Chip could hum the tune "Silent Night." Maybe he could or maybe his mother has an active imagination, but what is important is that Chip Davis heard and remembered that story.

Maralee's aunt and uncle spent a lifetime as missionaries among native people of Indonesia. Some of those people were cannibals. They tell about approaching a cannibal chieftain while holding their first-born daughter, Janda. The chieftain asked if he could hold her. Janda would grow up hearing the story of her father handing her over to a cannibal to be held.

We have all been marked by the stories we have been told about birth and childhood. My uncle and Dad ran around the room like chickens with their heads cut off when Mom told them she was in labor. It was all they could do to get out of the apartment and they almost left without her. Dad said I looked like a cross between a tomato and a monkey.

My son Jay was adopted at the age of three weeks. We would tell him how we drove away from the adoption agency and then stopped the car just to hold him and look at him. We then drove for over an hour to where my mother was sitting with her mother as she was dying of cancer. We loved to tell how Mom took off his booties and counted to be sure he had ten toes. When Jay was four his sister Angela was born. Jay's grandparents brought him to the hospital to greet us as we left. They parked in front of the main doors. Jay hopped out of the car ran into the hospital and through the lobby to where we were leaving the elevators.

Later, when Jay was about ten, a neighbor learned that Jay was adopted and she asked when we were going to tell him about his adoption. Jay has always known that he was adopted. Our earliest stories always began with "We're so glad we adopted you." She told us that her son had never been told that. Soon after that her son began fighting with Jay and saying ugly things to him. Apparently, she had told her son about his adoption and sugar coated the news by saying that Jay Self was adopted too.

Your drawl, your laugh or smirk, your attitude toward life, how you say hello and your wave good-bye – you've been birth marked.

Take a trip with me in your imagination. Let's go to a twelve-year-old's birthday party. At some point in the festivities the mother will tell the stories she has on eleven previous birthdays. Part of the story will be about his circumcision. Now there's a story guaranteed to embarrass any twelve-year-old boy. Then there would follow the story about the trip to the temple for the ritual of purification for the new mother. "An old man named Simeon," she would say, "took you in his arms." And she would mimic an old man's shuffle and his gravely voice as she would tell him of the old man's words declaring their son to be special. Then she would wrap a shawl over her head and shoulders and pretend to be Anna.

Familiar stories. He has heard them every year of his life. He doesn't remember ever not knowing these stories, but he hears them anew. He is twelve. He is becoming a young man. Jesus hears these stories regularly. Notice how the text runs immediately to the twelve-year-old. These stories tell him of prophecies of his ministry, tell him of parental pride, tell him of the hope of his people and of all people. Over the years the texture of these stories will shift from pure joy and celebration to expectation and responsibility.

Perhaps for the first time his parents think he is old enough to hear about their escape to Egypt. Perhaps for the first time he hears overtones in the story never before noticed. These stories are not like the ones he hears at his friends' birthday parties. Similar, of course, but not the same. His friends' parents tell special stories, stories of love and pride, but their stories have nothing about people falling or rising. The friends' stories never mention a sword in their sides or piercing their mother's hearts. Perhaps the stories chase him to Jerusalem at Passover time, chase him to find the elders, the rabbis at the Temple, drive him to ask piercing questions. "What does this mean?" he demands. "And what does your answer mean?" "Explain what Micah said, and how about Isaiah and do you know what the Psalmist meant?" And then he would have also said, "Do you know what I think? Here's my opinion." He would have badgered the rabbis telling them, "I have birthmarks and I want to know their meanings!"

Two questions, at least, that we ask of every text: What did it mean then? What does it mean now? Or, if you prefer, what did it mean to them? What does it mean to me? Excuse me, what does it mean to us? – Assuming you are still listening. What does it mean? I didn't know.

I told Maralee I had everything for a sermon except for one thing. What's the point? I asked her what she thought. That shows how smart I am: I asked for her opinion. She knew immediately and told me, showing that she's smarter than I am. It's when the light goes off in your head for the first time telling you that you are blessed. That's it! The point of birthmark stories is that somewhere through your pilgrimage you will hear them as you've never heard them before and you'll feel the love.

And at some point, listening to all of Luke two and the chapters that follow, at some point in Bethlehem, or Nazareth, or in the Temple, or on Gethsemane, or at Golgotha, or Joseph's tomb, at some

point the light will go off in your head and you'll see
this is what it meant to Jesus. And in that same
epiphany, that same realization, you'll have new eyes
to see: This is what it means to me. Maybe this year,
during the season of lights, the light will dawn in your
life.

Preached at Immanuel Presbyterian Church,
Albuquerque, NM 12/31/2017

GPS: APPLEBY ROAD TO OTHERWISE

While they were talking about all this, Jesus himself stood among them and said to them, "Peace be with you." They were startled and terrified, and thought they were seeing a ghost. ... he said to them, "Have you anything here to eat?"

Luke 24:36-48

Each of the four gospels deals with the resurrection in their own way. Only Luke and John tell stories about a Jerusalem room where Jesus appears. John tells the Thomas stories. Luke tells stories that seem to compress forty days into one day. They each have their perspective. What if you were the story teller today? How would you treat fifty years of otherwise, differently from Jim, Roger, Kyle or myself? I've had this role at the tenth, twentieth, and twenty-fifth anniversaries.   I'm honored to be here today.

Luke's final chapter tells us three resurrection stories: women find the tomb empty, Jesus, appears to two disciples on the road to Emmaus, and then they all end up as a group in Jerusalem. The third story is picked up in verse 36 – our text.

We are, perhaps, not unlike the first disciples who got excited but were also confused and unsure of what was going on. And so, we read of their meeting in a room closed off from the outside world and debating what they have heard, challenging the meaning of the reports they received. Then Jesus enters walking, talking, standing, sitting. And then, almost a scene from Seinfeld with George, Elaine, and Jerry arguing in loud voices when Kramer bursts into the room and asks the great Messianic question, "Got anything to eat around here?" Isn't this the classic sign of health and normality? "Got anything to eat?"

We are celebrating fifty years of Austin Heights Baptist Church by worshiping together on Friday evening where Jim Denham preached and then moved to Judy McDonald's to ask her, "Got anything to eat?" We met at the campus to hear Roger Paynter and asked, "What have they to eat, here?" and now you will put up with me for a few minutes until we can ask, "What's to eat?"

Google: Austin Heights Baptist Church <click>www.austinheightsbaptist.org<click> Pictures, Gatheredbygrace, Empoweredbylove. Nice.

Upcoming<click> Let's see. Mondays, Wednesdays. Here we are. March 25, Shared worship with Zion Hill First Baptist Church . . . followed with a meal. "I love to go to Zion Hill!" "Oh, why is that?" "They feed us well."

We are celebrating fifty years of otherwise. Here. At 2806 Appleby Road. How do we get to otherwise from here? On Appleby Road. Well, as the First People, Native Americans say, "The long journey begins with the first step." Or Taoists tell us, "A thousand mile journey began with a foot put down." Or, to quote Jesus, "beginning with Jerusalem."

They were startled, terrified, thought they had seen a ghost. Jesus says to them, "W-h-y-a-a-r-e-e-a-y-o-u . . ." or something. In their joy, they disbelieved and wondered. Jesus recognized their shock and bewilderment and met their humanity with sameness, humanity. "Got anything to eat around here?"

How do we get to otherwise from here? A first step. **Start where we are.** Before we can meaningfully claim otherwise, we must acknowledge sameness. The heart of the gospel tells us Jesus is the Otherwise. All of us are not. All have sinned and come short. The point of the Incarnation—God with us—Immanuel—He, the Absolutely Different, became the Same.

Maybe the most important thing I ever did was to knock on T. W. Berry's door. T. W. Berry became my mentor. I wanted him to go to the white ministerial alliance. He explained to me why that wouldn't happen, but welcomed me to his ministerial alliance. I wanted things to be different. He taught me I needed to prove Same before I had a valid Different. So, I became the white face in black meetings—for ten years. And it hasn't changed. That is still Kyle's role. Before you can validate Otherwise, you must prove Sameness. Can we do something heroic, outstanding, dynamic, world changing??? Maybe, you want to get something to drink?

I did teach Rev. Berry one thing. White people do respond to the sermon, just not necessarily vocally.

Jesus could read the crowd. They are human. Not the first time Jesus probed basic humanity with this question. "Look at the size of this crowd!" "Right, maybe four-five thousand people on this hill." "Hmmmm, got anything to eat?" "Not much. The young people have some hush puppies and fish sticks." "That'll do."

John's letters describe this. Before his readers will accept Jesus as the Otherwise, they need to understand, as John put it, "We saw him, we heard him, we touched him. He was the Same."

You are witnesses to these things.

A second step toward Otherwise is to **identify the players.** Look around the room. This room or that room in Jerusalem. We really don't know who was there. Probably the women who found the empty tomb. They gave him fish. Maybe a fisherman. An apostle, or several. A tax-collector. A prostitute? Different is not necessarily better or worse. Quite often it is just, well, different. I'm white, male, old, right-handed, hetero-sexual—I expect having two wives verifies that. I was born an American. I've been to Canada and Mexico and returned without being stopped at the border. That's who I am. I can't claim to have decided any of that for myself. People who are not white, male, old, right-handed, hetero-sexual, or naturally US citizens are different. Just different. Recognize and value the difference to be found among the same.

Within the community of the Same, we are all different. Third-Lieutenant George Burk wrote the words to "Amazing Grace." He could show the paper where he wrote the words.

The Love Class, a group of Downs syndrome young men were an Austin Heights Baptist Church ministry to one set of different.

In the forty years since moving from Nacogdoches, I have taught ethics and world religions to Baptist, Presbyterian, and Methodist college and seminary students before 2007. During the last decade in New Mexico, I have taught the same material to Catholics, ex-Catholics, Buddhists, Hindus, Muslims, Sikhs, Native Americans, DACAs, Dreamers, gays and atheists. Remarkably the same and yet challengingly different.

Most of the gospel, beginning with the Golden Rule, is not proprietary material belonging only to Christians:

> What you do not wish for yourself, do not do to others. *Confucius*
>
> Hurt not others in ways that you yourself would find hurtful. *Buddha*
>
> *Socrates* said it in the negative: Do not do to others that which would anger you if others did it to you.
>
> *Plato* used the positive: May I do to others as I would that they should do unto me.
>
> *Jesus:* In everything do to others as you would have them do to you; for this is the law and the prophets.
>
> *Muhammad* said: None of you will have faith until one desires for his brother what he desires for himself.

One way we value those who are different is by recognizing the sameness within the difference. At the end of the semester, my world religion students would comment that other religions are more like mine—whatever that may be—than different. They, those who are outside of this fellowship are different, but share the same humanity with us. Our testimony will be better received by those who sense we value their humanity.

You are witness to these things.

The third step toward Otherwise is to **cooperate in the march toward a better way**.

Some of those who very much like us are not marching toward that better way. Some of those who are very much different from us are moving toward a better way. It could help us to admit we didn't invent the good. We aren't the only ones who value the good. So, cooperation might be the better model rather than leading. Although, somebody needs to lead . . .what's an old white man to do? Here's a thought: follow the example Jesus gave us.

Jesus stepped into our lives as the same as us including death, death as the Crucified One.

Crucifixion was a common means of punishment and execution for non-Romans. Probably Jesus, as a youth, saw a hundred Jewish rebels crucified in a field close to his home in Nazareth. Had Jesus been a Roman citizen like Paul, he would never have been crucified. Peter, according to tradition was crucified, maybe upside down. Hundreds, even thousands, were crucified by the Romans. Other cultures have used the same heinous means of torture and execution and even in modern times, people have been crucified. There's nothing special about it, awful as it is. And yet, Jesus will forever be uniquely the Crucified One.

The crucifixion is part of our family history. It happened to one of us. If we are going to follow his lead toward Otherwise, it will be costly. It will require sacrifice.

Jesus steps into our lives as otherwise, as eternally the Risen One.

The gospel tells us that God planned this from before the beginning of time. The gospel tells us that Jesus somehow conquered death making it victory-less and un-stingful. The gospel tells us that Jesus died and yet lives. He is risen! Risen indeed! And therefore we need no longer fear death. The resurrection is part of our family history. It happened to one of us. If we follow the course to Otherwise, well, who knows, it should be a good thing.

Jesus came among us as one just like us to show us how to be Otherwise.

Volunteers sat in an adjoining room in this building, answering a phone for the Listening Ear, an anonymous help service on the weekends. One day, the phone rang during the afternoon. I answered, "Listening Ear." "What is this?" a woman's voice asked. I explained. She said, "I don't understand why this number shows up repeatedly on our long-distance bill." She gave me dates and times, and I saw by the log that her son just couldn't get a girlfriend. Of course, I couldn't tell her that. She hung up dissatisfied with my explanation. Then there was the evening a young man attempted suicide and called us. David Elkins overrode our rules, and went to rescue the man and got him to an ER. A lot of good things have happened in this room, in those rooms. In the kitchen. We're here for reasons.

The road to Otherwise will lead us to combat racism, and other isms. It will lead us to be accepting of people who are different in their same humanity. It will lead us to open our hearts and houses to widows, orphans, and strangers. It will teach us how to welcome others to our table.

You are witnesses of these things.

Preached at Austin Heights Baptist Church, Nacogdoches, TX 4/15/2018

TABLE OF CONTENTS

Doesn't the Table of Contents go at the front of the book?

Who says?

Well, that's just the way ... I mean if you look at the front of any book ...

So?

I mean there's a right way to do things.

Okay, so write your own book and do it however you like. I put together the book first and then did the TOC. If I put it at the front, I'll have to go through and add 2 to all the page numbers.

Oh. And you don't want to do that.

No. I don't. If you want to do it ...

Never mind.